THE
CW00541055

OMNIBUS PRESS
London/New York/Paris/Sydney/Copenhagen/Berlin/Madrid/Tokyo

Cover designed by Chloë Alexander
Picture research by Mick Middles & Sarah Bacon

ISBN: 0.7119.9762.4
Order No: OP 49335

Exclusive Distributors:
Music Sales Limited,
8/9 Frith Street,
London W1D 3JB, UK.

Music Sales Corporation,
257 Park Avenue South,
New York, NY 10010, USA.

Macmillan Distribution Services,
53 Park West Drive,
Derrimut, Vic 3030,
Australia.

To the Music Trade only:
Music Sales Limited,
8/9 Frith Street,
London W1D 3JB, UK.

Cover photograph: Joe Dilworth / S.I.N.

Every effort has been made to trace the copyright holders of the photographs in this book but one or two were unreachable. We would be grateful if the photographers concerned would contact us.

Typeset by Galleon Typesetting, Ipswich.
Printed in Great Britain by Creative Print and Design Wales, Ebbw Vale.

A catalogue record for this book is available from the British Library.

www.omnibuspress.com

For Lorraine and Carlhoun

In Chedzoy

Contents

Acknowledgements

Top of the 'Ta' list, of course, must be Mark E. Smith, for adding a sense of the surreal and loads of other things. Equally, huge thanks to Irene Smith, for trust and anecdotes.

To Chris Charlesworth, as ever, of Omnibus Press, for having the insight and/or blind courage to 'go with the flow'; Andy Neill and Sarah Bacon, both of Omnibus, for unwavering diligence . . . and for Sarah's band, The Rocks.

I am fond of so many people who have, in their varying ways, crammed themselves into my 25 years spent watching The Fall from reasonably close quarters. Here are a few of them: Kay Carroll – for the times; Marc (Lard) Riley – for not beating me up in The Hacienda (I never did write that review, Marc); Una Baines, Martin Bramah, Simon Wolstencroft, Karl Burns, Steve Hanley, Craig Scanlon, Elena Smith, Helen Donlon, Mike Leigh, Yvonne Pawlett, Arthur Kadmon (reborn now, as Peter Sadler), Andy Zero, Jon Savage, Paul Morley, Dave McCullouch, Ian McCulloch, Julian Cope, Andy Spinoza, Dave Haslam, Big Bad Brinner, Tony Michaelides, John Barratt, Ro Barratt, Dave Bush, Dean Bush and Emma, Jon The Postman, Julie Howard, Tony Wilson, Pam and CP Lee, Lindsay Reade, Kevin Cummins, Richard Boon, Dick Witts, Vini Reilly, Grant Showbiz, Ian Wood, Mike Nicholls, Tony Davidson, Colin Sinclair, Gareth Evans, Chris Seivey, Mike Finney, Karen Middlehurst, Carol and Jack, Ian Terry, Michael Bracewell, Terry Christian, Craig Cash, Eric Jackson, Mike Perry and Neil Sowerby at the *Manchester Evening News*, Alan, Liz, Margaret, Andrea, Suzanne, Stuart and all at *The Warrington Guardian* . . . the best local paper in the world.

And to the best web page in the world – www.visi.com/fall (Fall official site).

And the best magazine in the world – *Classic Rock*.

SOURCES: *NME*, *Q*, *Melody Maker*, *Sounds*, *Rolling Stone*, *Alternative Ulster*, *Shy Talk*, *City Life*, *Manchester Evening News*, *Vox*, *Select*, *Evening Standard*, *Daily Telegraph*, *The Times*, *The Wire*.

Introduction

Mark: ". . . thing is . . . this book . . . I think it will be rather good . . . but . . ."

Mick: "Yeah . . . hope so . . . but?"

Mark: "But I don't want there to be any of that retro crap . . ."

Mick: "Well, no . . . not much . . . well, there has to be a bit . . . a bit of retro crap."

Mark: "And I am not really into any kind of writing about rock music . . ."

Mick: "Er . . . no . . . not much either . . . well, perhaps just a bit . . . a bit of both . . ."

Mark: "Why?"

Mick: "Well . . . s'pose because it's kind of . . . like . . . a rock biography!"

Mark: "Yeah . . . yeah . . . I *know* that, Mick. But I don't want it going from album to album . . . and from band member to band member . . . that would be so dull. Don't want it to be another linear rock biography . . . on The Fall . . . that would be so dull. Who would want to read that?"

Mick: "Well, Fall fans might have an interest . . ."

Mark: "Well, I wouldn't have . . . I wouldn't read . . ."

Mick: "I want it to be more natural . . . off the cuff . . . going with the flow . . . which is what you do . . ."

Mark: "Yeah . . . yeah . . . that's why I agreed to do it . . . yeah. Only I can't stand tedious rock biogs."

Mick: "Won't be . . . will be a book about you . . . about The Fall . . . about what you do . . . about music . . . but it won't be a rock biography . . . but not about rock music and not a biography . . . and not retro crap but it will have quite a lot of stuff about the past in it . . ."

Mark: "Yeah . . . that's right . . . yeah . . . we'll do that."

Mick: "Right . . . that's that sorted then... good . . . glad we have got that pinned down."

"I hate the countryside . . . so much"

"Get out of my city you mediocre pseuds
And take those red-tie bastards
Who put up the Olympic flag with you
They walk around leering at young girls in packs
Worse than any yobs"

('City Dweller')

1

The Glen Rothay Hotel, Rydal, Ambleside. July 22, 2002

A thick yellow cloud of hollow gaiety had settled over Manchester and Salford.

Bulbous, ugly, dripping with synthetic PR; a celebration clad in Nike . . . in yellow and purple Nike! The full horror of The Commonwealth Games had, after a painfully extensive 'build-up', finally engulfed the populace, hapless and cynical alike.

It was finally upon us.

It was inescapable.

Large garish signs appeared overnight, screaming from the edges of the M60 motorway, taunting the grid-locked thousands, punching across the hype . . . tempting . . . tempting . . . miserable commuters to taste the celebratory air!

Manchester had won.

Something.

An event.

A major event.

Must have been . . . S Club would perform at the opening ceremony.

We all felt so proud.

And worse . . .

Little yellow bears clad in purple sweatshirts could be purchased in the petrol stations . . . and, to our horror, some would already dangle from rear-view mirrors.

Local news bulletins saw ruddy faced locals – and many not so local – leaping and hallooing in sub-Olympian glee . . . in Castlefield, down to Salford Quays. And soon the yellow cloud would drift outwards, rolling through Prestwich, encircling Winter Hill.

"Look at the alkies in Prestwich village in track suits, pretending to be sporty . . ." Mark would muse, a few days later, as we drove slowly and rather tentatively back into the city.

Decades of wearying political and fiscal hype had preceded the moment. The fervour of Olympic aspiration had receded to a Commonwealth Games reality.

"Think Commonwealth," Mark had noted ironically, a month or so earlier as we planned our mini escape.

"Yeah," I agreed. "It would be a good time to get the fuck out of Manchester. Let's go for late July."

It had been a *great* time to get the fuck out of Manchester! A *great* idea, I thought . . . Mark thought. And the idea had arrived, as Mark sipped lager and I cradled some head-crushingly bad wine in a pub in Sedgeley Park, Salford. Actually, for once, we were not fogged by the blue cigarette haze, or hammered by the prevailing banter . . . we were actually sitting outside, talking about September 11 while watching aircraft lights spin around the city, dipping slowly down to Ringway on our left.

We had been talking, on and off tape, that night. As, indeed, we had, on so many occasions peppered across a span of 25 years. And many of them will bubble up in the forthcoming pages.

But, this time . . . this time we would shunt it out of context. No Prestwich pub. No backstage area. No television studio. No place where one might traditionally enjoy the company of Mark E. Smith.

"The Lake District."

I think I had said it. It was, to be honest, an easy option. A mere kick up the motorway for both of us. Mark, who seemed easily capable of securing a lift from his native Prestwich and myself, travelling separately, from unlovely Warrington . . . a two-hour shunt in a Punto.

I had known, also, that Mark had spent time in this unlikely location. He knew the Lakes. He didn't show great fondness for them, not in the way he would speak about his curiously beloved

Blackpool, but he knew them. Had played football there. Had spent time, he told me, in a hotel called Rothay Manor.

OK. So I cocked up!

Two weeks prior to our escape to Lakeland, I had spent yet another week in the locality, jogging daily through Troutbeck, lounging in a fellside cottage reading Mick Farren's *Give The Anarchist A Cigarette*. And then, while I was enjoying that particular slip back to Sixties counter-culture, a rumble in my mobile had indicated the arrival of Mark's distinctive disembodied voice.

"Can you book us into The Rothay Manor?" he had asked. "It's a bit posh, though. I will help you out if you can't afford it . . . get me a double room. My wife will come with me . . . should be great . . . got that? Rothay Manor? Look forward to it, Mick . . . think it will be rather good, hah haaa . . . let me know."

And I fell back into my book and, I sense, into my wine. A mental note etched into the back of my head. Rothay . . . something or other.

But not, alas, deeply enough. The next day I scoured Ambleside, looking for the Rothay something Hotel. Problem was . . . most of the hotels in Ambleside were Rothay, something or other.

"Ha," laughed Mark, as we drove around, glimpsing at the multitudinous alternatives. "Lord Rothay . . . Rothay House . . . Brathay . . . I'm surprised you even managed to get a hotel in Ambleside, let alone the right one."

Actually, I hadn't. The Glen Rothay is technically in Rydal. Stunning spot, hinged at the sharp end of Rydal Water, glancing across to the bad-tempered humps of The Langdales and tightly clasped by a sharp corner of the busy Keswick road. Beautiful spot indeed. But not so posh.

And not The Rothay Manor.

Somehow I knew it. The moment I wandered in, intent on prebooking. It seemed right to me lacking, as it did, the unfriendly starkness of higher grade hotels. Indeed, a pub stretched to a grand scale, full of dark wood angles and deep red upholstery. It reminded me of Mark, curiously, and I could already envisage him sitting in the corner, grimacing at the ruddy-faced cherry hikers, striking up a conversation on world politics with the lone but somewhat perceptive Scotsman who always seemed to wander into the frame when Mark was holding forth.

The Scotsman would, no doubt, be completely unaware of Mark's celebrity . . . a sharply honed instrument that would leave him invisible, cutting directly through the masses before coming to rest with someone who treated him with almost religious significance. Nevertheless, blessed with belligerence and perception in equally large doses – as, indeed, is Mark – my mythical Scotsman, would know there is something unusual, if not special, about this angular, darkly clad stranger.

Two weeks later, I found myself sitting on a rocky outcrop that punched into the glass of Rydal Water. Years of acquaintance had taught me that I was different from Mark. Indeed, he would mock me gently, in the past and during our stay, lapsing into a chorus of "Ohhhh Country Boooayyyyhhhh," whenever he noticed my face enlivening to the sight of, say, Ullswater settling in the mist or, more strikingly, when I would talk of rural days in various northern backwaters.

"OK Mick . . . I've had enough country . . . get me back to Ambleside," he would goad, bringing forth, to my mind at least, a line from his glorious hit of the mid-Nineties, 'M5'.

"But ahm city, born and bred, too many car fumes in mah head . . ."

I had heard him punch that line across so many times, in darkened cellar clubs buried deep in Mancunia . . . in cavernous student halls in Essex.

Never had a line seemed to fit so snugly with its perpetrator. And from Mark, the line would always leap from the murk of a late night PA, from a sound muddied by the prevailing swirl of adoring studenthood . . . muddied too, no doubt, by alcohol and things that would be settling in my mind. But Fall songs were always like that . . . a dense backdrop from which a Mark line would surge and connect in some strange way, in a way that always seemed quite unusually profound.

And now, after all these years, it had all twisted out of context. I wandered back to the hotel, to be greeted by the owner's jovial and warming banter.

"The other two have arrived," he said . . . and something in his eyes threw a question at me, as if he hadn't quite grasped what he was dealing with here. It was a problem that I could understand. Mostly, I guessed, the Glen Rothay would be filled with the Berghaus marauders, all proudly displaying their muck-caked Zamberlan boots and fuelled by talk of ferocious weather and Helvellyn heaven! Or indeed, besuited reps en route to Glasgow, devouring hearty breakfasts in vain attempts to blast away that encroaching hangover.

Not too many guests, I sensed, quite like Mark E. Smith and his wife, Elena, who added a further dimension to our mini adventure.

"They are in their room," he added, again flashing that quizzical look.

I hadn't known Elena. We had met, fleetingly, from opposite ends of Mark's stairs a few weeks previously. Still, she held a charm that bridged that divide and, immediately, I had decided that I liked her. Cynics may scoff, partly because Elena is quite orchidaceously beautiful, looking for all the world as if she had stepped from the set of a Visconti movie. Being Greek but schooled in Berlin, she had about her that fascinating air of European glamour; well dressed, but possessing that natural style that would shine through charwomen's clothing. When I met her for the second time, in the hotel room at the Glen Rothay, I could clearly see the thick sheen of mutual respect and admiration. It was immediately good to witness. She softened Mark's edges, burred his attack. Intelligent – obviously so – and perfectly at ease. Of course I liked her; all the more because when I last met Mark there was a place at his side, a gaping hole, that she now seemed to fill.

"Ar yeh all right then, Mick?" asked Mark, clasping me tightly, smiling a crooked smile and backing to the door. The suggestion was to drop down to the hotel bar, loosen ourselves before the first interview . . . a few beers for Mark . . . bad red wine for me.

Only the ponytailed lad behind the bar, black T-shirted, Levi'd and overtly attentive, knew the score, leaping to Mark's assistance with cigarette lighter poised. Later when, rather embarrassingly, I explained that I had left my key inside my room, our ponytailed friend offered to climb up ladders and break in for me. It was the first of a number of staggered sightings that would occur during the next few days. Indeed, that night, in a downstairs disco in Ambleside, as the three of us huddled beneath the attack of the music, punching through the atmosphere, I caught glances from a gang drinking opposite. Initially fearing the worst, I soon noticed that Mark . . . Mark, this strange, huddled figure in black, was the one attracting their attention. Within minutes they would be buying him drinks and bellowing the usual truncated compliments.

"All right Mark . . . great Mark . . . see you Mark . . . keep it up, Mark . . . wanna nuvver beer, Mark?"

They couldn't have been older than 20 . . . 21, which surprised me.

"Good lads," exclaimed Mark. "Squaddies . . . I always get on well with squaddies."

Later . . . hours later, I was still trying to grasp that connection. Twenty-one-year-old squaddies, I mused, surely wouldn't be Fall fans, despite the continuing efforts of John Peel on the World Service.

"Well, that's the fucking great thing about The Fall," Mark had explained. "Because I am with a young band now, we don't get a load of old saddoes like you at our gigs. In fact we got rid of most of 'em. They grew old and tired, wanting to hear 'Totally Wired'. It was something that I was always against. You move on. The Fall stay at the edge. Always have and still are."

Later that night, deep into the black of a Lakeland night, while I slept in a strange room, Mark left the hotel, intent on walking the two miles back to Ambleside on a fruitless trail of a packet of cigarettes. It was then that he saw them, down by the river, deep in the woods. Two figures cloaked in white. Druid-like, hovering. They saw Mark, too, and followed him for a while, before darting back into the black.

"They could just have been a couple of students having a laugh," I shrugged on hearing this tale.

"Yeah, right. Yeah, yeah, of course," agreed Mark, although I strongly sensed that he didn't really believe this.

I believed him, though. I believed Mark. He offered the story almost sheepishly, as if expecting me to begin wondering about the amount of Jamesons we had consumed during our first lengthy interview, earlier in the day. It had been a curious day, really. Even those moments in the Ambleside Thai restaurant seemed . . . yes . . . curious indeed. Mark had shunned the beckoning Bistro and had, I rather strongly sensed, set his heart on rather more British fayre, something served up rapidly in one of the local fish'n'chip shops, all unfortunately closed. Though no fan of the stuff myself – having not touched a chip for several years – I would have been happy to be able to oblige. The compromise was a light calorie Thai meal which, though profoundly unsatisfying on any nutritious level, saw the three of us – Mark, Elena and I – touch common ground. Then came the cigarette incident. Three times, the waiter, hovering in increasing anxiety, explained that, "This is a no smoking restaurant sir," to which, Mark grunted, sniffed . . . proffered, "Oh yeah . . . all right," and stubbed his cigarette out.

Five minutes later, with Elena casting nervous glances to the kitchen, another one was lit . . . and so forth . . . and so on. It was curious because it wasn't an act of defiance at all. In fact, Mark was genuinely courteous – as I had always found him, actually – and, perhaps, ever so mildly embarrassed. It was just instantaneous . . . habitual. No real offence meant . . . none taken really. At one point, as Mark started to waft smoke away from my eyes, in respect of my non-smoking position, I thought. I noticed him glance towards the waiter with curiosity etched in his features. We had, after all, paid for a meal, and somewhat over the odds. No other diners fell within those mild smoke clouds. Like Mark and Elena, I had met, on numerous occasions, those whose revoltingly PC attitude towards smoking verged on the hysterical.

It would happen again . . . and again in Ambleside, two days later.

This time I missed the incident.

This is as Mark saw it.

"That fuckin' cunt . . . I mean. He grabbed his kid and said, 'Ooooh, you aren't goin' to smoke, how awwwful!' I mean, what a twat. He fucking backed straight into me as well, like he had no idea that someone else might be there. And he had his baseball cap on fucking backwards. Notice, I didn't say anything about *that*!"

Well, I was definitely with Mark on this one. People wearing backwards baseball caps! I thought, at that moment, and for the first time in 15 years, I fancied a fag! (Note to editor . . . must change that line for US publication.)

The next day hung in a damp mood, as days in Cumbria often do. I sat alone, at breakfast, chatting to a rep en route to Glasgow from Portsmouth, to two hikers and four Americans. All this was conducted in the library-like silence that usually prevails in British hotel breakfast rooms. I almost hoped that Mark and Elena wouldn't join our little throng. And, of course, they didn't. It would have been a savage cultural tug, that's for sure.

"And how are your *friends*?" enquired the hotelier, in the manner of Donald Pleasance.

"OK, I guess . . ." I shrugged.

The one with the ponytail hovered nearby. I sense that he wanted to ask a question but, fearing that he might break hotel protocol, he sauntered wearily into the kitchen.

To be honest, I didn't quite know what to do with Mark and Elena during the day. This was truly out of context. The time for interview would dawn but surely not before four-ish. A long day loomed.

I decided to take them to Keswick, tripping through the swarmed-about prettiness of Grasmere on the way. I had seen Tom Paulin, the poet and bizarre reactionary, unwittingly entertaining, though likeable as a crumple-shirted *Late Review* pundit . . . I had seen him in Grasmere, firing out a reading, two weeks previously. Mentioning this as I drove by Wordsworth's intensely touristy Dove Cottage provoked little reaction.

"I don't watch television Mick," proffered Mark. "Don't know who he is . . . don't read papers either. None of them."

This being the heart of literary Cumbria, I mention Melvyn Bragg, as one does.

"Oh yeah . . . you know what. They wanted to do a feature on

The Fall for *The South Bank Show*. It was a nightmare. They sent out this huge, thick pile of questions in the name of research. Stuff like, what colour are your father's eyes . . . and which members of the band do you get on with the best. All for Bragg . . . he wanted to tag along . . . kind of shadow me for a while. Can you fuckin' imagine that. Salman Rushdie was going to do somethin' too . . . I mean, fuckin' hell. Shoved it in the bin, I did. People kept telling me that it would have been such a good thing for The Fall . . . but we have never cared about that kind of thing. If it doesn't feel right, don't do it. That was always the rule with The Fall, no matter what the consequences."

True. Had I not known Mark, then I would have put this down to empty braggadocio. But I had seen it many times. Like this.

Why have you never done *Later With Jools Holland*, Mark? Have they never asked you? Always wanted to see The Fall on that.

"Never fuckin' appealed, Mick. You know. I wouldn't wish to put the lads through that. It's that musician thing . . . all getting together and jamming, you know. I never had any truck with musicians. I have never had musicians in The Fall. I don't like them as people. And that's why The Fall were formed originally, to get away from that. I mean . . . we have had classically trained musicians in The Fall. But they always had to unlearn their stuff. I know they found this really refreshing, after years of doing that carefully measured musical learning. No . . . fuck all that. Fucking musos all getting together. Those people have nothing to offer. The Fall have never been about that and any member who showed signs of it was fuckin' out. And that's why we have survived. That's why The Fall are still different and why people see something that is genuinely special about The Fall. It's just a pity that some of the younger bands haven't seen this. I see them all the time, making the same old obvious mistakes. Wanting to be in some scene. I think . . . also . . . you find that strange people seem to connect with me. Whether the squaddies or just some old guy in a pub. They are people who are not represented by the whole celeb stuff . . . they are far too intelligent for that . . . they are that sussed. In Salford especially, people are that sussed. They know what The Fall are about and they respect it. Fuckin' marvellous. Ordinary people, plumbers and that, can be very, very clever . . . they can see the surreal . . . all that *stuff*. That's where we have always been."

And so to Keswick . . . and all that implies. The pace drops, the average age rises . . . the tourist element alters. Plenty of Berghaus and Lowe Alpine . . . for sure. But something else, too.

Mark seems to like Keswick.

"Yeah, it's OK . . . let's stop . . . park over there."

'Over there' was actually an unwelcoming private driveway flanked by severe 'no parking' signs.

Later Elena would admit, "Mark and cars are not quite on the same level. It's just one of those things. He is the brightest person I have ever known. But he doesn't understand cars, or driving, or roads, or parking."

Finally opting for the town centre car park, we were soon wandering somewhat uneasily around the town, Mark pausing to purchase a sculpted rabbit for Elena, to admire the Cornish pasty shop, and to purchase a bottle of Lagavulin single malt. All of which might seem fairly mundane and, perhaps, not the stuff to be crammed into the opening pages of a conventional rock biography. Except, as I am sure you will have grasped by now, little sense of the conventional will drip through these pages . . . and quite right too, as so little of it drips through Mark's life or the story of The Fall (much of which, frankly, is a rather dull train of musicians adding two penneth of disgruntlement into the pot). What's more, The Fall fans of my acquaintance, and I am on grunting terms with many of them, would be rather intrigued to know that Mark prefers the traditional meat and potato pasty to the cheesy ones . . . and, undoubtedly, he would hold little truck with the veggie options that would better suit my particular diet.

But that was Keswick High Street and, before too long, the teeming pub had been located. This, too, remains an interesting factor because, despite the fact that it had been overwhelmingly commandeered by retirees from Lancashire who, having sold the family soft furnishing business in Accrington, had opted to spend the remainder of their lives dillying around in some pebble-dashed bungalow.

I had no real evidence of this theory . . . but, nevertheless, write with confidence.

Mark agreed . . . to a point.

"Yeah . . . many of them but there are still a lot of younger ones. I mean, what the fuck are they doing here? Why aren't they out at fucking work? Look at them . . . it's the same in every town in fuckin' Britain . . . people out spending money all the time . . . never fucking actually working . . . never actually 'making' anything. I mean, I work, fucking hard and so do you Mick . . . I know that. But most of this country isn't. It's going to all fucking collapse one day. It happened to the fucking Romans, man. That huge society just became a mass of false pleasure. Just bland hedonism . . . and then one day . . . it just fucking goes. And that's what is going to happen here."

"Yer damn right there mate," said the Scotsman. See? I knew he would pop up soon. He had been sitting, alone I think, observing the clientele. Knew he would crop up sooner or later. He didn't disappoint, either, loudly casting his perception of the world around for the benefit of anyone within earshot. But he was, naturally, keen to grasp the instant affinity he seemed to share with Mark.

"Yer right . . . it's goin' to all collapse . . . but not in my lifetime . . . I'm retired . . . I'm OK."

"You just got enough money to sit here drinkin' each day," stated Mark.

"Aye, right enough . . . not bad is it?"

I think I stretched Mark's patience, just a little, by pushing the Punto up and out of Keswick and along an old favoured scenic detour, taking in Ullswater and Glenridding, the Kirkstone Pass and Troutbeck before eventually sliding back into Ambleside.

Back in the hotel, amid the swirl of cigarette smoke in my room – which I didn't mind in the least – and cradling two large shots of the Lagavulin procured in Keswick, Mark told me a great deal about the early unfoldings of The Fall. Intriguing it was, too, to hear it from this direct angle for a young version of myself hovered in the darker shadows of the story, and there was much I didn't see.

It was probably the best interview we have ever stumbled into. With Mark, mischievous as ever, stretching the tale and pulling back sharply, hurtling in an uninvited attack. Good fun, sharp tactics.

"I will tell you stuff that I have never told anyone . . . mainly 'cos I trust you," he said, huffing strong, casting me one of those wicked looks and laughing . . . tugging on the cigarette and laughing again.

Sitting temptingly on my bedside table, the magnetic allure of *The Wire* magazine . . . not just any old copy of *The Wire* magazine, complete with its teasing balance of intellectualism and hearty memorabilia . . . but *The Wire* magazine from May 2002, with the leering pasty face of John Oswald shining from the cover and, of rather more relevance, a five page article written by Simon Ford, destined to tumble into part of a diligent Fall book that would skim around the edges with, it might be noted, considerable prowess though not, of course, getting to the heart of the matter: Mark E. Smith.

It would have been more elegant, everyone reasoned, not to have mentioned this at all. But I found it difficult to let it go . . . especially as, until this hotel room meeting, Mark had steadfastly refused to peruse the said article.

"Do you really want to show me that, Mick?"

"You don't have to read it, Mark . . . I'll chuck it away if you want . . . but I just thought you might like to sneak a look . . ."

And, indeed, Mark sneaked a look. Just one look. A speed scan and then, holding it away in disgust, offered:

"NO . . . no . . . take it away . . . take it out of the room. I don't want to read what those people – early Fall band members – have to say. It's not relevant to anyone . . . it's boring . . . and it's also a load of lies. That bit I just read . . . about me an' Una being at St John's College.

"I was working as a clerk, in town. Then I went to St John's College for about three weeks, doing A levels. Una wasn't there. She wasn't at St John's College at all. That just isn't true.

"They are all fucking liars, you know. They all are. It wasn't like that, at all. Una never went to any fucking college as far as I can recall. All this 'Mark and I' shit. What is she fucking talking about? I find it really fucking sad, you know, that people suddenly start clinging to The Fall after these fucking years, like it was the only important thing that has ever happened to them. I mean, I'm proud of the early Fall, as it happens, but I have done a fuckin' lot since then. And so have they. I'm not talking musically. Just their lives . . . pity they have to dig back to telling lies about that time. Ahh . . . I can't fucking read it. It's like Spinal fucking Tap. All that lot, Tony Friel, Martin, Una . . . all saying how great I was . . . I just got rid of the bastards . . . it's horrible . . . horrible . . . horrible . . . promise you will throw that away!!!"

OK. So I kinda promised.

And all was cool.

With whisky.

And wine.

And beer.

And later . . .

We had a curious moment.

When the three of us hobbled across the road.

And down the dip.

To the stream . . . with Rydal expanding to the north . . . we stopped and gazed . . . longingly.

"Stuff of poetry, Mark,"

I had said.

But he was shrugging . . . looked uncomfortable . . . uncertain.

I hadn't really seen him out of context.

Out of town. Out of the city!

Apart from the Deeply Vale Festival . . . but that was different.

And drugged into lunacy . . . but more of that later.

"Yeah, well . . . whatever . . . very nice, Mick, very nice er . . . er if you want to stand here, looking at the green . . . fine . . . we'll be in the bar though, right?"

"Yeah . . . right!"

I stood for a while. Dreaming into the glass lake. Soaking in the apparently unhealthy countryside . . . when a dark presence appeared silently beside me . . .

Like a stealth bomber . . . with a ponytail . . .

His face adorned with that half smile of embarrassment.

The kind a fan gets . . .

(I tell you . . . it would drive me nuts if, wherever I would travel, people would keep approaching me, armed with that same smile . . .)

"Do you know your mate? Yes? Is it . . ."

"Is it who?"

"Is it Mark . . . thingy? Him from The Fall? Mark?"

Sighing . . . "Yes . . . do you want to come across and say 'Hello'?"

Horror creased his features.

"No . . . ooh. No . . . no . . . no . . . God no! . . . Not at all. Just wondered . . . that's all."

It was, Mark had swiftly decided, about time we sampled the hotel cuisine. This immediately made me rather nervous, knowing, that is, Mark's apparent dislike of elements of the bourgeois. I had, however, wondered about attempting to sample that nice little church–cum–bistro thing in Ambleside. Would have been tricky though, and the signs had not been that great when Mark had opined, "Am not fucking goin' in *there* mate . . ."

So it was down to the hotel . . . shabbily lush and comfortable . . . hardly bourgeois, though friendly and not without aspirations to cuisine . . . and Mark, to my astonishment, settling down to devour a plate of mussels . . . with myself and Elena lagging in vegetarian options. In case you are beginning to wonder about the apparently inconsequential minutiae I am conveying at this moment – I had a mushroom risotto, by the way – I feel it necessary to point out that this rather pleasant little hotel scene served to precede one of the few moments during the 25 years that I have known Mark E. Smith where our communication had crumbled through, I sense, misunderstanding on my part. Never happened before, frankly. Nor was it, in any way, shrouded in any kind of antagonism. It was me, wholly misreading the situation and plunging into an alcohol fuelled confusion.

For two hours, the conversation had bounced along with effortless zeal. Indeed, now that we had snapped out of 'interview mode', it was a delight to usher Elena into the heart of the chat . . . a task to which she wholeheartedly applied herself, asking a variety of questions on all manner of subjects from a spectrum fringed by English football hooliganism on one extreme to the Californian based spiritual 'master' Maharaji on the other.

Only when the rather thornier subject of Blackpool emerged did the conversation darken a little. Not that I have anything against Mark's love of Blackpool at all . . . and found his desire to take his mum on holiday there quite touching . . . it's just that, ever since I spent a frustrating evening failing to succumb to sleep while crunching around on a bed topped with standard blanket before a midnight knock on the door preceded an enquiry into whether or not I wished to partake in the hotel's 'famous 4 am curry' . . . ever since that moment, I have been less than fond of the hotels on Blackpool's South Shore.

Which is why I told Mark, "I'll drop you off in Blackpool if you like . . . but you don't want to go to the South Shore . . ."

And just as I was about to explain about the blanket and the 4 am curry, Mark responded with:

"Been round the fucking world Mick . . . I don't need you to tell me which shore to stay at."

Fair enough, I reasoned, secretly wondering how Mark would feel when that blanket starts to crunch! But . . . no worries. I departed dutifully to the bar . . . and, on my return, a curious thing happened. As I sat, cautiously placing the drinks on the table, Mark and Elena silently rose from their seats and filed stealthily past me, offering not a single utterance. Had I offended them? Surely not, I reasoned. Although there had been blocks of years when our paths had failed to meet, those 25 years had seen a tight and enjoyable friendship forming . . . which, indeed, is represented in the flickering core of this book . . . so what was this about? It was an intriguing moment . . . knowing Mark, knowing that it is always better to 'go with the flow' – which is exactly what is about to take place within these pages – I immediately sensed that I had misread the signs, and that Mark and Elena would be waiting for me in the adjoining room. Now, I have no way of knowing whether it was the alcohol fog, or my failing eyesight or, indeed, hearing loss . . . but a swift shufti around The Glen Rothay failed to deliver me to the elusive couple. Five minutes later, face down on my bed, I fell into a slumber . . . convinced that I had somehow pushed the conversation too far . . . surely not so sensitive about Blackpool?

A huge rap on the door at 3 am convinced me otherwise. Though I felt unable to respond, paralysed and marginally conscious as I was – and dreaming about a Fall gig at Stockport College in 1980, when Mark had rather gloriously informed an obnoxious member of The Distractions to "Fuck off and learn to play . . ." – such sweet memories – I failed to respond. I don't know . . . it transpired that Mark and Elena had been waiting for me to travel with them – via taxi, presumably – to Ambleside.

"Are you OK Mick?" quizzed Elena, gently, as the morning dawned.

"It's just that Mark was worried where you had got to last night. He was upset . . . he thought he might have offended you!"

Manchester City Centre. December 22, 1940

The portents were bad, the city black, the anxiety heavy. All around Manchester, deep into the Lancashire conurbation . . . the ground had already thundered frequently as a most uneasy Christmas period dawned in terrible uncertainty.

The night blitz had already arrived.

As 1940 rumbled to a dreadful climax, the ports of Britain shuddered beneath waves of Luftwaffe attack. In Bristol, on December 2, over 100 tons of explosives, some 22,000 incendiary bombs, were unleashed, reducing civic buildings to rubble, but, incredibly, failing to block the main port and factories of Avonmouth. Southampton and Coventry also famously faced the seemingly unstoppable onslaught.

Liverpool, Britain's most important port on the west coast, with installations stretching six miles, with whole dark masses of power stations and dry docks at Birkenhead and across the Mersey, proved an even more appealing target for Goering's Luftwaffe. Indeed, beyond the obvious lure of London, Liverpool was the number one target, perfectly placed, as it was, to receive vital goods from "friends across the Atlantic". Liverpool was hit frequently between September and the end of December, literally lighting the way for two sharp attacks on Manchester. Throughout this period, Mancunians and Salfordians scampered nightly through soot blackened streets, gathering for staunch, though tentative camaraderie in the lavish peppering of pubs.

"Any night, now," was the cry. "Any night now."

For three elastic months, Manchester and Salford were gripped by the terror of this expectancy. As both cities contained many factories locked in the ferocious struggle to produce all manner of war materials, and at great speed, and as the area boasted the heart of the northern print industry, the threat of serious attack was nothing less than a bleak inevitability.

But the anxiety stretched into the winter, and began to warp into an unlikely braggadocio. The pubs – Salford, in particular, was lavishly furnished with pubs – remained full of defiant inebriation. Not, of course, exactly *jovial* inebriation, for flippancy is unwise, even after eight pints, when the true horror of warfare genuinely rumbles nightly in the distance. It wasn't easy, in Manchester, knowing that Liverpool was taking the full weight of Luftwaffe fury.

"That's the fuckin' truth of it, innit, Mick? When the media talks about the Blitz . . . when the Blitz is depicted in films, or even newsreels, all you ever see is cheery fuckin' cockneys in underground stations . . . they never show the full horror . . . of hospitals being blown to pieces . . . they never show what it was really like."

The true horror of war was real enough, if you lived in a city centre, or in any blitzkrieg tempting conurbation. But just a few miles away say, in Ashton-under-Lyne, tucked into the Pennine foothills, the blitz was to be viewed from vantage points, not in any kind of voyeuristic manner, but in curiosity spiced by the excitement of genuine terror. But even these people, in Ashton, Oldham and Rochdale, were not necessarily privy to the true horrors of what exactly transpired.

But in Salford, they knew.

Manchester was, as it happens, the last of the large industrial cities to be attacked by the Luftwaffe and it suffered the long anticipated *'double raid'* on the successive nights of December 22 and 23, 1940.

In the initial raid, 375 aircraft each dropped an average of one ton of high explosives, backed up by 37,000 fire bombs. Flares had been dropped to mark the target zone although, with gruesome irony, the

German aircrews were helped by the fires still burning in Liverpool after the previous night's attack.

The colour of the city changed violently. The black night of a Manchester December flashed into blinding whiteness as the flares lit the sky above the city, from Ancoats to Stretford, from Hulme to deepest Salford.

Then, with equal violence, white turned to red as the incendiaries took hold and the clouds reflected the crimson of glowing fires, 400 in total, surging through the city centre and blistering outwards, towards and into Stretford. The damage, particularly to the factories and commercial premises, was heavy. At its most dramatic, at about 9.30 pm on December 22, the dark huddle of buildings leading from the corner of Deansgate down to Victoria Station were hit by a ferocious wave of incendiaries. As many of Manchester's large fire-fighting force had been deployed to help the continuing blaze in Liverpool, they were caught light-handed and fires raged from Piccadilly, Market Street, The Shambles and around Manchester Cathedral, rising up and along the arch of Shude Hill. A grotesque horseshoe of fire rampaged through the lavish scattering of pubs, punching horribly through the walls of Cheetham's Hospital.

During two pre-Christmas nights, Manchester's heart was broken, albeit temporarily. War had arrived and it wasn't anything like any newsreel that had ever been seen and wasn't like anything that appeared in any newspaper for the time and it wasn't anything like the WW2 that would later occupy the pages of history books. It was sharp, black and satanic. It was lavishly indiscriminate. It was insane. It contained no trace of romance and it embedded itself into the psyche of Manchester where it remains, deeply etched into the creased eyes of ageing Deansgate drinkers. It remains deep in the shadows of a city that would suffer industrial collapse and commercial and cultural resurgence 50 years later.

Mark E. Smith: "Me granddad Smith was totally great, in a way. He was the opposite of me dad, Jack Smith. My granddad was a draft dodger really, whereas me dad was a Sergeant Major during the war, so there was always a conflict going on. But all this boiled down to a story that happened in December 1940, when my dad did the decent thing and joined up. It was a strange moment for them both, because they had never really gone out together drinking, which was always a shame. But, at this point, my granddad decided to take me dad out for a drink . . . he took him into town, y'know, where Marks & Spencer is now. I was always told it was on Christmas Eve but it must have been a couple of days earlier. My dad was really gobsmacked about this gesture. He thought it was fantastic. Out with his dad . . . such a rare thing, really. I think my dad thought he was set for a long session, going until closing time. But it wasn't like that at all. After about an hour in the pub, me granddad said: 'You bloody idiot, joining up! You are just trying to impress your girlfriend' (my mam).

"So after about two pints my granddad stood up, belligerent as ever and said, 'That's it . . . I want to go home now.'

"I mean this really hurt me dad. This was the first time they had ever had a drink together, and he was leaving just like that. Me dad said, 'You bloody old git. I am going away to war and you take me out and, after two pints, you want to go home at 9 pm . . . you fucking old bastard.'

"But me granddad just walked straight out of the pub, no apologies, nothing. He was a stubborn old git, really . . . which is where I get it from, I think. My dad sat in the pub and stewed for about five minutes. Eventually, furious, he stood up and ran out after me granddad, trying to get him to come back to the pub. What happened was, he saw my granddad getting on a bus out of Victoria and me dad tore after it and jumped on the bus just in time.

"And it was at that precise moment that the Luftwaffe came and plastered that particular pub . . . the whole fucking place went up. But it's so fucking ironic . . . if me granddad hadn't been the bastard he was, I would never have been here."

2

Tesco Store, Prestwich, Manchester. April 1, 2003, 6.30 pm

I was nervous.

Doesn't happen that often.

Hasn't happened with a pop star for a long time.

Being nervous before an interview, that is.

Not that I exactly flit from pop star interview to pop star interview these days.

Not that I ever did, frankly.

Well, not that many.

And, even then, interviewing the guitarist from The Drones.

On a Number 53 bus.

Wasn't so intimidating.

Though I was scared.

There were bigger moments than that.

I don't have them any more.

In fact, it's years since I have downed champagne in the New York Hilton.

With Bob Geldof.

Years.

Those moments don't happen anymore.

And not in Warrington, where I live.

Mark says that 'Warry' is better than Stockport.

Which is where I come from.

"Warry's only four stops from Prestwich."

He says.

And people don't wear deerstalkers.

In Warrington.

They don't in Stockport, either . . . though Mark once seemed to think they did.

Anyway . . . this is beside the point.

The fact is that I do not meet any pop stars anymore.

But even if I did . . . still . . . even if I did, I wouldn't be nervous.

Not now.

Couldn't give a monkey's anymore, to be honest.

Pop stars! Hah! I am 47, for God's sake.

Though I don't look it.

As it happens, no pop star lays waiting for the snap of my Dictaphone this evening. No weary "You are the tenth journo of the day, let's get it over with . . ." awaits to greet me, as I trundle aimlessly around Tesco, my head spinning with a barrage of 'must asks'.

Although I was on familiar territory . . . increasingly so, as I exited the store and guided my car down through Prestwich to the district known as Sedgeley Park. Normally this would be the preamble to a meeting with Mark which will swiftly carry to a local hostelry . . . and such meetings will, fittingly I believe, make up a large percentage of this book . . . naturally.

But not on this night.

And I really was . . . curiously . . . nervous.

On this night I would meet Mrs Irene Smith for the first time. Mark's mum. Curious thing, this. When I mentioned the meeting, rather casually, to a couple of acquaintances who were reasonably well versed in matters Fall . . . they both responded in exactly the same way. "Mark's mum? He has a mum? You can't imagine him having a mum, can you?"

(And another aspect about this does actually strike me as slightly odd, as I have been trundling back and forth . . . from Stockport to Prestwich . . . latterly from Warrington to Prestwich, for . . . it terrifies me to note . . . nearly 25 years, although there were periods . . . years in places . . . where our paths would not cross, either literally or culturally. Perhaps it was remiss of me to allow such absences to take place. However, it is, I have recently discovered, a Fall thing! Long-term Fall fans often tell of 'dark years', more often than not following a marriage or period in exile, when their lives were not punctuated by the release of new Fall product. But Fall fans who drift from the pack in a hail of "Oh, I've given up on all that music stuff . . ." do tend to return to the fold, two or three albums later; quite possibly never to return to the missing area. Arguably this is simply due to the band's enduring longevity . . . long-term fans have passed through several stages of life and yet do like to find themselves back in some darkened cellar club, 15 years on. The situation is especially poignant because the story of The Fall is far from the traditional rock'n'roll young buck to big books tale. No trashed Radisson Edwardians litter their back pages and, for the most part, the influx of financial splendour is conspicuous only by its absence.

Always different . . . always the same. A friend of mine, balding and jovial, works by day in the financial industry and spends his dubiously grasped earnings travelling the world to catch The Fall. Fanatical, he is. (Mark, naturally, would loathe this . . . should they ever meet.) And yet, to this day, he has never heard *Shift-Work*, *Middle Class Revolt* or *The Unutterable*. "There is no point in hearing them in retrospect," he states, inferring that you have to be there to live the moment. If an album is missed, it is best to be allowed to drift into some individual abyss. I quite agree. While I have always been happy to return to, say, *Live At The Witch Trials* or *Bend Sinister* . . . a Fall album is something that sits in a particular point of time and, when revisited, evokes that particular feel.)

And then there's Mark's mum.

Unseen by me.

In a Prestwich semi.

For 25 years.

And so I parked my car – meekly, the Punto – betwixt a raggedy oversized Ford plucked from the Seventies, and a gleaming Aston Martin. It was a fitting mix . . . typical of a disparate area where not only religions and cultures mix in reasonable if distant harmony, but 'money' and 'lack of' have also maintained a respectful relationship, often on the same street, often in adjoining semis.

Tesco Store, Prestwich, Manchester. April 1, 2003, 6.30 pm

I was greeted with a smile.

And by a mum.

You would know this, even if you were merely calling on some optimistic door-to-door mission. Somebody's mum, at the door. A winning smile. A welcome. I was ushered in, amid a flurry of greetings, and a splurge of words, immediately indicating an unusually active mind. Irene Smith, settled for the evening in dressing gown and slippers, turning the telly down to a soft purr, watching me from the sofa . . . and familiar too, breaking off from occasional sentences to lean forward, catch my eye and break into an endearing laugh . . . familiar and very, very . . . Mark!

And like Mark . . . and like this book . . . and like The Fall . . . and like Mark's life and, perhaps, everybody's life . . . the questions in my lap represent a rigid format that can't possibly match the flow of words. Irene Smith wishes to talk about Mark . . . and about lots of other things. I nudge, here and there . . . and gently interject, but am happy to succumb to a benevolent stubbornness, almost entirely in keeping with the time-honoured interview technique of her son.

Of course.

It could be any meeting.

With any mum.

Anywhere.

Except for statements such as this: "I noticed there is something on television about that Leigh Bowery. When is that on? I like that Leigh Bowery. Nice . . . very nice."

Which might strike you as a trifle unusual.

As would: "I remember when Mark brought that Alanah around. Did you know her . . . or . . . him? Alan Pillay was his name . . . did you know him . . . before he became her?"

"Yes . . ." I replied. "Have taken tea with Alan Pillay . . . or Alanah. (Noted alternating sex comedienne, diva, quality drag act, disco songstress, occasionally in the recording company of Gary Clail, flittering in and out of the Comic Strip gang, known to physically assault tabloid hacks in London scene clubs . . . powerful but kind . . . and, like Mark . . . psychic . . . once saw a man, standing behind me . . . handing me roses . . . thought it was my late father . . .)

"I liked Alanah. Mark and Kay, I think, used to stay with Alan Pillay in London in the early days. When I was about to meet him, Mark warned me . . . said he might be a bit emotional because of the steroids . . . but I remember him being very sweet."

And, naturally, Michael Clarke!

"Oh yes . . . Michael Clarke . . . the dancer. I remember my husband and a lot of our friends were here, watching it on television when Michael Clarke was dancing to The Fall. And the neighbours were watching . . . it was very exciting because it was the first time that many of them had seen The Fall . . . and then it came on and Michael Clarke was dancing with no bottom in his trouser . . . Didn't know where to look – and then, in realisation – Oh yes, perhaps I did . . . ha haaahh. It was a bit embarrassing. Don't know what the neighbours thought. But I like people like that. Michael Clarke was very nice . . . it's funny but this is something that I noticed from way back when I was very young. People would warn me about the drunks in pubs . . . but drunks are often very nice people. Very sensitive and caring people. Much more than many pious disapprovers, don't you think?"

I told her that yes . . . I do think exactly that. And from this rather unexpected launch, the conversation hurled back to childhood days. There were drunks then . . . apparently . . . in Fleetwood, where Irene was evacuated during the war. Where, pulled from the black realities of a life on the edge of a blitz city, Irene was cosseted and plunged into a quiet life of unreal simplicity, of respectful subservience, a confusing break from childhood normality . . . surreal and dreamlike . . . the memories would still linger. A few of them . . . just a few moments captured within the book on her coffee table, in which evacuees would offer their memories. Just a few. Just a few teasing, tempting memories . . . just a few!

Irene Smith: "When you think that those children were only five or six and, well, to leave their parents at that age, it would be unthinkable today, wouldn't it? I went to Fleetwood, and it was fine . . . there were some very good people, some very kind people who took in evacuees. By and large they are warm memories, nice memories, which is odd, isn't it? We didn't have any idea about what was going on. How could we have any concept of war? It was like a big holiday but, having said that, you were plunged into a different world. It was very, very odd and very unnatural. Mostly, very good. Very good memories. But there were also problems. At Fleetwood there were the trawler men . . . and they were often drunk. Very drunk . . . very drunk and fighting and lots of things like that. Also, there would be a lot of stories about that. About the behaviour of the trawler men and nasty things that went on. I never really saw it and it was never reported in the press, of course, but it carried back by word of mouth. My mother heard of it and she became very worried . . . well, you would be, wouldn't you? It was only years later that I realised how difficult this must have been for her. Imagine if your six-year-old is taken away from you. Imagine how difficult that would be . . . doesn't bear thinking about, does it?"

And, again, came that beguiling smile. Irene Smith, huddled in her dressing gown, smiling and looking to the ceiling, as if ushering the memories back down . . . then smiling again and turning to me.

"But you don't want to hear about me, do you?"

I told her that, to be honest, it was fascinating and yes . . . if that is the way the flow would go – and this book is all about the flow – then yes, I did . . . I did!

She smiled again, only half in belief. I understood her reticence and respected it. Mark had always been extremely careful to keep barriers in place around his family, allowing them to continue to filter happily within the Prestwich community . . . vital to their existence, in many respects. One of the definitive upsides of The Fall's unique position in the scheme of things would mean that, despite a few notable exceptions – when writing 'Powder Keg', which seemingly predicted the Manchester IRA bombing and the famously explosive time when he was bizarrely charged with assaulting his girlfriend and band member, Julia Nagle in the States – the band existence had continued to roll along beyond tabloid exposure . . . and beyond tabloid pressure. Only the *Manchester Evening News*, though ferociously devoured in the community, would occasionally breach that barrier, and then only softly, as news would filter gently into the daily 'Diary'.

Respectful of all this, I helped guide the conversation towards Mark's childhood . . . in fact, I tried to hold the subject over his schooldays but, as I have done so many times with Mark, decided to sit back and allow Irene full rein, to travel where the memories would tug!

Irene: "The thing with Mark is that he can be very stubborn. His father was just the same. Mark's granddad was very Victorian and that meant that they would expect the women to stay at home, do all the housework. Be subservient, really. It got a bit weaker with my husband and then weaker still with Mark. Down the generations that aspect tends to fade slowly away. But the Smiths are very stubborn and, I think, less able to change with the trends. There was something inbuilt. I wouldn't call it 'hardness' although it sometimes might strike people that way. But it would be considered old-fashioned now. Yes, I am sure it would.

"But it is still in Mark, to some extent. There is no doubt about that. I recognise that streak all the time. Not in a bad way now, he is very respectful and very loving of women . . . he is very passionate, Mark. He used to spend hours gazing at women in photos but in a loving kind of way. It's hard to describe. But there is still a bit of his granddad in him, there is no doubt about that. The Smith family . . . yes, it is very much within Mark and you can see it in the way he goes about running the band.

"He was the only boy, you see. We had three girls and one boy. Mark was the oldest. He was our first-born. It was very different to when I was a child. I was one of 10 children. Nine girls and one boy. So when I took Mark around to my mother's when he was young, they would call him "the Boy". They would say, "The Boy's here . . ." It gave him a kind of unique status, I think. It seemed strange for a boy to go around there . . . a place that had been so full of girls, really, so Mark was a bit different. It gave him a unique status. I think that everyone was fascinated with him in a way they weren't perhaps with the girls. Because, the thing is that the girls were the norm and Mark was . . . well, he was different, wasn't he?

So I think he always had a slight sense of being different from the crowd, partly because of him being a boy. Possibly this made him ever so slightly distant. You know. He had that air of being a bit different and still has. And that is possibly where all that began. His father never really had that. His father always seemed to be . . . and to want to be very normal. That was the thing, wasn't it? To fit in. To be ordinary. Nowadays nobody wants to be normal. But, back then, everybody did."

Mark: "I was born in Broughton. My mum's maiden name is Brownhill. She was listening to 'Stranger In Paradise' when I was born.

"We moved when I was about five or six, up to Prestwich. I have three sisters, Barbara, Caroline and Suzanne . . . Caroline is the youngest . . . I'm the oldest.

"They were a big family, the Brownhills. Me mam has eight sisters and one brother. As regards the family, I can't keep up with it, to be honest. It's just a waste of time. Every time I go into Broughton . . . If I go into a bank or something I will find that I am related to a quarter of the staff. They came from Broughton but many moved out, all over the place . . . Ashton, Moston . . . some even in Warrington. Not me though. I stay around here, Prestwich and Sedgeley Park, because I like it. Not because of roots. I do have all these aunties . . . can't even remember all their names . . . and they have all got kids. They are everywhere . . . but I am not much of a family person, to be honest.

"I had a very happy childhood, really. I just got left alone, which suited me completely. Me mam and dad were too busy looking after my sisters to be able to take much notice of me. I could basically do what I wanted. But this was a positive thing. I didn't run riot or anything. We lived down by The Cliff . . . Manchester United's training ground, in Broughton.

"My dad was from Higher Broughton. The Cliff . . . the front of the Cliff was precisely where his family were from. Me mam was from Lower Broughton. My dad was called Jack. Jack Smith. He was a plumber. He was a Lance Corporal in the army, going in at the end of the war, really. That's where the story of him and me granddad came in."

Irene: "Mark the eldest, then Barbara, then Suzanne – Suzanne, not Susan . . . I got that name from a magazine . . . actually, we weren't going to call Mark . . . Mark! In the hospital he actually had a tag on him with John Malcolm on it. That is what we decided would be his name . . . yes, John Malcolm on it . . . oooh, do you know I am not sure I have told Mark this. But I had some Jehovah's Witnesses come round one day, like they do and they were talking to me. I wasn't going to be that way inclined but, nevertheless, I found them so interesting . . . and I was thinking about this in the hospital and it suddenly dawned on me that I wanted a Biblical name . . . well, I suppose John is a Biblical name . . . but it suddenly didn't seem right. So I told the nurse, 'Hey, take that tag off him . . . I have changed my mind. I want Mark Edward.' I don't know . . . anyway . . . sorry, our kids. Yes they are Mark, then Barbara, Suzanne and then Caroline . . . and that [points to picture] is the grandson . . . Jack . . . named after my husband.

"But Mark still seemed to blend in all right. I don't ever remember him having any real problems at home or with relatives or friends. It all seemed very natural, very happy really. I might be wrong, to some extent. You don't always notice these things. You know, when children are growing up, you tend to stand back a little and let them grow naturally . . . grow in their own way and make their mistakes. I was always a great believer in that, in giving my children freedom. Freedom is a big thing with me. I wanted my children to enjoy life and develop naturally. Some of it was just the way things were. Mark's dad wanted a lot of attention. He was a plumber . . . had his own plumbing business and, to some extent, I would be waiting on him. Getting the meals ready, that kind of thing. It was fine . . . it was a happy house, really. I never resented being in that situation because that was just the way things were. We never had lots of money but none of my children were ever bored. Never. That is one thing I wouldn't have stood for and my husband agreed. Children have very active minds but they have to learn how to make the most of them. That is what makes children happy and fulfilled. I think that perhaps we were lucky because our children were all bright and were always doing something."

Tesco Store, Prestwich, Manchester. April 1, 2003, 6.30 pm

Mark: "I went to primary school in Broughton. I am not from around here . . . everyone keeps on reminding me. In those days people aspired to Prestwich. It was leafier. We used to go to Rhyl on holiday. It was fucking terrible. I was lucky, really, 'cos me sisters took all the attention. I liked to be left alone. It was great having a name like Smith. Kept you anonymous. I knew it then but, the older I get, the more I appreciate it.

"We went to Rhyl in me dad's plumber's van. I put a stop to that when I was about 11. I'd say, 'There's no way I am going on holiday with my family anymore.' They would say, 'Oh alright,' and leave me behind. I hated going with the family . . . not because I hated them, I just hated the idea of going to some poxy fucking guest house, which was 10 times worse than our own house and wandering about on Rhyl sands . . . and all of us in some small room. It was just fucking horrible. Couldn't understand how that could be perceived as fun. All seven of us cramped into his van . . . and then in the guest house. It was really fucking horrible. Just some cheap holiday . . . weird things happened to me, as well . . . weird things in Rhyl.

"Well . . . the thing was that I started speaking in tongues. I started speaking in different languages. Real languages too. Obscure ones. And languages like Russian. I would start speaking Russian in Rhyl. It just happened. Just like that. Don't know why. Don't know if it was the trauma of being away from home . . . or what it was. But it was the real deal. I have no doubt about that.

"I took O levels. Do you want to know how many I got? Don't think it matters a bit. I did OK. Nothing spectacular. But it doesn't matter because I was learning a hell of a lot in my own time. My own curriculum was always far more educational than the official one. Kids, today, should be encouraged to learn out of the curriculum. Will never happen. But it should. I suppose the intelligent ones, not the ones with 15 fucking A levels, but the really intelligent ones will understand what I am trying to say. It's not that fucking difficult. Don't get me wrong, I am not saying that I am massively intelligent. There were lots of kids smarter than me, but I learned how to learn on my own. I still do, to this day. Not sure today's kids can manage that. Some can. Most just lose it. That natural instinct. Poor sods . . . they haven't got a chance, let alone a clue."

Irene: "Mark was quite independent. He was always completely happy on his own . . . at ease. Later, when he got to about 17, he wanted to go out to parties and things. Well, my husband was not keen on letting him go but I argued for Mark, really. I always said, 'It's like letting them out on a rope . . . you have to give them more and more rope and ease them out.' I strongly believed that they should go and experience the new world for themselves . . . but, of course, we worried. But the thing was that, when I was young, I was like a little mouse, really. I never even wanted to go anywhere. I was probably too obedient, if that is possible. I was bright, at least I think I was, but I needed more sense of adventure. When I look back at my childhood, there were definite periods, especially later, as I grew into my teens, that I knew that I wasn't being allowed to fulfil my potential . . . not that I knew what it was.

"So when I saw that all four of my children were very adventurous, I quite liked it. Times had changed. The world now belonged to them and there were many things that I didn't understand, so I was really pleased when I realised that they all had the courage to go out and see for themselves. They were all very strong in that respect and I saw it as a good thing."

Mark: "When I was young there used to be this thing where watches would explode on me. Watches used to blow up and break when I was around. It was all extremely disturbing, to be honest. They would get water in the middle and no one could ever work out how the water got in. But I realised that it was a bit pointless, being a psychic. The one thing I noticed with psychics, and I used to hang around with them when I worked on the docks . . . there were many of them around for some reason . . . and I noticed that they were all very clever and their watches would explode and they could say, 'Oh, he's going to die over there . . .' or something. But they could never back a horse, could they?"

Irene: "Yes, you would have to say that independent was the word for Mark. He was never any trouble, really. I mean. He may have been a bit mischievous, like any young boy but certainly not excessively. You would never call him a naughty boy. At school he was always very good, very attentive apparently. You see he was always interested in things. We had all these *Encyclopaedia Britannicas* . . . and Mark would sit for hours looking at those. I remember him vividly, lying down there reading up on the French Revolution. Checking all the facts. I think he had watched a programme on it and was following it up. I'm not sure if it was actually to do with schoolwork and that is how he was. He always wanted to find things out for himself. That was a very important thing with Mark. He had a natural interest in things. He did his schoolwork but he seemed to understand that it was good for him to discover things for himself, rather than just pleasing a teacher. Yes. He liked his books; very much . . . he always loved books . . . always had a book on the go. Still does. Yes. Even later, when he was in the band and went on different gigs, he became well known for his plastic bag with books in it. He wrote a song about that, didn't he? Plastic man? Or something like that. That was Mark, carrying a book everywhere. He's not like the children today, is he? Can't imagine them getting on a plane, carrying a book, can you?"

CARRY BAG MAN

I'm in love with the Carrier Bag Man
I love the Carrier Bag Man X2
Carrier bags strewn all around the room
Ah, the Carrier Bag Man – I am him
Coz I am the Carrier Bag Man – I am the carrier bag man

I've no time to sit comfortable down
But I still need armchairs round my home
To put carrier bags on

I am the Carrier Bag Man
Carry a bag man!

I don't make waves, I hide bags in graves
No cash is earned straight nowadays anyways
Please all you onlookers understand
So make gangway for Carrier Bag Man

I am Carrier Bag Man

[*megaphone rant*]

When in town I keep head down
Kneel on the croft when the Mariah comes round
Fat-assed workmen, I scurry around
There's few good places to hide bags behind

Coz I am Carrier Bag Man.
Carry a bag man!

No, I agreed and thought of the Nike clad generation . . . and, more immediately, of a clutter of youths that had clotted the corner of the street, as I had pulled my car to a halt . . . not just a general teenage clutter, but on a more disturbing level beyond that, where the curious grey skin pallor strongly indicated some kind of abuse. And I had wondered, as they began pushing each other around, and as one falls backward through a privet hedge, and as they all bounced away, leaving a flurry of discarded fish'n'chip cartons, if my middle-aged disgust was really harboured in hypocrisy. Here I was, let's face it, writing a book about somebody I first met when we were both classed as 'punks', even if neither of us would be particularly punkishly garbed. But we, too, believed ferociously in some kind of teenage rebellion. That was the very point, wasn't it? And, filter back 30 years, to a time when the young Mark would be skulking along these very streets, boisterously looning among these very privet hedges and, frankly, grasping the rather softer drug culture of the day with equal glee. Was Mark really any different than the Nike clad oiks of today? Despite that, I had to agree with Irene Smith. I couldn't see any of these reading up on the French Revolution.

Mark: "Trouble today is, well, they can't get a bloody job now, can they? So they play football on the street where I live. My problem is that I have turned into the bloke who goes out when the kids are playing and gives them hell. 'Put that fuckin' ball away . . . you've got the biggest park in fuckin' Europe around the corner.' But they answer back, now. We never did. We ran off. A year or two ago, when I was on my own, I did get a bit crazy with them. Well, they would be playing on Saturday morning, say and, perhaps, I had been out on tour . . . and I might not have slept for a week and they would drive me mental. It would have been all right if they were four or five, but they would be 14 . . . 15. When we were that age, the last thing we would do would be playing football on the street. We had more important stuff to do . . . wouldn't have degraded ourselves. But, at like, 14 years old and they are threatening to send their dads round. But you just know the dad isn't going to come. He's slumped in front of the telly watching the girls on *Neighbours*, or something. So the mum would come round, asking if I remember being young. Tellin' me that I think I'm a big rock star . . . completely missing the point, of course, but at least the mother cares enough to come round.

"Funny thing though. When I shouted at those kids they actually seemed to like it. It was like the only time anyone of a different age had actually talked to them. They don't get talked to at school . . . not really. Well, only in some patronising manner. I just thought someone should get those kids up and going . . . get them doing something . . . they would enjoy it, it would do them a world of good. But all they ever get is patronising gush, call it political correctness, whatever. It's brainless crap and, the thing is, the kids know. They are not stupid. Kids never are. Not really. They know a damn sight more than some local school inspector knows. It's just a pity that they can't stop fucking patronising them. It's so obvious . . . but no one sees it. Learners? But if you shout too hard, they start crying.

"You know, going to school . . . you never really got to read the books that you really wanted to read. So the trick was to dig them out for yourself. I could read before I even went to school, funnily enough. Before I went to primary school. But, when I was there, I would read anything that wasn't on the school syllabus, really. Edgar

Allen Poe . . . newspapers . . . anything. At school they would just give you *Jane Eyre* and all that. I didn't read James Bond books at the time like a lot of people did. They are good though, aren't they? I never really got to read them until about 10 years ago when we were doing this mix in this bloody studio. Turned out the studio was owned by Ian Fleming's daughter. She wrote as well. Detective novels. Pretty good too. They had all the James Bond books there. So, when I was waiting around, which is how you spend most of your time when you are in studios, I would sit there reading all the James Bond classics. Fantastic books.

"When I was at school, like, the teachers couldn't understand a word I said – but that was because of my accent. And they used to laugh at me, and stand me up in front of the class and made me read something and made out that was exactly how not to speak. But I came top of the class two years in English.

"I remember when we were learning graphs at school you had to vote for The Beatles, The Rolling Stones or The Monkees, right, and I hated music when I was six, we didn't ever have a record player so I voted for this one. The school graph was like a stack of votes for The Beatles, Stones and Monkees and then Fred And The Playboys which was me. They said, 'Who do you like, Beatles or The Stones?' and I said, 'I like the mad one,' and they're going 'What about The Monkees, Smith?' and I'm going, 'I don't know them, we don't have a record player in our house and my dad doesn't allow the radio on,' and they were going, 'must be mad'. They started calling me a freak. It was like *Lord Of The Flies*. It's a Northern Soul record. There's no bourgeois content, that's why it's good."

Then again.

You never know.

Irene: "Of course he went at 18. Left to set up with his girlfriend . . . Una, wasn't it? Again, I had what he would call 'observant neglect'. You don't interfere too much in what your kids are doing . . . but you are watching all the time and are there when needed. You see in my family there were just too many of us. I could have got away with a lot if I had been that way inclined. My father used to say, 'You have got to set an example'. Well, I set it by the way I was . . . and my kids were completely different to me, I am very happy to say."

Mark: "We never really had records in our home when I was young. We had a record player but, if we did play a record my dad would say 'You are breakin' the fuckin' record player. Take that off!' It would just be some rock'n'roll record . . . Elvis Presley or something, but my dad would never have it. 'You think you are being funny, playin' that, don't you? Take it off. Take it off, now. It's breaking all the equipment.'

"I was into Northern Soul first. That was what was happening around Broughton and Prestwich. You would go round to your mate's house and listen. Funnily enough, quite often they would have an older sister or something who would be into Velvet Underground or Pink Floyd. So you would hear a bit of that as well. But, generally, it was all Northern Soul. Motown was basically looked down on. They are a bit like that in my area. Not so bloody daft and they are still the same today. A lot of the old guys, they haven't got fuckin' Beatles records or any of that. They will still have Northern or the Velvets or something like that. Something a little bit more sussed.

"I was in the dark generation. That strange sort of age group in Britain. I was thinking about this the other day. We are dispossessed, the middle-age group. The group that wasn't completely musicfied, it's now eight- and nine-year-olds who are the main pop buyers, but when I was a kid we didn't get a record player in my house until I was 14. My father wouldn't have a record player in the house; it just wasn't a necessity. There were no pop shows. Radio One only started in '68 when I was 12 or 13. What I remember . . . I remember the Sixties because my father used to make me work with him when I was about 11 on summer holidays. Every kid had two months holiday, and I'd be sweeping up after my father, which was great 'cos he had a lot of apprentices in this big plumbing shop. All of these apprentices would be listening to The Kinks and The Move, always playing the radio full blast. And I'd only hear it downstairs [cups his ears]. When I got my first record player, I remember the thing that was happening was T. Rex. In school before that everyone was into

The Beatles. I remember we used to have polls and I was the only one in my class who didn't vote for The Beatles, The Rolling Stones or The Monkees, because I didn't even know what it was. I voted for John somebody and his Playboy Bunnies* just to be awkward. The weirdest name on the paper got my vote. I always hated all pop music when I was a kid. The Beatles, The Rolling . . . it was more of a girls thing when I was brought up. I suppose it is now. But then, the generation of mine was the one that started off the new wave, punk. The generation that rejected all the singer-songwriters, which is a strange thing. It went back to real bone-crushing guitars. In Britain, it's the generation that's going around Europe killing off foreign football fans. These guys, they're just like me, see, because we were getting teenage in the Sixties, when it was boom time, and we came to manhood in the fucking real bad recession and it's gotten worse since then. I was one of the last of the working class to get a really good education . . . all the ideals of the Labour Party fused in the Sixties. It was unusual for kids like me to go to real good schools, so we had a real good education, and then we end up in the middle Seventies and there's no jobs or anything. So what you've got is a *Clockwork Orange* situation. You've got all these pretty clever guys with nothing to do. But the kids younger than me, they're OK because they're used to it. They're a different breed altogether.

"I came from Broughton. It was very much a red area. Very Man U. I was the only one in my class who was a City fan, naturally. I had to be contrary. Me dad took me to football. Not just to Maine Road, but everywhere, Oldham, Bury, Stockport County, that's how it was in those days. He would say, 'Bury are playing tonight . . . do you fancy it?' That's how it should be now. It's really stupid how they section supporters. But it was great because it was a spur of the moment thing . . . Oh. Let's go and see Oldham vs Charlton. These days you have to book like three weeks in advance. Takes all the fun out of it."

Irene: "But I am not sure any of the kids really know what they

* Doubtless John Fred & His Playboy Band whose sole hit, 'Judy In Disguise', reached number three in January, 1968. Bloody good single it was too – Ed.

want to do. I am not sure that Mark had a clear idea. Perhaps he always had an inkling that he might be some kind of writer but you didn't really think in those terms back then. Being a writer wasn't exactly an option, was it? I'm not sure it is now. There was a period when he became really interested in politics and used to say that he wanted to be a politician, which I did think was unusual at the time. He took a great interest in politics, did Mark. Always and, the thing was, that he seemed to be able to see the full picture, too. I could tell that he was interested in the personalities . . . in the kind of people who would get into politics. Yes, he definitely had a period where he was seriously thinking about how you would become a politician.

"I suppose he must have been about 16 at that point and, thinking about it now, not many 16-year-olds would express a desire to be a politician, would they? I don't think he really thought too much about it, Again, it wasn't something that seemed possible at the time. Mark didn't go to university, you see. But I remember the teacher saying that he should have gone to university. That he was definitely bright enough and would certainly have done well there. But my husband used to say, 'The only letters I have after my name are my initials on my hammer!' That was his rule, really and I suppose it was very old-fashioned . . . it certainly seems so now. He really wanted Mark to go into his plumbing business and follow on from him. I think he really expected that and was a bit shocked when it didn't happen. But the point was that, deep down, Mark's father had originally wanted to be a chemist. But, again, there just didn't seem to be any way that that could happen. Getting to university was certainly unheard of in Higher Broughton, where we came from, back in the Fifties. But I knew he expected Mark to follow him but I could also see that Mark's heart was never into it. I knew that from a very early age. His brain was in all these books all the time. I sensed that, maybe, his father was a bit jealous, which was only natural, because he hadn't been able to do what he really wanted to do. Looking back, more and more, I really do sense that now. He used to say that he really didn't believe in university. And he did have a point. The kids are at university for such a long time now, aren't they? I remember when I used to work in the Post Office, some people there had kids at university and they were always having to send all kinds of money and things. Mark's dad used to regard them as being really lazy . . . well, I don't know about that. But it is coming out now that some of these kids are there too long and still don't know what to do [when they leave], perhaps it might have been better if they had got jobs sooner. Having a degree doesn't mean so much these days, does it? They all seem to get them but it doesn't make more jobs. I sometimes wonder what might have become of Mark if he had gone to university. Would he have become a politician? Who knows . . . but he hasn't done so badly, has he? He has made an impression on the world . . . he has certainly achieved a huge amount and, of course, I am proud. I am as proud of Mark as I am of all the kids."

Mark: "My dad was alright. He was strange . . . I get on better with him in later life . . . I left home when I was 18, I couldn't stand it. But after I moved into the house in the next street to my parents after 10 years away, I got on really well with him, it was strange. I'd suddenly go to bars and drink with him. There are lots of things I learned when I left home about things he taught me that made me a lot more secure in myself. Like, my dad had never given me money, just never gave me money. He wouldn't even . . . I wanted to go to college when I was 16, so I did for a short while, but he gave me no money . . . [laughs] . . . so my ribs would be sticking out. I'd hate the bastard. I'd go, 'You bastard. Other kids are getting money.' But when I thought about it I didn't really like college anyway. I educated myself a lot better. I don't have any real money problems . . . I never have. I've been in real bad debt with tax due to the group. But I've always been able to live on anything. Some kids go through life and because their parents gave them a lot of money they are in a permanent state of debt and personal insecurity . . . they totally depend on a certain amount of money coming from . . . somewhere. I think it's great that parents, especially American parents, are generous. I think it's great. But what you think is a handicap comes in real useful when the band's got no fucking money . . . like my father always said to me, 'Look, if you've got £5 in your pocket on Friday, your life's made,' which is great. That's the ideal. That's a real English working class . . . They were brought up during the Blitz. They don't throw anything away. They're that type. I was the first child of four. My father wasn't well off when I was born. He was working for his father then. That's a lot of why I left home, because the idea was to carry on the plumbing business in the family . . . one of your stereotyped stories. Which I wish I'd done, I really [laughs] wish I'd done a plumber's apprentice. It'd be great to be able to do your art and have that back-up. Plumbers make fortunes. They never used to when I was a kid. They used to get nothing. Now, they're so in demand. But I just don't have it in my hands, you gotta have it. I can't even change a plug now, it's real hard."

Irene, again, casting her gaze up towards the ceiling and then down and then to me: "Oh I do hope I am making sense here. Is this any help to you? I hope so . . . I know you would say it is because you are a nice . . . but I hope it is. It's funny, but The Fall have become part of my life, in a sense. It has never been intrusive at all. In fact, we have had so many fun times . . . times at Fall gigs and travelling . . ."

I glanced around the room. Though it had been muted upon my entry, the television still hurtled disturbing images from the build-up to war into this ubiquitous living room. Any living room . . . any living room, anywhere. Blessed by a squat coffee table and a mantelpiece adorned with postcards from Mark . . . Greetings from San Francisco . . . New York, New York . . . Greetings from Hitchin . . . Beautiful New Zealand . . . missives from the four corners, gentle reminders from an extraordinary life . . . and Mark E. Smith touching base, dipping a toe back into homely reality, grasping a root.

"Yes he has been good," continued Irene, noticing me glancing across the cards. "Always writing to us . . . always writing. Always finding the time. I think it was always important for him, too . . . to be able to write back like that."

Picking up on Mark's theme, I asked Irene if she, herself, had ever seriously longed to write; if, as Mark had suggested, a ghost of an author lay within her background, if she resented the lack of artistic opportunity.

"No, no, not really," she replied, though none too convincingly. "Well, I always did think that I would like to write a book, but it was never a big thing for me. It was just a thought. I mean it never seriously entered my head so I didn't end up feeling disappointed. I think it would be different if I was young today. I mean, it's a completely different world now and I think I would probably want to get out there and do something. But it was never even there to think about and, anyway, I am proud of the way things have turned out. I don't have any bitterness about that even if Mark's dad never really allowed me to kind of grow in my own direction . . . but I don't know what that might have been. It's hard, isn't it? I really don't know if I could have written or not. It's something you never know unless you try. The fact that the opportunity was never there also helped me in a way, because I feel that too many people are doing things like that now.

"I think more of other people, other women I knew from those days and I certainly think that was the case. That they were held back and not allowed to fulfil their potential. I think, in those days, a lot of the Jewish women, and there are so many of them around here . . . I think that they certainly felt trapped in the family and I am sure there was resentment there. It was always so obvious with them because they often tend to be very artistic, don't they? Very talented and I hate to see talent held back.

"No. Not me though. Perhaps it was just meant to be this way . . . because it made me give freedom to my children. But, when I think about it, it is actually a better world now in that respect. It's great to see women breaking out and being assertive and doing things. My daughters have all done that. All very determined. Just like Mark, really. You could say that he had to break tradition very determinedly, or he would have been a plumber . . . not that there is anything wrong with plumbers.

"It was my father who told me what I had to do. He told me that I had to go and work in the raincoat factory. That was what happened back then. You didn't have the choice. I remember when I was at school, the headmaster told me that he always thought I would make a good teacher. I mean, I was only 14 and I couldn't believe that at all. I knew that I would have to go to work as soon as possible, full stop! Imagine me being a teacher! And yet . . . sometimes when I think back, I probably could have made a good teacher. I was probably brighter than I realised or than I was expected to be."

Mark: "Me mam's attitude is that she could have written and all that. Books probably. But unfortunately she had four children, so she couldn't. But she keeps tabs on what's going on. Not so much on me, but what is going on in the pop world. I may go and see her and tell her that we have a new record out or are about to go on tour . . . blah blah . . . but she will say, 'What about that Eminem? I know about him and he had a problem with his parents.' She tells me all about his problems . . . all kinds of stuff that I don't know, stuff about his new producer, fascinating stuff. I quite like Eminem, anyway. So it's OK. She's pretty sussed, in the Salford way. She might ask if 'dance music is like Joe Loss' but she knows, really. She susses out Robbie Williams straight away. I mean, anyone of our generation who knows anything knows that he is a pub singer. But she grasped that straight away. She saw that he was a Blackpool act."

It is, I noted, generally acknowledged that Mark inherited his infamous work ethic from his father. But I asked Irene if that notion might be slightly unfair on the extent of her influence. Could some of that work ethic have stemmed from her own determination?

Irene: "I never really thought of it like that but, in a way, maybe you are right. I suppose there is a certain female stubbornness. I mean, women had a strength that wasn't acknowledged, didn't they? Yes, that might be correct to some extent. I enjoyed leaving school and going to work, to be honest. But just going to work was exciting in itself, back then. Working in a raincoat factory or a Post Office indicated that you had reached certain adulthood, even if you hadn't. It was part of growing up and that work ethic you speak of wasn't something you either had or didn't have. The difference was that you just didn't have any choice. You just had to get on with it and that was that. There was no two ways about it. There was nobody else involved, you see. You simply had to survive and, if you didn't go to work, you didn't survive. It was that simple. So it wasn't a question of wanting to . . . you just had to. You couldn't even be ill in those days. You just had to go to work and bear it if you were ill. Nowadays, they would take a few weeks off, but you didn't dare do that then. I remember being very ill and having to go to the Post Office and thinking that it would be OK because I could sit on a chair . . . so that's what you did. I suppose it was a work ethic . . . that was on both sides of the family . . . well it was instilled into everyone and it was just driven by fear. Fear of losing your job because you couldn't afford to let that happen."

And, one would imagine, such a natural drive to survive would filter down to the children. However, as we are often all too aware, this isn't necessarily the case. It was intriguing to note how one thing Mark would refuse to tolerate within the ranks of The Fall would be the encroachment of laziness . . . so often a factor of young musicians and, at times, the very reason that some young people become musicians in the first place.

Mark: "Correct. I have never held any truck with the notion that rock'n'roll is an easy option for people, because it isn't. Not if it is done correctly. Not if it is done for the right reasons . . . and the right reasons are to create the kind of music that comes from within, regardless of what the record companies or fad or fashion might dictate. And that is never easy. That is always hard graft and that is what I have always done and have always demanded."

Irene: "I actually thought Mark would be . . . err . . . perhaps a journalist. I could see that he had that natural curiosity and I could see him asking questions and getting stories. It was only a thought, I don't really recall him ever saying that himself. But he was a bit guarded about that kind of thing. Even if he had said that he wanted to be something, you wouldn't know if he really meant it. It was as I have said. They have got to do it themselves, really. That's the only way it should be. He always had very good school reports, right through school. I never recall a single disappointment when reading his reports. I'm not saying that he was one of these brilliant kids, who came top in everything, but he was obviously bright and, more importantly, he applied himself. The teachers always recognised that. He always got As and Bs. I suppose there was the odd teacher's comment that would say, 'Needs a bit more concentration . . .' but not many. And that was the worst thing that was said. Having said all that, we didn't really take much notice of school reports with any of the kids. We knew that the teachers had no idea, really, how a child was developing because of the sheer amount of changes. Children develop in many different ways and at different times. So how can a teacher, with a class of 30 or so, really understand how a child was developing? The main thing was that they all seemed generally pleased with Mark and we were because we would see him at home, always doing his homework. He knew exactly what he had to do and he did it. It is difficult for the teachers, when you have a classroom full of kids, isn't it? And, as always, the noisy ones always get the most attention, regardless of whether they are bright or attentive or whatever. The shy or reserved ones might have far more potential. I think that people still rely too heavily on teachers' comments and should observe their kids more out of school. I have always believed that and I am sure that Mark picked up on that. You see, a lot of the kids today, all they are doing is getting a qualification to get a job. They don't have the ability to look beyond that. To see the wider world. I don't think they are encouraged to do that. But that is what Mark always did and, I suppose, that is what he has done with the group. He has done totally his own thing and it worked out for him. So I take a bit of pride in that, in encouraging him to do that.

"He went to the primary school . . . then to the big school. The Grammar School and then St John's College. I remember first starting off with him, saying, 'Come on Mark, sit down and we will test you,' and all that. Studying French and things like that. But he always tried very hard. He worked hard in other ways too. He did a paper round and he would always come in from his paper round and revise really hard. I think his father urged him into the paper round, to toughen him up a bit. You know they would have to get up and go out in the early morning, it could be freezing cold or pouring down with rain and they would have to get up and get out there. Nowadays I am not sure the kids would do it . . . or perhaps they do. I think that parents understandably worry about their children being out in the streets now. But Mark was really remarkable in that way. He seemed to thrive on having to do a job and he knew why he had to do it. He understood the value of what he was doing. He understood the value of money. He still does, actually. The pop world certainly hasn't changed him in that respect. I know he doesn't have millions of pounds or anything, but he has been to an awful lot of places and he has done a lot and yet he still seems quite level-headed when it comes down to the important things. Yes. He did that paper round. In fact, some of the time he would do a round in the morning, go to school and do a round in the evening. You never had to tell him to do it . . . never once. He never let the newsagent down. Mark would never even think of doing such a thing.

"Mark never caused any trouble at all. He was always very respectful of you and of adults in general. I think he gets a bit upset, sometimes, when he sees what the kids get up to, today. It's funny that, isn't it? Because I suppose being in the group and all that is a rebellious thing and he was rebellious in the sense that he knew what he had to do and knew what he thought about things and nothing would budge him. But that didn't mean that he didn't respect you. Quite the reverse. I'm not suggesting that he was a saint, of course not, but he knew right from wrong. We didn't even have to show him that. He would do the right thing."

Mark: "I remember at school, there'd be these paintings, with just a brown blob and a green blob and this sixth former said it was about the economy, the death of Jesus and the Third World, and he'd obviously been thinking about all that before he started. I did something in art in the fourth year and sixth form kids would say, 'What does that mean?' and I'd say, 'Nowt.' And it'd be, 'How dare you do things like that?', and I'd say, 'Well, it looks better than your brown blob.' Turn of the century, all this started. No one had this attitude before 1900."

Irene: "I remember when his father died, Mark came round to see me and asked me how much his father had been giving me for housekeeping. And I don't think that Mark was going through a particularly good time at that point. He knew that I was overcome with grief, because I was, because his father died very suddenly and it was a great shock for everyone. And, no, Mark wasn't having a good time for a variety of reasons at that point. Marriage breaking down and things . . . and yet he made sure I was all right. I would open a draw and find that he would have left £50 there for me. Because the money was frozen in the bank and I do think I would have struggled. But he always looked after me."

Mark: "As it turned out, me dad died before me granddad. I had to break the news to me granddad when he died. Not funny really, but by that time my granddad was getting away with it, as everybody thought he was senile. He was upset, actually. 'I told him he was carrying too much weight around,' he said. 'Bloody told him, our Jack.' As if he was dead fat, which he wasn't. The vicar was with us, as well. Which was a bit of a mistake as me granddad had a psychotic hatred of any clergy. He was terrible. When he saw nuns in the street he would shout, 'Look at them, they should be killed.' But the vicar was there . . . and me granddad just snarled and said, 'What der you want?' in a really aggressive way. 'I'm here to arrange the funeral,' said the vicar. 'Oh yeah . . . well, that's what you are tryin' ter make out. How much do yer want? Open the draw and give him a fiver to bugger off.' "

Irene: "When he was in the group, he never failed to send those postcards, letting us know how he was getting on. Wherever he went, he would make time to write cards to us. I have them all now. Right back to when he first went with the group . . . to San Francisco, I think. We were absolutely terrified because they were only kids . . . but the cards started coming and still do, which is very reassuring. And when he came home he would always come round and tell me about the places he had been to. I used to have to say to myself, 'Irene, don't start worrying . . . don't get all worked up about it.' It was difficult when they first started going away with the group because the pop world is very strange and I worried about the kinds of people who might be around The Fall. I mean, if you think about it. We were just two normal people in our semi in Prestwich and our son, who was only 18, was in places like New York and San Francisco and living in a world that we knew absolutely nothing about. So if you actually sat down and started to think about it, you would get all worked up. You would be thinking about drugs and the like . . . and you would hear things. So it wasn't as easy as people might think, especially in the early days. But Mark was bright and, to be honest, pretty sensible in many ways . . . that might surprise a few people, but that was the thought that helped me. That he wasn't daft. Not like a lot of people his age. I can certainly understand how people in the pop world get into trouble.

"Having said that, it was very exciting. He would write to me a lot and tell me all that was going on, the places where The Fall had played, who they had met, how the recordings were going . . . he would write and tell me all this stuff, which is quite remarkable, isn't it? 'Great,' he'd say. 'Oh . . . I am in a hotel in Chicago, drinking a mint julep!' I mean, can you imagine how that seemed to me! It was a million miles away from anything that I had ever experienced. A mint julep in a Chicago hotel? What on earth was happening? Both myself and my husband were astounded by it at first. It didn't seem real and we certainly worried about whether it would last.

"But it was always quite an adventure for us as well as for Mark. It's a pity that sometimes when they go to these amazing places that they don't often get a chance to have a real look around . . . well, I don't think that they would have been interested in the early days, but Mark would be now. I knew from quite early on that, if Mark didn't do anything else in his life, then at least he's been to interesting places and has done something very interesting. It's more than a lot of people can say, isn't it?"

It is.

I agreed.

More than many people could say.

But The Fall.

The Fall are not just a pop band. Or a rock band.

They are not really like any other band.

They are just, The Fall.

This is a difficult concept.

Even for people within the music industry . . . sometimes.

But how could a couple such as Irene and Jack.

Who never really acknowledged the existence of pop music.

How could they be expected to grasp that concept?

Irene: "I always knew that The Fall had something that appealed to an unusual type of fan. Not your average fan, perhaps a more intelligent fan. I knew this because of the subjects and things that

Mark puts into his songs. It is not like watching *Top Of The Pops*, is it? And sometimes I do watch those things. But The Fall work on a different level to that. I always understood that. Obviously, there are a lot of things that I don't understand because I don't know about many of the things that Mark listens to. So I only ever heard the end result. But, I always knew that it was something different . . . something that not everybody would like. I understood that much, right from the very beginning."

Another paradox
With The Fall
Another myth
That they are a male thing
That girlfriends always hate The Fall
That it is fat,
Sweaty
And male.

But there were always women. Always women.

Irene: "Mark was always passionate. He always adored women, you know, and in a very positive way, as I said. I always like meeting his girls. First there was Una. She came here first and I remember that she had picked Mark up from a 'do' at work. It was a Christmas 'do', I think and Mark had drunk too much. And I will never forget that Una was wiping Mark's brow very tenderly and looking after him because he had been sick. So I thought, well, he'll be alright with her. There had been one or two before Una but I think she was the first serious girlfriend and, of course, he moved into the flat in Prestwich . . . in Kingswood Road with her. They were only 18. It seems very young now, doesn't it and it was a big step for Mark. Of course he was working at the time and, at that point, it all seemed very conventional. Then there was Kay . . . yes, I got on very well with Kay and that lasted for quite a while, didn't it? . . . Oh yes, that's right, he went to America with Kay, didn't he? And they split up over there . . . yes, I remember all that. Trying to work out what was going on from Mark's postcards. Then he met Brix in Chicago, didn't he . . . in Chicago? We knew something was going on. He hinted at it in his postcards. And when he came back with this lovely blonde girl, well, it was amazing, wasn't it? I liked Brix, too . . . she was very friendly, you know in the way that Americans are, very forthright, but very nice. And then there was Saffron. His wife after Brix. Again she was very nice . . . and Julia, I think there was something there, wasn't there? I wasn't ever quite sure. He doesn't tell me everything, you know. I don't know all of it. And now there is Elena and she is lovely, isn't she? Absolutely a lovely person for Mark to end up with. I can see how Mark adores her. He won't let it show, which is how he is . . . but I can see it. She is very beautiful but also very kind, very intelligent. And she brings out something else in Mark, which I think is very positive. I think it will last this time, but who knows? But, to be honest, they were all very nice at first and I got on with them great but, of course, if they fall out with your son then I understand that they wouldn't want to speak to me. But they were all lovely and I really do think that Mark adored them all, you know. But, the thing is that I don't think that Mark's job is very suited to keeping relationships. It must be so difficult to maintain a relationship in that situation because there are all kinds of pressures, aren't there? When they go over to places and there are girls here and there. People are always demanding things of you. It takes its toll and I have seen it in Mark's eyes before now. He sometimes seems so tired and I worry. I worry because I know what he is like. He can be his own worst enemy, Mark, but I think he is always at his happiest when he is in a relationship. He may seem like a loner but he isn't, you know. He might be tough, but he really needs women with him. But in his job there are so many things going on and the girls are all round . . . it must be very hard. I wouldn't have liked it myself. But he's a romantic, Mark, you know. He always was. He always loved poetry, right from a very early age. Thinking about it now, I suppose that was quite unusual too. He loved poetry and he loved girls. Yes, there were a few before Una but I didn't see any of those. I think his father didn't encourage him, so he never brought them home."

He never brought them home.

And then there was Una. Mopping his brow.

And a job.

And a band.

How strange it all seemed.

Irene: "It was all down to him reaching the age of 18. His father always made that clear. 'When you are 18 you can do what you want.' And, of course, that's when he started going to all these alternative clubs and pubs, with bands on and things . . . it was a strange time, that. Because it all came so quickly. Suddenly, at 18, Mark was out of the house, in a flat with a girlfriend and then came the band. And all kinds of possibilities appeared to be opening for him. And I thought about him going out to all those pubs and clubs and it suddenly dawned on me that he was actually a lot older than I had been when I was going out a lot.

"And it reminded me a bit of when I was young. My mother used to say the same things that I was feeling with Mark. And I used to go dancing at the Devonshire Ballroom on Devonshire Street in Broughton. It would start at 7.30 and you would come home at 11.30. My mother thought that was very late although my sister Christine would go out at 10 pm . . . my mother found that impossible to understand. She always went to bed at 10 pm and couldn't understand why anyone would want to be out later than that. Different generations, you see.

"We used to go dancing and to shows. We would go to see talent shows . . . at Wythenshaw and we would be coming home through town and I would see them all queuing up to go in the clubs. We would go to pubs and shows that finished early but never the clubs. There were hundreds of clubs in Manchester in the late Fifties . . . far more than now and it spoilt a lot of jobs that, I think. It was an age when suddenly people discovered going out to clubs and staying out late at night. I suppose there hadn't been much fun in the years after the war so it was one of those periods when having fun and going out suddenly seemed so important. These things go in cycles, don't they? I remember when I worked at the Post Office. Oh, there was one girl who used to go to clubs and she never turned up on Saturday morning. She'd be out Friday nights till the early hours . . . but yes, it was funny to us . . . as we were travelling home and I would say to Jack, 'Look at that lot . . . they are going in clubs, they are . . . look at them!!!'

"We did go once or twice. We used to see stand-up comedians in those days. That used to be the big thing in those days. Ivor Davies, the comedian . . . you don't see him on television now. He was the compere at this pub called The Fusilier in Pendleton. We would go in there first and then go on to a talent show at Wythenshaw. And there was this big woman called Bella and she would wait for Ivor Davies to finish. He always ended his show and Bella would be waiting at the side of the stage . . . and he'd say 'Right . . . come on, Bella!' And he would get her up on stage and it would just become part of the act! The talent shows were great, too . . . they were full shows and hardly cost anything to get in. Oh, we saw all the comedians . . . all the ones who would be on television later on . . . in the Sixties. They were all in these talent shows in Manchester in the Fifties. Who was that Liverpool one . . . on *The Comedians*? It didn't always work out. I remember going to this beautiful club once and there was all food and about 40 staff and they would be expecting crowds and there was about 10 people turned up. We had a marvellous time. Then next week there would only be five people because it didn't take off. I remember seeing Ken Dodd a lot. We would see him at The Hippodrome in Ashton-under-Lyne and he was always a problem because he wouldn't finish. You had to leave at 11 pm to catch the bus back to Salford and Ken Dodd would go on and on and on and nobody liked to leave because you thought it wasn't polite just to get up and leave, but Ken Dodd wouldn't stop . . . he was relentless. With his tickling stick he used to point out people in the audience. We saw him twice in Ashton. We saw a lot of good things at that Ashton theatre . . . that's where one of my daughters lives, down in Ashton so we would go over there quite a lot. The pubs are nice in Ashton, aren't they? Very friendly people, Ashton people, very friendly.

"Oh, we saw a lot of shows. Jack Hannon and his band . . . things like that. And it were £1 16*s* to get in and we would collect vinegar bottles and take them back to the shops and with the return money we would be able to go to the shows. We would scrimp and save and get all those bottles out from under the sink. Yes, we would go to

The Devonshire. I think they changed its name into The Devonshire Sporting Club. I don't know why. Oh, and these Americans came there, one night . . . all chewing gum and looking the way Americans do, you know . . . because we had never really seen them. And everybody was talking about them because there were two black ones there . . . I mean we were only about 15 you know and we were fascinated and terrified by these Americans . . . they were slouching and had that funny look. It's terrible to think of it now, but we hadn't seen black people so we were very ignorant. We didn't understand at all. And we came out of The Devonshire and these two black men were standing in the road and we just flew past them, terrified. I know that seems terrible but we didn't know any better, back then. It was a strange time . . . I mean, there is one little story about Mark, when he was very, very young. We had a black milkman. He was great, actually, a big Jamaican . . . and Mark went to answer the door . . . he must have only be a tot and he had a dummy in his mouth. And the milkman looked at him and said, 'Take that out of your mouth' . . . and Mark was terrified and he ran into the house and threw his dummy into the coal fire . . . did us a favour really, because he was getting to the end of the dummy stage. So he did us a favour . . . the milkman, the Caribbean milkman.

"The Devonshire Street dancehall was a very, very good one. There was never any trouble. I don't think people even thought of that. There were no drinks there, no alcohol at all. There was just a little soft drinks bar in the reception. I mean, I was only about 14. Of course, I was working . . . that seems odd now, doesn't it? It seemed old at the time. But it was great fun. There were cakes and things . . . they all did the jive . . . throwing us over their shoulders and all of that. But if the men wanted to get a drink they would get a pass out . . . a ticket to get out and they would go to one of the pubs on Great Cheetham Street. I went once . . . I was frightened to death and worried that my father might find out. I mean, we didn't drink or anything. Generally people didn't drink, not like they do now . . . mostly though I wouldn't go out. There was no point because you knew the boys would come back in after they had had their pint. So you waited until you saw one that you liked. That's where I met

Jack . . . at the Devonshire Ballroom. I remember he asked me to dance and he said that he could dance but he couldn't turn. So when we got to the corners I would have to say 'Nooowww!' and he would turn. Anyway, we started talking and he seemed like a really nice guy . . . and he showed me photographs of his sister who was in America. He only had one sister, and he showed me the photographs. We just got talking. It wasn't an instant thing because I met all my boyfriends there . . . not that there were that many, I hasten to add. But that was where you went to meet boys. I once met a chef who worked at the Grand Hotel . . . and he got me and my friend some tickets to see a band there. It was a beautiful night. I will never forget those times. Nice things we did, back then. Those places were designed to help you meet people. You could sit and talk and dance. Nobody bothered about the lack of licence. Nobody ever fought . . . although, there were places where trouble did happen. Where was it . . . near The Rialto, where the Teddy Boys went . . . it was called The Assembly Rooms and that was where the Teddy Boys went, yes . . . Teddy Boys . . . they had razors around their necks. They had the blazers and shoes . . . I suppose a lot of them went into town as well. To The Plaza where the bands would come and play. Lots of bands on one bill, playing rock'n'roll. They were all good places, for the money we paid. I don't know how they manage it these days. Everything is so expensive. We didn't have much money but it always seemed enough. Nowadays, nobody ever seems to have enough money to get by and that, I think, is the cause of a lot of the trouble, I really do. That is one thing that we instilled in Mark, the respect for money. We made sure that he understood the value of money and respected it. He still does. He's not tight or anything, not at all. He knows what money can do and I also think he understands how it can corrupt people. He's not rich, by any means, but I think he values the fact that he works hard for money . . . because he does. And we all did. It was necessity and it was built in. You don't waste money . . . so many people just waste money on things they really don't need and then they find that they have no money, don't they?

"And we weren't tight, either. We all smoked in those days. All the time and we would hand them around. Everybody had a cigarette case with their initials on. Because you wanted to be like Bette Davies and Humphrey Bogart, you know? So you went out and flashed your cigarette case around. I bought my husband a nice one, with his initials on for Christmas. Funny about cigarettes, isn't it? Fourteen, I was . . . puffing away. Terrible, really . . . Have you ever smoked?"

It had been a fascinating tirade. Glorious indeed. Click the Dictaphone, settle into the chair, enjoy the evening. Not a drop, not a hint, not a flicker of ego . . . and if a mother's natural pride might cloud the objectivity a little, well that could be forgiven. Interesting, too, to note the difference that lay between, say, The Fall and The Smiths. While many people reading this book will, I strongly sense, agree with the notion that The Smiths, during their short lifespan, would be playing a completely different game – a watered down version of The Fall, it has been mooted – they were playing in pop's big money league. The Fall, by contrast, would always be on a different plain. Lesser in commercial terms. Greater . . . far greater, in terms of forging the idiosyncratic; in terms of creating a lone genre . . . unprecedented . . . but not without cost. And here was a real cost. A big cost. The biggest cost of all. I flashed back, at this point . . . to a different place, in 1985. I recall standing in plush Hale Barns, plush and set deep within Cheshire, and standing on a lawnmower street, a street of gentility, where the norm would be a BMW and a place on the board of several companies. And a white haired lady, looking at me kindly from over the hedge of a house called Ventnor . . . and the lady was the mother of Morrissey . . . just a trickle of years into The Smiths' existence and yet enough, it obviously seemed, to transport her from her native Stretford – which might parallel Prestwich in terms of social strata – and transplant her in the heart of Cheshire. I remember it seeming striking, even back then, to see the fruits of Mozzer's labour manifesto within Cheshire bricks and mortar and noting the difference, right then, right at that moment, between The Smiths and, my favoured both then and now, The Fall. How could this be? I thought, in my naivety, that The Smiths had been ploughing a similarly indie vein – of course, they had been doing no such thing – but that debate, where Rough Trade segued into London, is not the point here. The point is the basic human difference that a fairly modest trickle of chart hits can make. I must admit, that is perhaps not the best comparison . . . think then, of the difference between The Fall and Atomic Kitten!

OK . . . I am stating the obvious . . . but would this be so obvious to Mrs Mozzer and Mrs Smith?

I don't know.

It still strikes me now . . . as rather odd.

Because The Smiths, for all their undoubted brilliance, were a short, sharp shock . . . and one that has worn reasonably well, though not as well as we believed at the time.

And The Fall roll on and on.

And still make a vital noise.

And *Country On The Click* is among their best releases.

Imagine that.

Imagine if The Smiths were still making records on a par with *The Queen Is Dead.*

And imagine if Mrs Mozzer was still living in the community of Stretford.

Would she be happier?

And yes, I told Irene.

I did smoke.

Thirty a day.

And I gave up, aged 30.

Just like that.

I was proud of that.

'Cos I am an addictive sort.

Can't say the same for red wine.

But I defeated smoking.

Irene: "Did you? Well done. That's the right time to stop. I have only just stopped now!!! Last June. And it has been difficult. I mean I would like to have a smoke every now and again . . . but my chest isn't good . . . no good smoking with a bad chest. How did you stop? Suddenly . . . wow . . . oh yes, I cut down gradually, went down to five a day. I would buy 10 and make them last as long as I could. But

I did like one . . . I mean I've never been a drinker but I did like a cigarette with my vodka on a Sunday. But it's funny how you get used to it, don't you? Are you more than 30, now?"

"I'm 47, Irene. Your son came to my wedding when I was 24!"

"Are you? Well you don't look it. You don't look anything like 47! Good heavens. How do you do it?"

"Good women and wine, I think . . . and I have slimmed . . . massively!" (There is a point to this . . . honest.)

Irene: "Mark drinks too much, doesn't he?"

"I don't know, Irene. Mark wouldn't be Mark if he didn't. The Fall wouldn't be The Fall. I wouldn't be here, talking to you. This wouldn't be an interesting story. I am not saying that the drink is the fuel . . . it's just that it is an important part of the story and shouldn't be undervalued. It's there. It's part of Mark. It's part of many great writers . . . and I strongly believe that without it Mark would be dead . . . or a plumber. Whatever, I repeat, The Fall would not be The Fall."

Break time . . . break time in Manchester.

Irene: "Smoking is outlawed now, yes . . . people are all outside now, aren't they? If you go to town at lunchtime, you see them all stood outside, puffing away outside The Arndale. I remember at the Post Office. When I first started, at 14 . . . we all had ashtrays and nobody used to bother, did they? Everybody smoked at work . . . then they had this mandate, saying that smoking was banned. It seemed terrible at the time. Now, smoking is very anti-social, isn't it? I don't think that Mark likes that. I know he likes a cigarette and that's the way it is."

I smiled at this. I have noticed this absurdity, too. I dislike the puritanical idiocy of non-smoker fascists . . . and have noted their hypocrisy, too.

So I agreed with Irene, who had recently, reluctantly given up the dreaded weed . . . and our eyes drifted to that television set, as eyes tend to do at 9.30 pm on a Tuesday, and allowed a cruel world of war to soak in. The sound didn't need turning up. The images were all too obvious.

Irene: "I was watching that war today! Those American Marines. They are so aggressive. They reminded me of the Americans we used to meet when I was 14. Yes, so full of themselves and shooting at anything. They seem bolshy . . . oooh, I must admit, I like the way the British Colonels talked . . . absolutely marvellous, very intelligent. But it's going to get really bad when they get to that Baghdad . . . oooh, with the street fighting. I think the Americans thought it would be so easy and Blair thought they would all jump up and down and welcome us but, it stands to reason, if you bomb somebody's house, they are not going to turn around and thank you, are they? And they are so lovely those Iraqi people . . . the ordinary people . . . it must terrible . . . terrible. That Bush, I don't like him . . . he looks really sinister. I think he is trying to get back for his father. I really do. But Blair, he wants to save the world, doesn't he? He's got enough problems going on here. And he will have all kinds of trouble when this is over. He won't be able to stop the terrorism. It has opened a Pandora's Box, this lot has . . . where everybody's against us and we have got all these in the country and they will be stirred up as well. I think they have made a very big mistake. It may take a few years for everyone to realise that but, one day, people will look back at the start of this war and say that was when the trouble really started. Getting rid of Saddam Hussein is one thing . . . but they will be paying a price for many years to come. Oh but those people are so nice . . . and they haven't got a lot. I always think that, when I look at the poor people . . . what they have got would be precious, wouldn't it? I was only reading today, in the *Mail*, about the things we did around 1918 . . . around Basra . . . we did a lot of bad things in the old days and they have all come back to haunt us, haven't they? Like Northern Ireland, yes. I know . . . it always comes back. I never expected Blair to go the way he has . . . I don't think Mark is too keen on Blair but I thought he was alright. I am not so sure now.

"Mark was very interested in other people. He always was . . . he would watch people very carefully, although he wouldn't ever come to rely on them. He is his own man, as they used to say and knows his own mind and won't let anyone else near. But he would observe people. He still does. I mean, that's what he does in his songs, isn't it? . . . Observing people. I don't think that Mark is too proud to learn from other people, not at all. He likes talented people . . . he likes artistic people. I think he respects them. My husband was a bit different in that respect. He didn't take much notice of other people at all. He wasn't really interested in them. Now Mark . . . some people may think that Mark can come across as a bit hard but he isn't. He is strong, rather than hard. But he does watch other people.

"I did go to The Hacienda once. Did you go there? I remember meeting Tony Wilson at G-MEX that year [1986] and he came up to me and said, 'I am very privileged to have known your son.' That was nice, wasn't it? And then I went to The Hacienda and there were all these marvellous men in black overcoats with hair brylcreemed back. I was so excited by it all. And I met one of them from The Stone Roses there . . . where were we? On the balcony at The Hacienda. That was quite exciting. I had a write-up . . . they wrote about me . . . with my bouffant hair. And our Suzanne was holding my hand, taking me to the toilets . . . looking after me. I watched The Fall, it was quite exciting. And I went to The Ritz to see The Fall. It was good, The Ritz. I had been there before. It was funny . . . there was a blind man there, listening to the music . . . listening to The Fall. That was a good night. I danced at The Ritz in the old days, on the sprung dance floor. But it was a bit different with the young ones . . . jumping up and down. But I remember our Barbara, she told me this . . . she went to a concert of Mark's and she said there were three skinheads and they were jumping up and down and shouting and she said she poured a pint over their heads. I said, 'What did they do?' She said they did nothing . . . just laughed. But there was never any of that with the usual Fall fans, was there? That was one thing I noticed. That Fall fans did all tend to be nice . . . perhaps they were a bit more intelligent than other youngsters. I don't know . . . Oh, but I went with my husband to see them . . . one night. I think it was at Jilly's, in Manchester. And my husband had his suit on and the bouncer told him that he wasn't allowed in because he wasn't properly dressed. And he had his suit on . . . and inside they would be sat all over the floor with beer all over them. I took my sister to the gig at the Free Trade Hall. Yes. Did you go to that one? Yes? I was downstairs and these boys from Liverpool were there. And my sister told them that I was Mark's mother . . . and they were asking me if there was a chance of me getting them backstage. I said, 'I am sorry . . . it's like getting an audience with the Pope.' Even I couldn't get backstage that night.

"I have had some wonderful times because of The Fall. A lot of the fans, you know, have been very kind. I have met a lot of very interesting people, too . . . all kinds of people. Lovely people. I don't go out much, these days . . . but now and again I might. I don't suppose there are many people my age who can say that they have been to an 'alternative gig' and were afterwards dancing away to The Rolling Stones? Ha . . . not many people my age do that, do they? Can only manage it now and again, though. I am happier, really, being here. But it has been good, very good . . . very good times."

Good times.

I was no longer nervous.

I lingered, awhile, repressing my journalistic glee while pouring over old photographs . . . of Mark and the sisters . . . holidaying here and there . . . encased in striking normality. And how curious to see the young, smiling Mark E. Smith . . . as a schoolboy, scruffed hair and smiles . . . young and gleeful and soaking everything in. Like every photo album in every house in every Salford street. The area in which he would drift . . . drift and soak in the local character . . . the local colour.

Mark: "There was this mad Irish guy . . . Thomas . . . who was a big influence on me. He was an influence on me when I was growing up. He had that great Irish thing. All the kids I was brought up with always did what their parents told them to do; Irish kids never did what their parents told them. They'd always take the piss out of kids who really had nice clothes and stuff . . . it made me more secure in myself. I had great parents, but Thomas was one of those guys who could reduce you to tears and laughter just by talking. That's why I had a really nice childhood, because of Thomas. He was a few years older than me. His sense of humour was completely absurd. Like there was this guy, he used to call him 'Simon of Diarrhoea' and he used to invent these stories about what Simon's house was behind the doors, and how he lived off diarrhoea . . . you know, disgusting stories that would go on for ages. He'd throw in some real cheeky things. It's strange about Thomas, I haven't thought about him for a few years. I don't see him at all . . . he's gone completely . . . he was too tuned in."

At the door I paused. Boxes lay at the foot of the stairs. In the hallway. Boxes of mementoes, trinkets, ornaments, vases.

"I am leaving here soon," said Irene. "I am getting ready to leave . . . been a long time in this house. Many years . . . many years."

But I didn't sense sadness there.

Not at all.

If anything . . . a curious release.

An acceptance that things move on.

That things change.

And in change there is life. Adventure. Challenges.

The whole point, really.

Is to understand . . . and move on.

3

Dirges In The Dark: Manchester/Salford 1976/77

Not a drop, not a hint, not a flicker of genuine evocation permeates Michael Winterbottom's 2002 film, *Twenty Four Hour Party People* which, in charting the rise and fall of Factory Records, claims to focus on the Manchester 'scene' from the mid-Seventies onwards. Although entertaining, in a breathless, pacey and shallow manner and fleetingly humorous, it narrows down to one tight, wholly inaccurate view of the times, with a script that drips from a small huddle of egos and floats around a tight bundle of insular anecdotes. While this is of little consequence to Mark E. Smith, who expresses no desire to revisit the dark days of mid-Seventies Manchester and certainly refuses to romanticise that moment, let alone drift along lanes of sepia-toned nostalgia, it seems important, as far as this book is concerned, to establish the backdrop in front of which the notion of The Fall would unfold.

In a meeting, in October 2001, between Michael Winterbottom, *24 Hour Party People* writer Andrew Eaton, Tony Wilson's ex-wife Lindsay Reade and the writer of this book (I was merely there as support for the understandably aggrieved Ms Reade, a close friend), Andrew Eaton openly stated: "We have made history here. It is a pity that we had to cut a few people out of the film . . . just because of the way the film was cut, they missed out on being a part of history."

Although not particularly caring a jot about the film and, indeed, fully sharing Mark's ambivalence towards the very idea, I still found the arrogance of that statement rather shocking. This was the precise moment when it dawned on me that he might well be correct;

that people might not correctly view the film as an absurdly warped slice of comedic fiction chiselled from any era at all – despite Tony Wilson's constant litigation wary claims that it stretched beyond reality . . . how very naive of you Tony – but they would actually believe that that is how it happened. What's more, the notion that the entire Manchester scene mushroomed from those two pivotal Sex Pistols gigs at the Lesser Free Trade Hall on June 4 and July 20, 1976, has been wearyingly overplayed in the music press over the years, a snowballing effect that culminated in David Nolan's Granada film – and resultant book – *I Swear I Was There* and Winterbottom's little ego orgy . . . and, indeed, Wilson's supporting book.*

Mid-Seventies Manchester

The concept of a 24-hour party person would have been quite absurd in the mid-Seventies Manchester that Mark remembers as ". . . the most miserable fucking place on earth . . ."

It was a curious spell for a city where, 10 years previously, a thriving if unholy necklace of nightclubs ringed the city centre, when the glamorous fringe of the 'George Best Set' languished in boozy camaraderie, surrounded by harsh go-getting press boys and full-time floosies looking for a way out. Indeed, in 1970, it was still possible to grasp fading traces of a city once dubbed 'the nightclub capital of Europe'. Infamous names still screamed from neon nightclub signs – Jackie's Explosion, Nice'n'Easy, Rowntrees Sound, a scene that segued uneasily into Northern Soul and the continued success of the legendary Twisted Wheel. However, as the Seventies progressed, one by one the great clubs would fold, either at the hands of

* Of particular interest here is Mark E. Smith's appearance in Tony Wilson's *24 Hour Party People* book, which clearly depicts a curious exchange of opinion between Lindsay Reade and Mark E. Smith. Rather bizarrely, Lindsay is portrayed accusing Mark E. Smith of being 'middle class' (bizarre indeed, as Lindsay hails from the large abodes of Gatley) while Mark deflects the criticism . . . if, indeed, that is what it is. When asked about the alleged exchange, neither Lindsay nor Mark could recall ever meeting each other. Mark: "I've never even heard of Lindsay Reade . . . I barely ever really met Wilson." Lindsay, levelly, replied: "I wouldn't have really known anything about Mark."

merciless authorities or equally unsavoury downbeat hoodlums, squeezing small change from the city's dying nightclubs, bleeding the centre to a close. There was a blackness to Manchester-By-Night that encroached deep into the heart of Piccadilly, with long silent shadows and blackspots, and that silence was infamous too, and never seemed to be quite so evident in, say, Liverpool or Sheffield. By night, mid-Seventies Manchester held a rare kind of menace.

In terms of culture, no city could least resemble the burgeoning city of café bars, theme bars and clubs of today's Manchester. Eating out, in the city centre, was an experience far from exotic, the lavish peppering of steak bars competing with tired English-owned pizza emporiums and, down the scale, a heady mix of Formica greasy-spoon style caffs and, in the ancient sense, Wimpy Bars crowded with remnants from the glam era and ageing Crombie kids, reluctant to leave behind their wildness and hazy memories of football skirmishes.

As to rock, the Free Trade Hall still reigned as the city's chief venue, with hints of the oncoming punk rush beginning as far back as May 31, 1974, when a riot greeted the conclusion of a Lou Reed set on his 'Sally Can't Dance' tour. It seems extraordinary to note this, given the disparate cultural climes of today, but whenever the polar extremes of glam and progressive rock would meet to watch an artist with dual appeal – Reed was a good example, Dr Feelgood and Roxy Music also performed to overtly raucous hoards – a sense of danger would hang ominously in the air.

Mark's record collection was eclectic, to say the least. Although well acquainted with the swirling vortex of faceless artists who found unlikely success on the dance floors at Wigan Casino, Blackpool Mecca and The Torch in Stoke-on-Trent, Northern Soul failed to permeate his collection. Much has been written about the Velvet Underground and Doors records that would languish there although, in truth, they would mostly settle dustily to the rear while more esoteric and contemporary sounds, most notably from Germany, would gain repeated plays alongside snatches of reggae and rockabilly. While it doesn't seem quite so unusual to note this in 2003, in mid-Seventies England such rarefied tastes would be considered elegantly refined. I can personally validate them, too, as Mark once excitedly allowed me to borrow a copy of Can's 1971 opus *Tago Mago*, which punched improvisational beauty around my bedroom for a number of years, and such tracks as 'Paperhouse', 'Mushroom', 'Peking O' and 'Bring Me Coffee And Tea' would echo rather too obviously into Public Image Limited's 1979 success, *Metal Box*, at the time regarded as a great leap forward for the English underground. In *Muze* magazine, in 1985, John Lydon would later admit, "We took a great many ideas from Can but, if I am to be honest, it was The Fall who first turned me in that direction. I may never have been a huge Fall fan but I always liked reading Mark's interviews. He seemed to have the same ideas as me. He always seemed to voice the things that I was thinking. There was some kind of link. We were both working class and both a lot more intelligent than people gave us credit for. It didn't surprise me that Mark would listen to Can and reggae."

Una Baines did not enter into the circle that would become The Fall via a love of eclectic Germanic experimentation. Her early Seventies was spent typically flitting around the obvious pop references although, like so many involved with the punk generation, she continued to carry affection for Marc Bolan and David Bowie, two artists who managed to transcend the seismic shift into punk with elegant ease. Nevertheless, by the time she met Mark, initially at the summer fair at Heaton Park, Baines had grown slightly uncomfortable with the cloying commerciality of fading glam and, though unwilling to sink into the unappealing and ironically named area of progressive rock, had already started to long for something more challenging. Mark provided the answer, introducing her to a raft of books and records. Much time was spent devouring these new cultural avenues.

Although Mark has no recollection of Una Baines ever attending St John's College, it is no doubt true to state that the swirl of poetry and prose that existed in Mark's head, and had already started to filter onto myriad scraps of paper, began to gather pace with his liaison with Baines. In the pre-punk mid-Seventies, bored by both the echoing shallowness of Radio One-fired pop and the deadening musicianship of the more serious rock scene, Smith and Baines were seeking some kind of way out.

It was Mark's sister, Barbara, who first introduced Martin Bramah and Tony Friel to the couple. Bramah and Friel met at Heys Boys Secondary School. Both bright and brimming with ideas, despite falling from an education system that failed to identify their talents and left them in a post-school daze, armed with one solitary qualification between them – Bramah's Art O Level. Time was, therefore, spent bumbling through the city centre, dipping into the Underground Market, into Paperchase, into the tiny and lovably smoky Bohemia of the Virgin Records store on Lever Street, where they would huddle in the rear, soaking in sounds through a rack of headphones, their enthusiasm fuelled by musically astute assistants, quite the antithesis of the stark, chromed commercial cathedrals that sneer at you in every town centre today, bearing the name Virgin Megastore.

Bramah and Friel were, like Smith and Baines, simply lost, adrift in a mid-Seventies city that was, itself, unhinged from any kind of cultural intensity. Ageing ex-Granada executives might argue otherwise, stating the continuing success of *Coronation Street*, which was already a depiction of a lost Salford where neighbourly values still gathered tightly around terraced street life . . . somewhat removed from the stark reality of life in or around, say, Liverpool Road during that period, where omnipresent fear of violence had already stifled any trace of neighbourly affection.

Kingswood Road

A flat, like any flat in Prestwich. You would drift down Kingswood Road, never quite sure which would be the right one. Slabs of fallen affluence, plaster crumbling into tufts of nettles, tell-tale clusters of doorbells with numbers or names scrawled in biro. Everywhere, the prevailing transient air of bedsit flatland. Hunched, shadowy figures scurrying into the night, hurrying back, laden with 'takeaways' and off-licence bags. Faces behind curtains, surveying the land for the Jaguars of prowling landlords . . . or worse. Occupants too immersed in their fantastic youth, blinded to any signs of outward near squalor, be it the rusting carcass of a Ford Capri or violent cracks across living room windows. Unremarkable perhaps, it was an area that slumped into downbeat studenthood, where eclectic music seeped from front rooms, where the faint whiff of cannabis seemed to hang in the air, where books would be read and taps would drip. It was neither particularly vibrant nor did it settle into deadening somnolence.

The flat was a perfect base from which would rise Mark's burgeoning imagination. A perfect base too, perhaps, to nail the ragged early stirrings of The Fall, where vision and perception would emerge from the slightly shambolic, definitely naive early music, where Tony Friel's jazz pretensions would clash heartily with Bramah's raw punk heart.

In retrospect, it seems that wandering into that flat was rather like wandering straight into a Fall song. In retrospect, it seems also to have had an air of austerity that, perhaps, wasn't quite so pronounced at the time. If one wishes to read a certain romance into hessian walls, grubbed up woodchip wallpaper, wood-effect vinyl coatings, drab paint, swirl rugs and flower-patterned armchairs, with cigarette ends exploding from ashtrays, with coffee cups and, here comes the escape route . . . books and records. The books lay everywhere . . . temptingly. In the toilet you might stumble across, as I did, a psychological thriller by Colin Wilson set in the Lake District.

"Take it, read it . . ." Mark would say, preferring books to be 'out there', in circulation, rather than gathering dust.

A Ronco Records display stand dominated the room. Fresh, one suspected, from Woolworths record department, where it would have been used to exhibit budget-priced albums, cheaply assembled *Top Of The Pops* albums, proudly housed behind the vision of a grinning, bikini-clad slice of cheesecake. Now it was arguably put to better usage. A Kim Fowley album. A Kasenatz-Katz album. Lou Reed's *Berlin*. The Groundhogs. Can's *Tago Mago*, of course . . . offerings from Faust and Gene Vincent, from Eddie Cochran and Max Romeo, the Virgin reggae sampler *The Front Line*, and several Doors albums.

Initially it would be Mark and Una who inhabited the flat, offering slices of cake, coffee, beer and dope to passing near-strangers.

Mark: "What you have got to remember about me, Mick, that I

am a bit . . . er not with you, because I trust you . . . but with many people . . . like when the BBC ask me to give my Top 10 records, I just select 10 randomly. I am not going to tell them what I really like. Not my serious records. It is something that is precious to you. I don't want to know what anybody else's favourite records are. Why should I? So I just give them the expected ones, really, Velvet Underground, Philip K. Dick book. You know, good stuff but it is the stuff that everyone expects me to like. I like Bo Diddley and that. I like rockabilly and reggae. Some very obscure stuff but, if I let that out, other musicians would pick up on it. So I just bung in the Velvets who, frankly, were a bit passé, especially in North Manchester. But you wouldn't know that, Mick, 'cos you were from Stockport.

"I didn't educate The Fall. They were all into stuff. Tony Friel was into jazz. T. Rex was listened to, as well. Our band was like a bedroom thing, anyway. For an awful long time, really. Me, Una, Martin and Tony. But in those days the concerts that people went to see were like Led Zeppelin at Earls Court. I hated all that well before punk. Funny though, as the years pass you kind of see the beauty in some of the stuff you hated . . . and vice versa, I suppose. Loved The Pistols, of course, but hated punk generally."

What was unusual about this was the sheer passion involved. Although trips to the nearby Forester's Arms were frequent, the talk rarely veered from its central musical core, with all four adding snippets of poetry and writing into the mix. Evenings would be wildly experimental and, fuelled heavily by beer and the sundry mild drugs that circulated quite openly around Salford at the time, this unlikely Bohemian quartet soon started acting like . . . and indeed, looking like . . . well, some kind of band.

It was, to say the least, a loose gathering. Mark's spirited guitar stint faltered and Bramah reverted to his Bolan days, and spent many hours practising the guitar. Una began by banging on biscuit tins before switching to keyboard. "Don't knock it Mick," Mark once explained. "Biscuit tins are very adequate for initial rehearsal sessions . . . far better than some ego crazed drummer with far too much equipment for his own good."

Notions of taking this musical ensemble into a situation where they might actually perform live were rarely expressed. It was, after all, 1976, and the kind of gigs that might have been appropriate for them had yet to be realised within the community that would become the force that fired the oncoming rush of punk.

Elsewhere in Manchester, things had started to gather pace. For a number of years, Tony Wilson had been filtering his – mainly American – pop affectations into the unlikely outlet of *Granada Reports*, a comparatively hi-tech local news/magazine programme that has seen Wilson climb into the hearts of mothers across the region, his local fame taking him no further, however, than rounds of local celebrity cricket matches. Not until his enthusiasm and wry delivery on Granada arts slot *What's On*, which brought the soft, already ageing Sad Café and Pythonesque Alberto Y Los Trios Paranoias onto the small screen, was there a hint of musical stirrings in the region. *What's On* caught the attention of Granada boss David Plowright who, openly challenging the monopoly of *Top Of The Pops*, commissioned Wilson to write and front six half-hour slots of comedy Bohemian chat mixed with marginally left-field music. *So It Goes*, named after the Nick Lowe single, gained instant infamy in the summer of 1976 and, although it was still drearily championing such acts as Dr Hook and Nils Lofgren, soon found itself under siege from the brash new acts of the south, Eddie & The Hot Rods and, most spectacularly of all, The Sex Pistols.

The events that illuminated Manchester's embryonic punk circle in 1976 have been heavily documented, not least by this writer, and there seems little point in reiterating them here. Nevertheless, it was a period that remains unsurpassed, and not because – as strongly hinted at in *24 Hour Party People* – there was any sense of pulling together, of punkish camaraderie . . . because, frankly, there wasn't. The prevailing sense was of sporadic change. At the start of the year, Manchester remained cloaked in the greyness of inactivity, at least on the local scene . . . a scene that was slightly enlivened by the existence of two crumbling former bingo halls, both situated in areas of bombsite-like clearance. To the north, The Electric Circus began its musical life as a pre-punk dope den, where second division exponents of prog rock would perform with dexterity, if not imagination, before a swathe of nodding heads and sweat-stained denim, where deals were negotiated in the shadows and doormen longed for action and invariably found it, where the walk home, or even back to the car, took you across scattered shards of broken glass and taunts from local kids, up too late, bricks at midnight hurled from the shadows.

To the east, adjacent to Belle Vue speedway, stood The Mayflower, parallel in every way to The Electric Circus, and at its best a showcase for the more eccentric fringe of prog rock. Classic evenings with The Sensational Alex Harvey Band and Gong would spice a generally rather tawdry, predictable gig list.

Before The Sex Pistols' Lesser Free Trade Hall gigs came a lesser championed event in unfashionable Stockport, when glam rock brats from the enormous Wythenshaw overspill estate Slaughter & The Dogs performed at an unlovely and long forgotten venue called The Garage, in the Portwood area. Wilson and his wife Lindsay had unwisely downed a tab of acid prior to the gig and subsequently fell into the romance of an alarming gathering of fading glam gangs, intent on dark mischief and a loose, barely pub standard rock outfit desperate to gain a foothold on some kind of scene. But it was significant, simply because Slaughter & The Dogs – whose unholy following included producer Martin Hannett – represented a tight Wythenshawrian gangland community who sensed that something lucrative was coming, specifically a means of prising money from some kind of artistic uprising. This is significant here because, frankly, one cannot imagine anything more dynamically opposite to the ideas that were floating around that flat in Kingswood Road.

Other acts of the time were also gathering momentum. The Drones, soon to be briefly managed by local *NME* scribe, Paul Morley, had emerged from a previous existence as clubland pop outfit Rockslide. By the dawn of 1977 they would be fully attired in a variety of slogan-daubed garments, mostly pertaining to the downfall of royalty or other dumb nonconformities. Quite what it was they didn't wish to conform to always remained unclear, as The Drones, despite considerable local success, soon became solidly, depressingly archetypal purveyors of parochial punk. Once again, the gulf in musical and personal terms between anything running through the heads of The Drones and the thoughts of Mark E. Smith and cohorts couldn't have been more profound.

Closer, arguably, would be Buzzcocks, particularly while Howard Devoto remained weirdly glued to their mike stand, as he was through 1976. Devoto's enigmatic ability to fuse a scattering of Beefheartian references through a spiky garage format plucked directly from The Seeds, MC5 and The Troggs did at least share a few reference points with Smith, who had already been alerted to the ironies to be found in west coast pop psychedelic. The simplistic flower power pop of LA's The Seeds in particular would be cherished by Mark, but even the fluttering of Buzzcocks wasn't enough to instigate a desire to perform in any kind of live arena. Of more influence, undoubtedly, was Patti Smith's extraordinary *Horses* album, which married vivid poetic imagery to a ferocious urban edge-of-punk swirl.

Mark: "Yeah, Patti Smith was obviously hugely important and continued to be so. It seemed perfectly natural for us to tune in with much of that New York thing . . . and some of the LA stuff from the Sixties. That was far closer to where we were than anything that would take place in Manchester. I mean, the fucking Drones! C'mon. A million fucking miles away from what we had in our heads. But it was still something that we did naturally, without really giving much thought to it evolving into a band, at that time, anyway. I mean, I would be reading poetry while Friel was trying this jazz stuff . . . and he was into Jaco Pastorius. Not quite Slaughter & The Dogs, was it? And that was the stuff that people were shouting about in Manchester at the time. We fucking hated the glam rock crowd in Manchester at the time, and Slaughter & The Dogs were pretty central to all that. There was a big split actually, between the people who were about to be attracted towards punk . . . because in 1976 nobody was really a punk . . . and the glam rock were seen as the enemy really . . . more so than the hippies, who we personally quite connected with. This surfaced in the second Sex Pistols' gig at the Lesser Free Trade Hall, when there was a lot of trouble."

Although the lasting influence of the two Pistols' gigs at the Lesser Free Trade Hall has been hugely overplayed, the members of the band who would become The Fall did indeed attend, and were immediately struck by the possibilities that were now presenting themselves. Most notable, perhaps, was the positive proof that The Sex Pistols, this band who had caused so much fury in the music press and beyond, conveyed a level of musicianship, and indeed a level of innovative ideas, that seemed remarkably within reach of the average Salfordian, licking his way through initial guitar chords. If nothing else it was an awakening of possibilities.

Mark: "Yeah, it was crap, the Lesser Free Trade Hall and anyone who says differently is lying. But what it did do was to break things down. That was perhaps the point. Actually, I'm not that convinced that it was, but that is what happened. It was very simple really. We came away certain that we could do a lot better than that. I mean, I loved the Pistols, really. I loved Johnny Rotten's vocals. I certainly connected with that. The way he used his non voice. That was absolutely fantastic even though, in many respects, the Pistols were a pretty bad heavy metal band."

The notion that The Sex Pistols were a 'pretty bad heavy metal band' was not confined to Mark, either. *Sounds/NME* writer Ian Wood, soon to champion The Fall's cause, noted at the time: "It was the most bizarre gig I have ever seen, not because of the band, but because of the audience. I mean, there were guys there who were pretty sussed in terms of music, and these sussed guys were going absolutely apeshit about a bad, out-of-tune heavy metal band who seemed devoid of any real ideas other than performing a weak copy of Alice Cooper. Rotten had presence, and that was a joy to witness, but that band was lumpen."

Such was the divide, following the twin gigs. Some scurried back to dope fuelled bedsits and sat cross-legged next to Dansettes blaring Gong and Man . . . and others opted for speed and Iggy. The Prestwich gang were taking the middle course, while swerving off into the unknown. Every weekend the heady cocktail of beer and drugs would take them to unusual areas. Unusual, one senses, because, in direct contrast to Richard Hell's proclamation of a 'Blank

Generation', entering into a state of blank apathy was never an option. Getting stoned with the people who would become The Fall was always an empowering experience.

Mark: "I was writing all sorts at that point . . . and before the band. Prose. Bits of prose. Just scraps, here and there . . . essays, poems, sci fi. Anything that came into my head. I had always done that. I had always written things down. Just thoughts, scraps. It is quite strange, actually. I have never really thought about this before but I hadn't really entertained any notions of being a writer. That wasn't the point. I would be jotting things down for my own amusement and I still do. Of course, now they tend to surface as songs, but the scribblings came before The Fall.

"I think, from that moment, we started to think on a different level than the punk thing. It was obviously going to be something that would explode and fizzle out very quickly, which is exactly what happened. Also, although we would go to clubs and gigs and things, I never had any sense of hanging out in any kind of scene at all. Never wanted to . . . and never did. I find that whole concept repulsive, frankly. But it was happening even then, you know. Members of Slaughter & The Dogs and The Drones hanging around together as if they were fucking superstars. It was just pathetic. But, yes, it was also empowering because we just didn't want any of that.

"It started with me on guitar and reading poems. Just as a hobby. That's where The Fall began. Me, a guitar and a few scribbled words. Yeah . . . a hobby. It's all very simple, when you think of it like that. Martin came in, did a few things. I never took myself seriously at all. I was just playing A and E on the guitar and obviously you would have thought Martin was going to be the singer. He was good looking and had a kind of charisma. But we couldn't get a drummer. The only drummer we got was that bloke from Stockport. The bloke who died. Little bald fella."

A band, then. A real band. From Prestwich. Naming the band wasn't too difficult. It would, surely, have to be something pulled from the mass of literary references that scattered the floor of Mark's flat. These included Jean-Paul Sartre, Colin Wilson and Albert Camus. Master Race & The Death Sentence – Smith's initial idea –

could have fallen from Nietzsche and was dropped for obvious reasons. As a non-gigging unit, they briefly adopted the moniker The Outsiders, which seemed to fit on every level. Colin Wilson's fading masterstroke, *The Outsider* (written on a park bench, legend tells) had been a Smith favourite for a number of years. Equally, Albert Camus' *L'Étranger* (*The Outsider*) had more or less created the blueprint for modern existentialism and the daft pretence of living outside of society. (Which is something, one strongly senses, that everybody feels, although more profoundly during teenage years.) For obvious reasons, as some kind of messy and disparate scene was unfolding without them, The Outsiders seemed to fit like a glove. Unfortunately, and not surprisingly given the obvious nature of the name, it was discovered that at least two other bands were hauling their equipment around under that name, so they decided to skip to the Camus' follow-up, *La Chute* (*The Fall*) which told the tale of Jean Baptiste-Clemence, a well-heeled Parisian barrister slowly peeling away all the trappings of success and falling down the social ladder while moving base to Amsterdam. The Fall . . . stark, simplistic, aloof, fateful, existential, blessed with duel literary references. Quite perfect.

By the close of 1976, the change had started to settle. The Electric Circus had played host to The Sex Pistols' 'Anarchy Tour' on two occasions; each one perched delicately on the very brink of violence; each one fired by Rotten's manic glare; each one reaching a level of intensity way beyond anything attained during those weird, soulless nights at the Lesser Free Trade Hall. Just attending The Electric Circus – a haunted former bingo hall, swirled in the yellow glow of street lights, encircled by broken bricks, shards of glass, and assorted rubble hurled from the derelict Forties flat blocks opposite . . . just walking towards it was enough to raise the anxiety to a state of paranoia . . . and all this before the speed, invariably purchased in one of the Circus' dark recesses, managed to kick in, transporting even the most mild-mannered punter into an absurd state of frenzied, wholly unrhythmic dance. These were the two gigs that truly altered the course of Manchester, when the dynamic shaded from the near violent reactionary stance of the prog rock regulars – who were still force enough to create a riot during a December set by The Damned – generally fell away, allowing punk's fresh breath to sweep through the club. The Lesser Free Trade Hall was comparatively irrelevant . . . these were the two gigs that kicked Manchester into the new era.

In January '77, Buzzcocks huffed and puffed and slammed down, bagged and posted out their classic *Spiral Scratch* EP, which caught the moment . . . a moment that seemed dipped in magic . . . precisely at the point when the rush of punk seemed genuinely revolutionary. It wasn't difficult to realise that *Spiral Scratch*, in Manchester if not the whole country, immediately became the hinge . . . after which all punk's genuine promise simply fell away, leaving little more than a sordid scramble for column inches. It was something that Mark E. Smith, if not the rest of The Fall, had no intention of joining. The Fall would be different . . . always different . . . and always the same.

It was a curious irony of the times, but the most positive forces on the Manchester 'scene' would, by and large, stem from the 'old guard'. While the young punks bickered and scrambled to gain music press affection, and as the downbeat punk promoters immediately started to resemble sordid downbeat sub-hoodlums, attaining a professional aloofness way beyond their station, any genuinely positive vision lay in the hands of those who could see beyond the initial blast. The listings magazine, *New Manchester Review* – a thoughtful precursor to *City Life* – occupied a neatly Bohemian office in Oxford Road's student-land . . . and the editorial office, swarmed about by bearded post students, loon-panted generals and assorted fringe writers, battled hard against the new wave of exciting but comically pretentious prose of new players like Paul Morley. It was a small battle, which Morley won, although the small power remained with the *New Manchester Review*. Upstairs sat Martin Hannett, or Martin Zero, as he liked to be known during the flickering infamy he enjoyed after producing Buzzcocks *Spiral Scratch*. Hannett sat, at all times, in a circle of smoke, bellowing monosyllabic Wythenshawrian into a telephone, running the local agency known as Music Force, ably assisted by his girlfriend, Susannah O'Hara. As 1977 moved on, Hannett had already started to enjoy a tempestuous, near violent relationship with Tony Wilson, and this brittle, old-fashioned duo would soon head the initial dynamic of Factory Records. Also, often to be found in the building was Dick Witts, a classically trained drummer, writer, agitator, music activist, avant-gardist . . . and lots of other things.

Mark. "I was the guitarist, at first. That much is true. Martin was the vocalist. Yes. It was right, in a sense, because he was a really good-looking guy and looked like a vocalist. Our first gig was . . . in North West Arts, just off Deansgate. It was a Manchester Musicians Collective thing. Dick Witts put us on. I am told that Buzzcocks were there, but I don't remember them being there at all, to be honest. What I do remember is the Manchester Musicians Collective being very good because I was really into avant-garde stuff at that point and they really encouraged that. I was listening to Can, Stockhausen, that was the direction that I wanted to take. It was Dick Witts, who was a classically trained musician, who got me into a lot of that stuff and I appreciated it because it carried me away from the fucking Manchester punk scene, which I was never into at all. And people knew that and wouldn't put us on. Those people pushing the punk thing, talking about being liberal and all that . . . they wouldn't let us play. But Dick would.

"I mean, that is the thing about all that 1977 shit. That's the thing that really annoys me, especially when people claim that we were a big part of it. The truth is that they didn't want to know us and we didn't want to know them. The only place we would be allowed to play was in Liverpool . . . in Liverpool they understood The Fall really well. I don't like playing in Manchester and I certainly don't like the concept of a Manchester scene. Never have done. We did play some gigs, of course, but it was far easier to play The Marquee or elsewhere in London after our first single. I mean, you know that . . . you came down to London often enough, didn't you?

"But that 1977 nonsense. There was actually a period of about two years where fuck all happened in Manchester. Every time you rang up a social secretary, trying to get a gig, all they would say is 'Send us a tape' and all that crap and I wasn't having any of it. That's why they all left the band. Or got fired. Because only fucking Eric's would put us on. It wasn't so frustrating for me, because I was working and they weren't. I was working in Urmston, at the container bases . . . I was working between there and the docks.

"I chose the docks. Rather than work in some fucking office in Manchester, I preferred to do some physical work. I was unloading on number nine dock at Salford. Right there where the Lowry Centre is today. That was my dock. It was great. Sometimes, I had to get on a motorbike and get over to Liverpool. It makes me laugh, sometimes. When you get Liverpool on *Granada Reports* and you get old dockers talking about how sad it is that the docks have gone. They always say how marvellous it was in Liverpool and then it all went away. The reason it went away is because they never used to do any fucking work, really. There were boats from Nigeria there, full of cotton or whatever. They would have sailed halfway around the world then have to wait two fucking days for the Liverpool dockers to get their fucking shit together. I have never, ever forgotten that. It was disgusting and cruel. It would take a week for those fucking boats to get to Liverpool and then no bugger would help them unload. And I know there will be lots of middle-class wankers getting annoyed when they hear me saying something like that . . . and I have nothing against Liverpool or Liverpudlians, who I like a lot. But the thing is that I was there. I saw it and no amount of ageing dockers on *Granada Reports* can persuade me that it was any different. It changed my views on life . . . well, certainly on that part of life. I was just a 16-year-old kid, really . . . or whatever . . . and I had to take the dockers on. It wasn't easy.

"Were The Fall a left-wing band? That's what it says in that *Wire* article/book, right? Well, I was never left-wing in the way it is perceived. I actually enjoyed my work, you know. I just couldn't understand why anyone wouldn't enjoy work. Especially the dockers. To me it was much better than being in college. I loved chucking bananas off boats. It was great. Better than being at St John's fucking college, that's for sure. But I would still write. I would write in my lunch hour. I would write in my head. Working on the docks freed me to do a lot of that."

Dick Witts was an instrumental player – quite literally, at times –

in a game, if ungainly circle of local talent that gathered under the umbrella of The Manchester Musicians Collective. Again, an irony of the MMC was the distinct sense of 'old wave' that would, from the close of '77, prevail at their Monday night gatherings at Manchester's premier jazz/pub venue, The Band On The Wall, on Swan Street. Once the very venue where 'killers' could be hired for £5 – I'm not making this up – The Band On The Wall was the one place in Manchester where the feel, the pulse, the atmosphere of a London pub rock venue would hang eerily in the air. The Manchester Musicians Collective were, throughout their existence, entertainingly rag-taggle, refreshingly aloof from any sense of prevailing trend or fad. Three bands a night would play, and never had such a disparate bunch ever been seen working together in inelegant partial harmony . . . and there was another thing, a big thing, an important thing. One would sit, on Monday nights, sipping too much appalling lager, smoking something rather dubious, falling into chatter with the assorted musicians . . . could be Frank from The Manchester Mekon or from Fast Cars . . . or even, rather ironically, Mick Hucknall . . . one would be speaking to all manner of musicians, none of whom exactly fitted the already cloying punk stereotype . . . and not once . . . not once would anybody mention A&R men or record contracts or the music press – apart from a few sly digs at Paul Morley . . . and hugely deserved at that. The talk would be simple. It would be of music and ideas. It would hold a collective intelligence that rose beyond the fad. It would be the perfect entry point for The Fall. It would be a level above.

Meanwhile, two doors away, in the Smithfield public house, in a foaming mess of bitter and chat, The Drones, Manchester's premier punk band, would spend the entire evening talking about record companies and television opportunities and journalists and 'enemy' bands . . . bands like Slaughter & The Dogs and Buzzcocks and that new one . . . Stiff Kittens. I mean no put-down, no disrespect, for The Drones were heading into a cycle of the eternally underrated – they could be invigorating and speedy, despite their name – but it was just something so simple. The Fall, moving into the Manchester scene, were simply playing a different ball game entirely. Punk was amazing, empowering and, above all else, great fun . . . for a while. But The Fall were about to take it several steps further. The word that sprang to mind at the time, and it still jumps to the fore in 2003 . . . is 'integrity'. That was an unlikely path to tread then . . . even more so now. Even more so, now.

Dick Witts then . . . an intriguing diminutive character, part punk rocker, part classical drummer, part plum vocals, part scuffed leather jacket and ripped jeans, part orchestrator agitator, part dumb skin pounder . . . big talker, relaxed, cool, nice guy . . . part writer and journalist . . . part PR man, part fan . . . a whole, lovely mass of paradox. Dick Witts kick-started the Manchester Musicians Collective . . . kick-started The Fall too, to some extent. Dick's vision, however, was not wholly suited to Mark. The very notion of a 'collective' stood absolutely against the aloof nature of the embryonic Fall. At least, that's how it seemed at the time. But Witts, who once told this writer, without a hint of irony that, "I like bands like Joy Division and The Fall because they fly between the black and the white," brought a wholly unexpected agenda to the circle. Pockets bulging from his Halle Orchestra pay, Witts and his erstwhile cohort Trevor Wishart, another tireless agitator who similarly lacked the kind of ego that was beginning to darken the punk side of the city, started to promote events of modern classical music, largely unlistenable to these ears. I can only recall the time when, stunned by the sheer horror unfolding before me, I fled such an event at, I think, the Royal Northern College of Music, that seemed to actively promote the kind of cacophony one might find at Snape Maltings, or some other cradle of contemporary classical filth. Nevertheless, Witts and Wishart were both accomplished musicians who found themselves facing an artistic cul-de-sac. Years of practice, years of theory, years of study had dulled their innovative edge. Witts would later admit: "The joy had slowly dripped from the music I would be playing . . . I was moving towards a high level of musicianship, but it was merely performing someone else's music and, to some extent, it was parrot style. I had lost the emotion."

How curious, then, to see Witts and Wishart re-energised, not by the guidance of their tutors, but by the equally cacophonous noise made by young kids who were, by any comparison, completely, utterly, musically illiterate.

Witts: "I just fell into it. I loved not just the energy . . . I soon tired of that, but the fact that the musicianship didn't matter a bit. It was like my mind was suddenly opened by these kids who just allowed their imagination to take them some place. It was just incredibly refreshing."

You could see the pretensions literally dropping from Witts at the time. In an instant he became scruffed and streetwise, prone to hanging around the offices of the *New Manchester Review*, an organ which carried his writings and, in retrospect, should have pushed him a little further, for Witts would later write an extraordinary and wholly underrated biography of Nico, who flickered briefly in the Manchester circle.

The Manchester Musicians Collective traded under the umbrella of the drably named North West Arts who, in turn, were a parochial offshoot of the Arts Council. Before they emerged drably in triumph at The Band On The Wall, the venue at which they are most fondly remembered, they camped out in an office in the ironically select area of King Street which, though not quite the Armani garrison it is today, was nonetheless strikingly up-market from any quarters normally occupied by sub punks and scene peripherals.

More fittingly perhaps, the subterranean confines of the cellar were used to showcase grubbily intriguing gigs on Monday nights. This writer recalls one such occasion which consisted of two apparently stoned guitarists playing a full and wholly unlistenable set while lying down and screaming at the ceiling. One strongly suspects they now run a pet stall on Ashton market. They couldn't have known it but, in terms of sheer force of attack, they were reasonable precursors to Discharge and, therefore, Slipknot. I only part jest. In contrast to the rapidly transforming Electric Circus, or the Ranch Bar on Dale Street – which was the genuine and long forgotten home of what might be referred to as Manchester punk, the North West Arts Cellar proved to be a decidedly dopey affair. How strange to note that, as one started to grow decidedly weary of the amphetamine push of the other venues, the Manchester Musicians Collective seemed positively refreshing, certainly lacking in prejudice. Nick Lowe's 'So It Goes' seemed to hang omnipresent throughout the night . . . punctuated perhaps, by the short sharp blast of The Damned's 'New Rose' and, naturally, Buzzcocks *Spiral Scratch.*

Perhaps it wasn't surprising to note that The Fall member most responsible for leading the band into the Manchester Musicians Collective was the jazz-orientated Tony Friel, whose musicianly notions for the future of the band had already started to clash with Mark's embryonic and rather more primal ideas. Nevertheless, the band did start to attend the meetings, and even joined in the curiously loose musicianly banter.

In a basement, suitably aloof and closeted, The Fall tentatively nudged towards their first gig. It was far from easy. Even the members of the MMC had to be persuaded – by Frank, soon to be the marvellously loon-panted member of The Manchester Mekon, as reactionary as it was possible to get without joining The Eagles – to let the Prestwich band 'have a bash'. Except, frankly, even that wasn't so easy. The Fall stumbled in their efforts to secure the services of a drummer. There would be the extraordinary 'Dave', pulled in after the band had seen his advertisement in the *Manchester Evening News*. 'Dave's apparent credentials, legend tells, revolve loosely around a penchant for right-wing extremism, which seemed rather at odds with the reactionary left-wing stance of the band . . . in image if not in actuality. The politics of The Fall began, and would remain, splendidly locked in ambiguity, fiery on individual issues, but dimmed in terms of actual stance. Mark – rather at odds with the others – immediately understood the power of producing strong, potentially political statements while deliberately casting them adrift from any recognisable state of party politics . . . which is the only reasonable stance of the artist.*

* This contrasts strongly with the other member of the early Fall. Bizarrely, the author of this book recalls a comedic 'run-in' with a latter-day Una Baines in 1986, when Baines was enjoying life as keyboard player of a ferociously active 'Rad Fem' outfit who turned out, en masse and ably supported by a plethora of seething cronies, to play the odd 'Battle of the Bands' contest at the Romiley Forum, in Cheshire. This

The first gig was suitably bizarre. In a restaurant. That fact, alone, was curious, partly because of the heartbreaking dearth of restaurants in Manchester in 1977 and partly because, by all accounts, the decor owed much to the vibe of an igloo or polar bear set, if, indeed, polar bears have 'sets' . . . well, I sense you get the drift.

Mark spent the entire gig hunched beneath the venue's low arch. In journals elsewhere, it has been noted that Mark's vocals took on a new and gloriously aggressive dimension, at once squeezing barbed rhetoric into the room while poking a finger into the astonished face of the watching Howard Devoto.

Dick Witts (1978): "The surprising thing about The Fall, from the outset, was that it was clear that there was something special going on there, but nobody could quite put a finger on exactly what it was."

Least of all the band. Partly astonished by the unexpected vocal power and curious stab of charisma of their singer, all five band members, including Una Baines, who as she had yet to be able to finance her new keyboards had to sit in the ranks of the audience, astonished and perhaps confused that audience who couldn't decide whether to applaud or deride the sheer attack of these Prestwich misfits.

It was different, too. One night earlier, had you taken the advice of Paul Morley, you would probably have travelled to The Electric Circus to catch a spirited and average set by the aforementioned Drones, who hurtled their way through speed-freak anthems advocating the beheading of royalty, the drowning of The Pope, attacking the poor commuting Mancunians and lambasting Southerners

was surreal in the extreme. I was assigned the grim task of announcing the winners, and found myself – despite having personally voted for Una's band – under savage verbal attack when it dawned that they had been beaten by some dumb punks fronted by a Debbie Harry lookalike. "Foookin' men . . . they are all the same," screamed Una. "It was the same when I was in The Fall . . . fookin' men takin' all the credit." This startled me, if only slightly, as I had voted for the band on the grounds that they had carried a certain intelligence into their craft. This was a theory I swiftly revised after the second glass flashed by my head. I felt as if I had wandered into someone else's war and wondered why Una Baines couldn't remember me as the sensitive young chap who once spent a full two hours in The Forester's Arms, convincing her that her contribution to The Fall was fundamental albeit, as it transpired, only in the short term.

. . . pretty much standard fair for the run-of-the-mill northern punk unit, devoid of originality and fired only by some vague notion about wanting to be a bit like Johnny Rotten. Already, such drivel had become the mainstay of the little Mancunian bands who swam off ineffectively in the wake of Buzzcocks.

To fully prepare for The Fall, even in this jagged embryonic state, where they were stumbling into situations – rather than any trace of a groove – that, frankly, astonished themselves, you might have been better spending the previous evening listening to Coltrane or King Crimson. Suddenly, here we found a band that, though structurally simplistic and hanging on the edge of a cacophony that wasn't entirely planned, still managed to carry a high level of intellectual attack. Mostly, and in direct response to the failing music, this intelligence fell into the hands of one Mark E. Smith who, from gig one, song one, used words to take this punish din to another place entirely.

Ian Wood, *Sounds* writer, taxman, real ale fan, and bearded mini guru: "The Fall were so obviously more talented than anybody else at that time. Their problem was, and it was an ironic problem, that they couldn't play as well as The Drones, who had been a cabaret band . . . or even Slaughter & The Dogs. But they just had more ideas. What they were doing was just so obvious . . . so obvious it was instantly brilliant."

It was rudimentary at this stage, with the two main men stooping and Mark E. Smith grasping his chance and surging to a new level. The songs dripped on either side of musical simplicity which would soon be exaggerated further by the addition of the toy-town cuteness of Una Baines' keyboards. Indeed, the Baines addition, warped plonkety and intriguingly artless, would actually help cement the tradition of 'dumb down' that would forever set The Fall apart from just about any other band, keeping them true to Mark E. Smith's unstinting desire to remain fantastically in the left field. At that very first gig, pre-Baines, that jagged determination was already in place.

Astonishingly, in retrospect, there was an unlikely surreal twist. The set list, such as it was, did contain a block of unusually disparate songs, occasionally soaked in natural punk bile. 'Psycho Mafia' was a tale of violence and late night terror, 'Hey Fascist' was self-explanatory to some extent, although Mark was already edging into unusual areas, and 'Race Hatred' looked beyond the simplistic sloganeering that was about to be adopted by Tom Robinson's band of psuedo politicos. These three songs, as performed in the anxiety of a first gig, remained shaky and neurotic enough to simply pass for punk bluff and bluster. But 'Bingo-Master's Break-Out!', an absurdly pretty jingle, carried things rather further. The song was written in surreal, tragi-comic mode, and involved Mark's observations about a downbeat bingo hall perched menacingly on a crossroads of Bury New Road. It was a place where bedraggled hopefuls drifted in on Friday afternoons to sink into the neon glow and bow to the absurd, repetitive and meaningless expressions of the Bingo Master . . . the God for the afternoon, although even as he suited his circle of bingo clichés, his control was wrestled about by the hand of chance. 'Bingo-Master's Break-Out!' took a leaf from Luke Rinehart, and commented on the twisting of fate and chance, of desperation and emotional stress, of life in the gutter . . . looking hopefully towards the pathetic. And there was something else . . .

"Checks his card through eyes of tears . . ."

Part and parcel of The Fall . . . right there, day one, grasping the audience's attention with something so stacked with obvious pop hooks, a trick already learnt from Mark and Martin's leanings towards the psychedelic garage scene of Sixties LA. Contrary to the latter-day scribbling of po-faced psychedelic aficionados it was a resolutely 'pop' scene and, in the case of The Seeds – another firm Mark fave and a teen pop scene at that – it contained emotionally surreal elements, soaked in sarcastic pathos. 'Bingo-Master's Break-Out!', although it was to emerge rather scruffily on the band's first single release, was the first great Fall song . . . great indeed because it sounded like no one else in 1977 . . . and nobody else sounded like The Fall in that most copycat of all rock years.

The song's greatness was defused though . . . disguised and usurped by the final elongated number . . . a vast, all too obviously punk twisted wrench of a song that grasped two lonely chords and stretched them to last . . . 10 . . . 12 . . . 13 minutes. The song was built around stories

Reflective by the pint. A lyric forms? (*Andrew Catlin/SIN*)

Irene and Jack Smith take time out in Fleetwood. (*Courtesy of Smith family*)

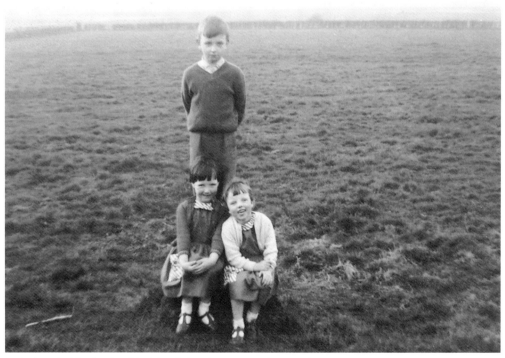

Mark, suitably aloof and lurking behind sisters Barbara and Suzanne. (*Courtesy of Smith family*)

Mark, May 1962, already among the books. (*Courtesy of Smith family*)

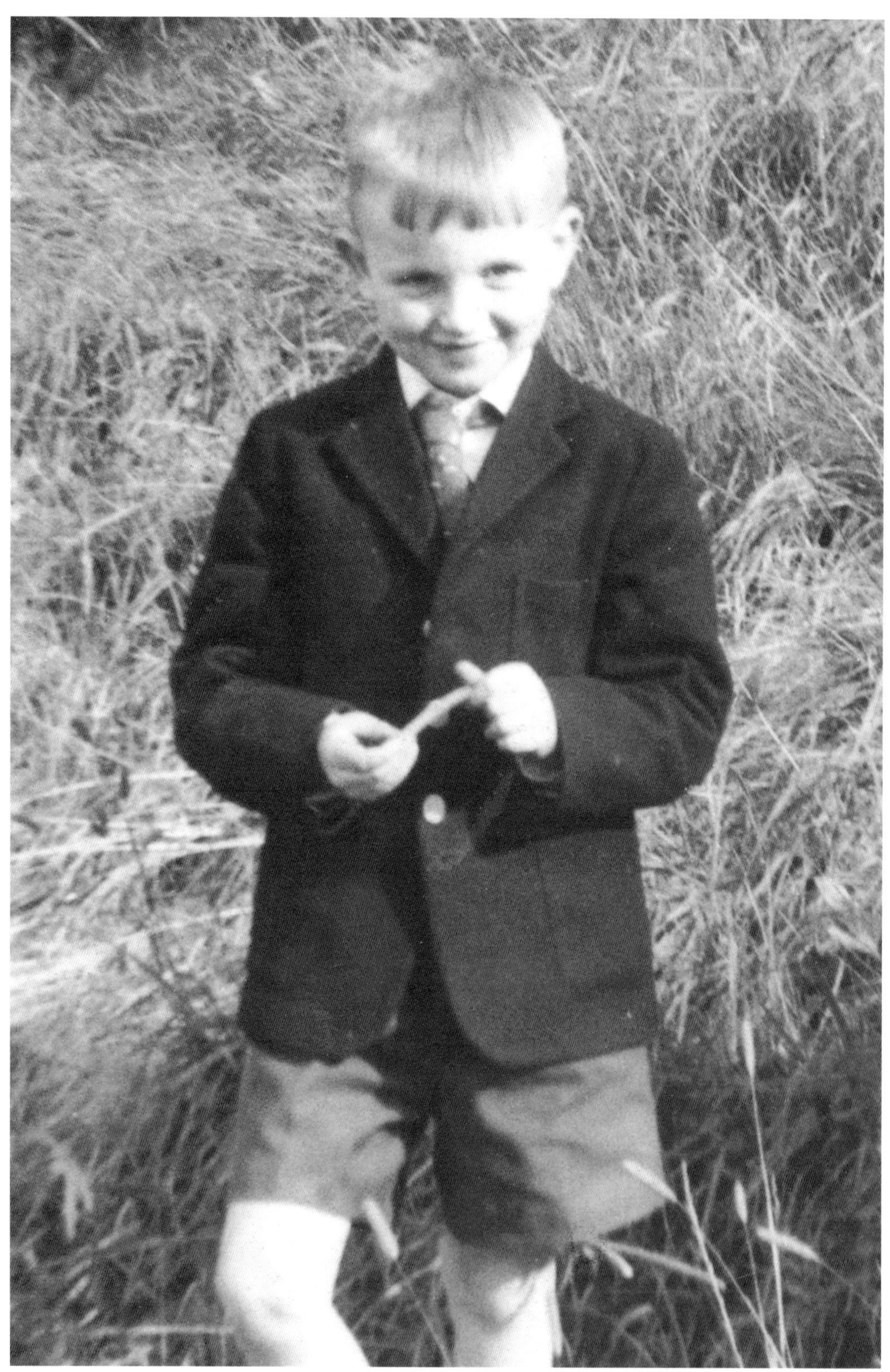

"I hate the countryside so much." Mark 1963. (*Courtesy of Smith family*)

Band meeting at Mark and Una's Kingswood Road flat, (l-r) Martin Bramah, Una Baines, Karl Burns, MES, Tony Friel. (*Kevin Cummins/Idols*)

Live At The Witch Trials, 1978. (*Kevin Cummins/Idols*)

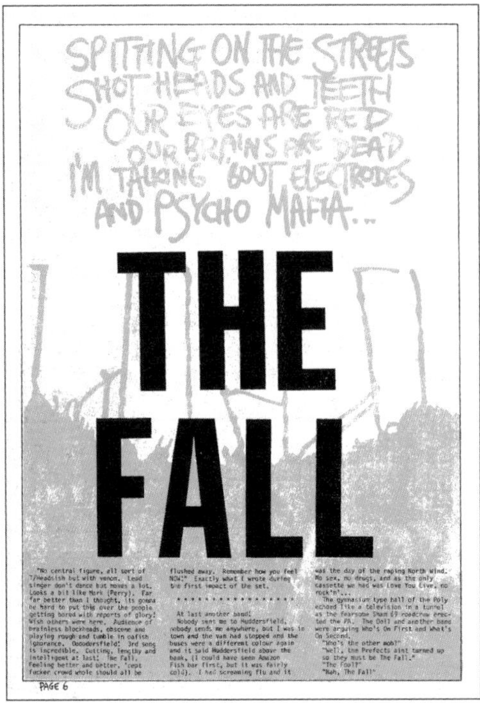

SPITTING ON THE STREETS
SHOT HEADS AND TEETH
OUR EYES ARE RED
OUR BRAINS ARE DEAD
I'M TALKING 'BOUT ELECTRODES
AND PSYCHO MAFIA...

THE FALL

"No central figure, all sort of T/Headsish but with venom. Lead singer don't dance but moves a lot. Looks a bit like Mark (Perry). Far far better than I thought, its gonna be hard to put this over the people getting bored with reports of glory! Wish others were here. Audience of brainless blockheads, obscene and playing rough and tumble in oafish ignorance. Ooodersfield! 3rd song is incredible. Cutting, lengthy and intelligent at last! The Fall. Feeling better and better, 'cept fucker crowd whole should all be flushed away. Remember how you feel NOW!" Exactly what I wrote during the first impact of the set.

* * * * * * * * * * * * * * * * * *

At last another band!

Nobody sent me to Huddersfield, nobody sends me anywhere, but I was in town and the van had stopped and the buses were a different colour again and it said Huddersfield above the bank, (I could have seen Amazon Fish bar first, but it was fairly cold). I had screaming flu and it was the day of the raping North Wind. No sex, no drugs, and as the only cassette we had was Love You Live, no rock'n'...

The gymnasium type hall of the Poly echoed like a television in a tunnel as the fearsome Sham 69 roadcrew erected the PA. The Doll and another band were arguing Who's On First and What's On Second.

"Who's the other mob?"

"Well, the Prefects aint turned up so they must be The Fall."

"The Fool?"

"Nah, The Fall"

PAGE 6

THE FALL (STANDING L-R) UNA BAINS - ELECTRIC PIANO, 20, ARIES, CHANGES A LOT; MARK SMITH - LEAD VOCALS, HYPOCHONDRIAC, 20; (SITTING L-R) JONNIE BROWN - BASS, YORKSHIRE; MARTIN BRANCH - GUITAR - LEFT-HANDED, B. VOCALS, 19; KARL BURNS - DRUMS, 19, MATERIALIST

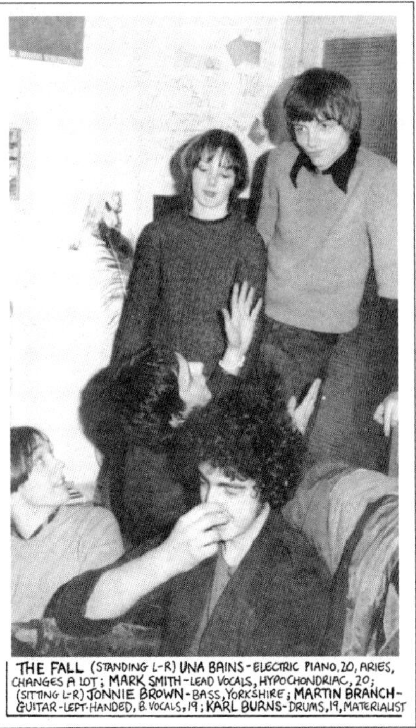

One of the band's first features in *Zig Zag* magazine, March 1978.

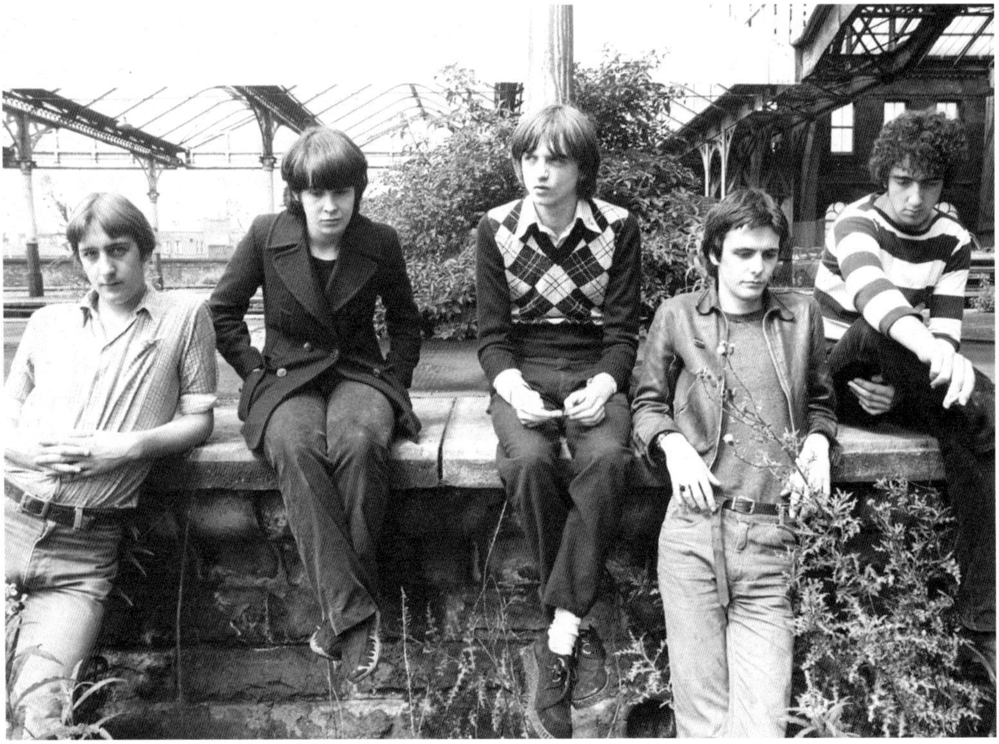

Marc Riley, Yvonne Pawlett, MES, Bramah and Burns hit the weed. (*Kevin Cummins/Idols*)

"I still believe in the R 'n' R dream." The Fall in rehearsal. (*Steve Lyons/SIN*)

SIDE, SOMETHING ALONG THE LINES OF "BABY WAS BABY 'COS SHE

I'LL END BY SAYING, IF YOU AIN'T GOT THE SINGLE IT'S YOUR LOSS ~ The Nosebleeds - pure fun for drunk people.

The Fall

BASSIST, MARC RILEY TO REPLACE THE SACKED ERIC. SO NOW THE NEW-LOOK **FALL** IS:

YES, YOU'VE GUESSED IT – THE PREDICTABLY UNPREDICTABLE 'FALL' HAVE HAD ANOTHER LINE-UP CHANGE! AS WE REPORTED IN THE LAST "A.U", UNA, THEIR KEYBOARDS-PLAYER HAD LEFT, BUT BETWEEN THEN AND NOW THEY FOUND ANOTHER YOUNG LADY TO TAMPER WITH KEYBOARDS AND RECRUITED A NEW 16-YR. OLD

Martin Bramah-Gtr/vcl.
Karl Burns Drums
Marc Riley-Bass gtr.
Yvonne Pawlett-E.piano
Mark E. Smith-Vocals

CRACKER FACTORY=Rehabs for no-hopes=Pre-fabs for jobless dopes.

Become Part Of The Music Scene with The Fall. So don't you forget it.

When I was at the Witch Trials of the 20th. century, they said: "You are white crap. You are an aesthetic anaesthetic. Your repetition will never be accepted."
The Fall 1979

E.P. RELEASED 11.8.78
on Step Forward records
A side: 'Psycho Mafia'
'Bingo Master'
B side: 'Repetition 1'

THE FALL – GETTING AS PREDICTABLE AS A NEWSREADER WITH FLEAS.

TRIP OUT + EXPERIENCE THE FALL: THEIR BLISTERING E.P. IS OUT NOW AND THEY'RE ALMOST CERTAIN TO PLAY BELFAST IN THE NOT TOO DISTANT FUTURE.

PHOTOS: LEFT, L-R, Martin, Mark, Marc + Karl. ABOVE RIGHT, Martin + Marc. BOTH PHOTOS FROM A RECENT GIG AT [illegible]

Excerpt from Dave McCulloch's perceptive fanzine, *Alternative Ulster.*

Outside the Codrington Mews home of Faulty Products with new drummer Mike Leigh (second right), March 2 1979. (*Paul Slattery*)

from the nearby Prestwich Mental Hospital, tales of controlling treatments, of bullying tactics in the corridors and the horrors of imposing a repressive 'boredom' on people already lapsing into mental illness. The song, 'Repetition', would become something of an early Fall anthem, although its emotional depth would arguably be exaggerated. The extended nature of the song owed more to the band's punk roots than any genuine artistic commitment.

"The psychiatrists must be killed . . . they put electrodes on your brain . . . and you are never the same . . ." spat Mark, and even through the venom of those early gigs, it was eerily possible to spot a large dose of irony hiding in the shadows. Was Mark – and I always wanted to ask this – hitting back, not just at the hospital tactics, but also at the exaggerated claims made by some of the patients?

Mark: "We used to invite the patients over for cups of tea . . ."

"Repetition in the music and we are never going to lose it . . ."

There were obvious problems and the biggest one of all was called Dave. When a face doesn't fit, let alone a political stance, and, indeed, a cultural leaning (Dave was known to have Beatles records in his collection), something would have to snap. Dave probably never realised it but, in being swiftly jettisoned in the wake of post-gig euphoria, he would set a precedent for the edgy dynamic and attrition that would soon become synonymous with this band, as Mark set out on his singular artistic mission which at the very least incorporated a genuine desire to keep the band's feet on the ground at all times.

His immediate replacement, a man who would drift in and out of The Fall for three decades, was a manic – though rather endearing – Stooges and heavy metal fan who still allowed his curls to unfold untrendily down towards his neck, who still allowed Black Sabbath on to his stereo and who, despite a marked fondness for The New York Dolls and Iggy & The Stooges, remained somewhat scathing about the unfolding Manchester scene. Karl Burns was his name, acidic was his nature. He carried a hint of menace that masked the fact that he was, by immediate comparison, a somewhat more advanced musician, proficient on both guitar and drums. Despite this musicianly deftness, he was allowed into the ranks as Una Baines took stage left on keyboards. Already, one gig in, the Fall dynamic was beginning to splinter.

Mark: "You know . . . I wasn't going to tell anyone this, Mick. But, the more I started to sing . . . when I got up and sang, or shouted or whatever . . . people fucking laughed at me when I sang, you know. And that sort of made me madder. Buzzcocks came to a few gigs at the start and I would overhear them talking. They would talk to the group. They would be saying, 'You are great but you have got to get rid of that fucking singer.' Not Pete [Shelley]. Pete was great. But the others were like that, totally. They kept on telling the group that they could get better. You have got to get rid of that crap singer. Those are the words that I heard over and over and over again and I knew that the band were taking notice of these statements. I knew that they were smiling to my face and plotting behind my back. Because they just didn't think I was good enough and they wanted me out. That is the reason that it pisses me off when I hear them all saying how great Mark was. Because they didn't see it. Some of the audience saw it. Dick Witts saw it. You saw it, to some extent, but the band were not seeing it. It's just out-and-out hypocrisy because they were never really part of The Fall. They were part of some other group. Blue Orchids was just about right. That's where their heads were at. I am not big-headed about it at all. It's just a statement of fact that The Fall, the concept of The Fall in those early days . . . was in fact me. It became more than me, later, when Steve Hanley and Craig Scanlon and quite a few others would join because, by this time, they would be in tune with the concept of The Fall and it would move on from there. But Friel . . . Una . . . Bramah . . . all talking about The Fall. Forget it."

Manchester 1977

The inevitability was that punk's sharp focus would cause it to rapidly develop musical orthodoxies – mostly prized from old Stooges recordings – that would effectively be far more rigid than the myriad styles it so sneeringly replaced. It might be noted, therefore, that while Mark E. Smith readily admired The Sex Pistols – "Are their lyrics fucking great?" he told me at the time, " 'Holidays In The Sun', man, fucking brilliant" – it soon became clear that he was not about to jettison his Can albums because of the length of Germanic hair involved. Sadly, to some extent, there were continuing signs that The Electric Circus was rapidly spinning into a grubby, unholy zoo, filled with followers rather than, as was noisily claimed at the time, genuine innovators. Spinning around in speed rush frenzy were, indeed, examples of the most submissive kind of fandom. Clash fans perhaps, with 'Sten Guns in Wilmslow' daubed meekly on the back of sub-Wrangler 'Sea Dog' brushed denim. For the most part, it remained fun, drifting down to Collyhurst on Sunday afternoons, to snigger in the shadows as The Adverts, Ramones/Talking Heads, The Jam, Buzzcocks endlessly and The Clash's infamous 'White Riot' tour hurtled the crumbly venue into a hazardous frenzy, and watch the increasingly adventurous, increasingly garishly clad clientele battling for the spotlight. It was a weekly ego fest that would spill out and onto the stage, allowing sub performers such as soon-to-be Fall devotee Jon The Postman and a cruel joke named The Negatives – featuring Paul Morley, Kevin Cummins and Richard Boon – all on board to increase their chances of making a mark rather than any kind of deliberately artless statement. You could sense a swell of desperation in the crowd too, in the lesser bands who had started to flicker in the shadows, more and more they adopted rock-star guises, tight brash red jeans, shining in plastic, wallowing in touches of make-up in a look reclaimed from the glam age. They wanted to be seen . . . seen on buses . . . seen walking to The Electric Circus . . . seen floating down to The Ranch on Dale Street, where their garish braggadocio would clash with steely Teds, all of a sudden in resurgence, all of a sudden offended (and for reasons that have never fully dawned on me) by the punks who so clearly longed to achieve the same state of oft-inebriated distance from the mainstream.

Mark and The Fall gang dutifully attended The Electric Circus. It was, after all, on their beloved north side of town, at this time dramatically crumbling to inner city decay to such an extent that it was almost evolving into a stark post-apocalyptic vision, rubble and decay awash in the yellow lights, as if brought to life by a particularly one-dimensional Clash lyric. At least it looked vaguely romantic even if the reality was somewhat less cinematic. In true Salfordian tradition, as the houses fell away, nicotine encrusted pubs remained and in many of these, on various days, could be found Mark E. Smith and his friends, conspicuous only by their utter lack of effort in regard to adopting any trace of unifying punk garbs.

Mark, in a letter to the author, 1979: "I can't understand people like them (indicates Manchester band V2, a glitzy assortment of spandex-clad glam punks, simply melting in make-up, screaming to be heard). I mean, why would you want to dress like that? You outlaw yourself by doing that and, in a negative sense, step out of sync. The point is that it is not a clever thing to do. It has no intelligence. Anyone can do that, regardless of talent or vision. It's utterly meaningless in this instance. I realise that they might point out that Iggy Pop and The New York Dolls adopted the same attitude, but they would have been heard and seen whatever . . . and it was original to them. I mean, I have nothing against these people . . . that one . . . is his name Mark? Your friend . . . he's a nice guy and all that. You meet far worse people in the music business than that . . . but they just seem to be going about things in a very clumsy and juvenile way. I could never do that."

And Mark never did, famously procuring his stage wear – as ever, exactly the same as his off-stage wear – from the stalls of Bury Market. It was a line in clothes that, though later championed as gloriously ironic, always seemed perfectly natural for Mark, be it the diamond patterned sweater he – again rather famously – wore for a gig at The Marquee or the knee-length boots he enjoyed at The Festival of the Tenth Summer in 1986, referred to as "an affectation" by a writer from style mag *The Face*, unwisely as it happens. Affectation never hovered close, never once descended on Mark E. Smith.

And certainly not in 1977 when, happy and resplendent in drab day wear, Mark would sink into those shadows . . . and he wasn't tapping up journalists, or promoters, or photographers and certainly not members of other groups . . . Mark would be doing nothing more than sinking into the evening. Soaking in the pre-gig reggae disco, glancing stage-wards and observing the stance of the singer, drinking, smoking and doing the things that everybody approaching late teens should have been doing. Around him . . . the members of the band . . . all of them, did those little careerist things . . . and they *did*, too, latching onto the coat-tails of many a lesser outfit, pleading for a spot. But Mark just watched and allowed it to soak in gently. The Electric Circus happened before his eyes . . . and he wasn't overly impressed.

'Stuff The Jubilee Festival', Squat Club, Devas Street, Manchester. June 3, 1977

It was duty rather than protest and almost wearying. It was, after all, the summer of 1977, when The Sex Pistols orchestrated a headline grabbing Thames boat trip and found their rallying 'God Save The Queen' mysteriously shunted from the number one spot. Punks, naturally, fell in line. In Manchester, on June 3, 1977, the members of The Fall trundled down to Manchester city centre where they met with the proprietors of Manchester's twin fanzines, *Shy Talk* and *Ghast Up*, plus a rag-taggle gang of 20 or so dubiously garbed punks which included, it was later noted, future cyber punk author Jeff Noon, keen to gain a foothold in the artless mode of fanzine production, Jon The Postman, two Buzzcocks, Paul Morley and Buzzcocks manager Richard Boon. In a typically forceful, typically stupid over-reaction to any kind of anti-Jubilee protest, the Manchester Constabulary forced a banner waving oik into the back of a police van from which he would later emerge proudly sporting a number of body bruises. Most of the other protesters dispersed rather too merrily into the city centre, to regroup at the Wimpy Bar in the stark concrete anachronism of Piccadilly Square, where the atmosphere sank to downbeat. The Fall drifted along to The Squat, a dust-encrusted theatre on Devas Street, deep in the heart of Oxford Road's student land. It was to be the occasion of The Fall's second gig.

Mark: "Is that true? I don't remember that gig . . . or do I? Oh yeah . . . yeah, that's right. That was the second gig, wasn't it? I seem to recall Ian McCulloch and Julian Cope coming down . . . or was that a later gig? I am not a retro person and don't ever really like looking back at all, so it's a bit of a blur, this. Funny thing is that, when I hear the other old band members talking about it I immediately start to distrust what they say because they have conveniently wiped out some of the memories. They were already against me at this point, you know. They didn't think I could cut it as a front man at all. I will come back to this point, but it really annoys me when they all come out of the woodwork and say how great the early Fall were. Because they wanted fucking out, man. Friel, in particular, still wanted to play fucking jazz at this point. So all this stuff about it being a united Manchester punk scene is just crap. We weren't part of any fucking scene . . . we weren't even part of our own scene. Loads of fucking bickering going on. And they had no fucking idea where they wanted The Fall to go. They might as well have been in Slaughter & The Dogs, or some shit like that. It wasn't a particularly happy time."

Nevertheless, The Squat 'Stuff the Jubilee' gig would sink into Manchester music myth . . . the very venue – an unsightly Victorian annexe, forever under threat of merciful demolition – had sunk its feet into local music legend in the early Seventies when the embryonic Manchester based – and London baiting – music promotions company, Music Force, had helped save the venue by staging a series of 'sit-ins', rather ironically aping more famous events in the capital during the Sixties. Music Force, was a loose communist-style huddle of local musicians and cohorts led by innovative Wythenshawrian Tosh Ryan, Albertos/Durutti Column drummer Bruce Mitchell, blues legend Victor Brox and, as the punk age dawned, Martin Hannett. Their importance cannot be overstated. Mark's understandable aloofness aside, very little would have happened at all in Manchester had this unholy gang not managed to wrestle the impetus away from the University Social Secretaries. The Squat, being cheap and, frankly, often rather nasty, did provide a base that kept Manchester musicians bubbling away through the early Seventies. At one time it was, again loosely, co-ordinated by Tom Robinson Band manager Colin Bell and had operated as an arts centre that staged the early ideas of Rik Mayall and Ben Elton.

None of this history seemed particularly relevant to the 'Stuff the Jubilee' mini-festival which was high on possibility, high on fun to some extent, and lacking any trace of finesse. Not that it particularly mattered. It was to be one of those occasions, sparsely attended in reality, vastly attended in retrospect. Mostly, the attendees flopped around the fringes of the hall, or ducked into the dope huddles in the toilets, if not physically breaking into one of the practice rooms beneath the main hall. Most of the serious practitioners were at the gig and, significantly, at the gig to witness The Fall, without any doubt the most interesting act of the day. Yours truly attended the event with *Shy Talk* writer Steve Shy. Earlier we had stalked Martin Hannett in the nicotine encrusted office of Music Force. Steve had two reasons to be in attendance: as manager of the ironical and profoundly unmusical The Worst – whose main claim to fame was the fact that their drummer owned a Chad Valley drum kit – and, as 'bass' player in the equally ironic The Negatives, who included Paul Morley on guitar, photographer Kevin Cummins on drums, the aforementioned Shy and, later, Buzzcocks manager Richard Boon on saxophone. Like The Worst – and, later, Jon The Postman's Puerile – The Negatives were little more than a barrage of in-jokes revolving around vocalist and Sex Pistols bootlegger, Dave Bentley. If there was, as has so often been claimed, a genuine controlling heart to the Manchester scene, then a large part of it would be on stage at The Squat Club on June 3. Both sets were largely unmemorable – apart from Steve Shy's athletic leap during a hilariously inept bass solo – and merely paved the way for the main acts of the day. One of them, Warsaw, an embryonic, and rather dark unit, famously formed in the wake of The Sex Pistols Lesser Free Trade Hall gigs, would later emerge as Joy Division. The headlining act – although they would denounce the notion of competition . . . the more the merrier – would be The Drones. Standard punk fare, still managed by Paul Morley and the biggest non-Buzzcock draw in Manchester. But to give The Drones their due, and nobody else has, ever since Morley turned nastily on them within the pages of the *NME*, their prodigious commitment proved an inspiration for all the other acts.

And then, The Fall. Belligerent and brimming with brittle

dynamism, Mark spitting the words to 'Hey Fascist' across with unnerving venom, with Jon The Postman, a central pivot in the audience, bouncing in mock pogo frenzy, with another infamous Manchester punk, 'Big Bad Brinner' by name, endearing if a little sardonic by nature, swirling around during 'Psycho Mafia', and members of The Negatives milling with intent.

Buzzcocks manager Richard Boon, in particular, had designs on this unexpectedly sharp young band. Realising that Buzzcocks needed help if they were to make serious inroads into London and put Manchester music, much derided (despite Paul Morley's efforts) in the music press until this point, he was openly searching for a regular support band. Realising that the post Howard Devoto Buzzcocks were softening rapidly into a potential chart pop band, he at once admired the contrary stance and uncompromising attitude of the young Fall. Speaking of one song in particular, 'Industrial Estate' (which began with the innovative Mark E. Smith rant "Get up for Ind Est . . . Get up for Ind Est . . .") Boon noted: "It was sheer garage, like watching The Seeds or Stooges. I immediately loved it and knew also that it would contrast perfectly with Buzzcocks. The idea was to help them, take them along to our gigs in London as support . . . it was just a way of saying that there was contrast in Manchester."

Boon may, of course, have been wondering about managing The Fall himself. It was an open secret that, though excited by the commercial possibilities of Buzzcocks, the band had evolved away from his personal tastes, which were rather more esoteric. This would finally be proven after Buzzcocks house label, New Hormones, became a landing pad for every Manchester band who had been suitably inspired by Can and Beefheart. As such, New Hormones might have been the perfect base for The Fall, although Mark E. Smith is relieved that the liaison never materialised.

The first development of a Buzzcocks-Fall axis was to take place a month later, when The Fall supported Buzzcocks at North East London Polytechnic at a Rock Against Racism event. Typical of a time when politics were dramatically polarised, Buzzcocks enjoyed the support of the more profound polemic of their support band.

Mark: "We were all for it, of course, but even then the warning signs seemed obvious to me. This was our first venture out of Manchester, let alone playing in London and there were certain journalists there. I remember thinking that we were sitting ducks, to some extent. White, working-class, northern band. It was obvious that sooner or later the London media would try and adopt us in a very patronising way. Which is exactly how it turned out, as it happened. But even before that, at that particular gig, we had these guys asking us to hold banners up . . . hold slogans up . . . stress this, stress that. I told them to fuck off. We had enough politics in our music. That was the point . . . it wasn't obvious sloganeering. We weren't fucking Sham 69 or Tom Robinson. I was completely opposed to all that. With us you had to put in a bit of thought. And, even though we were a very young band and obviously had no following, we did respect the ability of the audience to decide for themselves. I became almost instantly disillusioned with the whole thing. I didn't trust a lot of those people. I thought that a lot of them were in it for their own reasons. Seemed obvious to me, that."

July 1977 also saw a significant victory for Paul Morley at the *NME*. Throughout the year he had been campaigning to be allowed to write a large Manchester feature for the paper. It had been tough going. Mostly, as the older journos of the Afro variety had gained a large degree of control, and had already been fighting hard to fend off the brash advances of, among others, Tony Parsons and Julie Burchill, they remained spectacularly unimpressed by a spike-topped northerner, simply dripping in precocity and spinning yarns about big happenings in Manchester. Twice previously Morley's reportage had been resolutely rejected. On one memorable occasion, wandering round to his local newsagent in Heaton Moor, Stockport, and fully expecting to have been handed his first cover story, he was immediately insulted by the sight of BB King glaring from the cover. Though a King fan, Morley argued venomously that, in 1977, *NME* should be concentrating on affairs rather closer to home. Eventually, they relented and beneath a headline that simpered "Manchester. The truth behind a bizarre cult sweeping the nation's youth", Morley managed to squeeze all his friends into an article which surged across Buzzcocks, Slaughter & The Dogs, The Drones – being the big three – before handing out accolades to The Worst, The Fall and fanzines *Shy Talk* and *Ghast Up*. It was The Fall's first acknowledgement in *NME*, so beginning a famously tumultuous relationship that would, in the coming years, hover on the brink of mild violence.

Curiously, from the moment Paul Morley's article heralded a new dawn of Manchester music – though, in truth, he had been scooped by a similar affair in *Melody Maker* – the whole shebang started to retract and, following the enforced closure of The Electric Circus in October, the city all but reverted to its former, largely gigless state.

On the face of it, with The Electric Circus being the essentially ramshackle vortex of the Manchester scene, most bands and followers regarded this closure as authoritarian repression – it closed because it was refused a food licence – and duly raised their voices in suitably punky protest. The reality was rather different. When The Electric Circus was full, and it was increasingly swelling as word caught on, it became blatantly obvious that the place, rather haphazardly operated by grubby downbeat hoodlums, wouldn't be able to cope should anything untoward happen to the electrics, and it was a miracle that it survived until the autumn. Nevertheless, Manchester's youth, or at least the punky aspect of it, was desperately seeking some kind of cause to fight and this added frisson made the final two nights at The Electric Circus – over the weekend of October 1 and 2 – at least *feel* as though they held a special importance.

Backstage, things were rather different. On both nights, any trace of camaraderie between Manchester bands vanished horribly as young men, unable to cope with the pressures of very minor fame, succumbed to the absurdities of their own egos. As such, the two-day bill looked impressive: Buzzcocks, the first sighting of Howard Devoto's Magazine, The Drones, The Fall, Steel Pulse, V2, Jon The Postman, The Negatives, The Prefects, Manicured Noise, Big In Japan, although some bands – The Drones, in particular – reacted badly to the competition, and it was rather sad to see the bitching spilling onto the stage.

Mark E. Smith, still a relative unknown, retained a dignified distance from any of this . . . as did the rest of the band, who appeared on the Sunday evening and seemed gloriously at odds with the enforced local bonhomie.

There was one moment, as 'Big Dave', an ex-punk fighting Ted, latterly turned punk, emerged from The Electric Circus' inoperative and eternally flooded toilet, holding a spilling loo pan aloft, presumably in a display of rebellious braggadocio – nobody thought to ask him – at the precise moment The Fall launched into 'Hey Fascist'. The image is lasting and remains the best fun-time moment of the whole highly uncomfortable event. For the most part of The Fall's set, the band were subjected to continuing ironic taunts of "Right on brother . . . hey comrade . . ." the indication being that The Fall's local image was one of ragged communistic ranters. Curious, as Mark E. Smith's socialistic leanings were based on rather more intelligent ground than that.

Two songs culled unceremoniously from The Fall's set offered a glimpse of treasures to come. 'Steppin' Out' was a song about growing awareness and seemed to centre on Mark's having moved away from the kind of sheep-like closeness that was prevailing in Manchester. "I used to believe, everything I read . . . but that's all changed, now I'm steppin' out," he sang, firmly establishing his ferocious independence. He could have been referring to the Morley article. The other was 'Last Orders' which took an obvious bar room statement and twisted it into an apocalyptic metaphor. Both songs remained simplistic but were dominated by Friel's increasingly inappropriate bass lines.

Attrition within the band was quelled, for a while at least, by the prospect of recording material for the EP, funded by Boon, and curiously intended as part of a sub-deal with Buzzcocks, whereby The Fall would even share the label – United Artists – if not New Hormones. If nothing else, this situation of 'signed or not signed' increased the excitable chatter in the pub and back at the Kingswood Road flat, where, increasingly, Fall 'hangers-on' (which, if I am to be completely honest about it, included yours truly). The dynamic of this small social swirl was changing, as well as the powers within the band. The period hailed the forceful arrival of Kay Carroll who had met Baines at Prestwich Hospital, where they had both worked as nurses. A decade ahead of the rest of the band, in both years and experience, Kay was hurtling from a fall herself, having been through a tumultuous marriage/two children/divorce cycle which had left her with a sardonic chunk firmly etched in her endearing character.

For me, the arrival of Kay actually hails a slightly awkward phase in the story. Kay would enter the band circle, first as a friend who had found herself captivated by the sharp and unexpected pull of their music, and Mark's lyrics in particular and, equally one senses, by her closeness to Mark, whom she lived with in Prestwich for a number of years. Obviously, I didn't know Kay as well as Mark, but I did know her differently. During the oncoming years, we became close, not in any sexual way, but with a brotherly/sisterly feel, where I would ease her through and out of arguments in the local pub, much to the amusement of Mark, who thoroughly approved. It was a friendship which I feel it necessary to declare while respecting the fact that, in terms of her heavy involvement with the day-to-day running of The Fall, I had no real idea what was going on. I did, however, realise from quite early on that Kay's arrival – well before she had taken on the mantle of manager* – fomented some form of conflict. Once, as I travelled through Prestwich en route to the flat, I saw Una and Martin locked in near hysterical discourse in the village. I had no doubt that they had just left Mark's flat. I had no doubt either, that Kay had been the cause of the unrest.

Mark: "Kay became the manager. Yeah, erm . . . yeah . . . you can ask me about Kay . . . all that stuff . . . those people in the *early*fall. But you know what. All those people involved in the early Fall . . . including Kay . . . but *all* of them dumped me at one stage or another. I mean it's a fucking cheek to see them talking, now. They all walked out. Friel . . . fucking hell. They didn't give a shit. I sacked half of them. But the point is that they thought The Fall was a no

* The first I knew about this was following a particularly spirited gig at St John's College, Manchester, during which Mark had mercilessly berated the promoters ". . . yes, well, due to typical student idiocy, none of the fucking equipment works . . ." in a serious though most entertaining fashion, after which Mark stated openly to me that "Kay is now the manager and things will change."

goer. They had all these Manchester mates yapping in their ears. Saying how better it would be if they did it on their own. The thing is that musicians don't get to the heart of it. Also there was a North Manchester and South Manchester divide. North Manchester is supposed to be full of fucking beer boozers and South Manchester supposed to be all arty farty.

"To be honest, that pop against arty farty stuff . . . the thing is that The Fall have always had a problem because, on numerous occasions, the band have wanted to take an easy road and play pop stuff . . . which wouldn't have been The Fall but they just wanted hits or whatever. Even the last group did that.

"The first Fall were hanging round with the Buzzcocks. The second group was hanging round with The Smiths. The third line-up is hanging round with Happy Mondays. The fourth one is hanging round with Oasis . . . and they would say things like . . . oh this group have got a villa . . . and all that shit. And big sports cars. And you, Mark, are only giving me two hundred nicker a week. They think, being musicians who haven't worked a day's work in their fucking lives, haven't worked since fucking school . . . I still get annoyed about it . . . fucking cheeky bastards. I took them all round the world and they start moaning that they are not living like Oasis. My attitude is simple. If you want to be in those groups then go and join them. A few times it was me sacking them but a lot of times it was like . . . oh, all right, go and fucking do it. And they go. And then . . . I call it the two-year gap . . . 18 months . . . two-year gap . . . they come over and it's all, 'Oh . . . Mark . . . how are yer doin?' I mean it's fucking obvious, isn't it? Some people haven't got the intelligence you know. You have no idea how many calls I have had. Especially since that film came out . . . that stupid fucking film. They have all seen it and it's like, 'Oh, hi Mark, give us a ring' and all that."

The Fall's first studio recording took place on November 9, 1977, down among the tawdry low-fi teak of Indigo Studios, where an eight-track mixing desk helped to slot their instrumentation solidly into place.

Mark: "I was fucking terrified, me. It was awkward because we didn't know what the fuck we were doing and, as such, were completely at the mercy of the engineers . . . something which I learnt very quickly. The fact was we were paying them, they were working for us and they had no right to cock a fucking sneer at us or adopt any kind of attitude. You have to make that clear from the start when you go in a recording studio. You have to know what you want, in terms of raw sound, and simply go for it. That hasn't changed either because today they come across all techy and, because you are older and have no interest in computers, they think they are cleverer. So you make it very clear just what you want. You are in charge. It's your sound. If they want to use high levels of technology, then fine . . . just as long as it all leads to the sound that you have in your head. It's that simple. If we had listened to them we would have become a dumb chart pop cabaret outfit within three years. But I always knew what The Fall would be . . . way beyond that."

Four songs were to be recorded. 'Bingo-Master's Break-Out!', during which Una Baines keyboard edges an inch away from the painful and was allowed to stand because of Mark's determination to keep within a primal 'garage sound', would, with any kind of warmer keyboards, have touched a musical prettiness that would not have been wholly representative. 'Psycho Mafia' needed no such intervention. Solid, all-out attack, self-explanatory and simply brimming with paranoia, as, indeed, was 'Frightened', which trudged resolutely at a slow pace like a late night walk home from Manchester city centre, a 'beneath the yellow lights' tale of urban paranoia. 'Repetition', the final, elongated recording had already started to drift into The Fall's backwaters, if not by the recording, then certainly by the time of eventual release, in August 1978.

"This song . . . this song . . . is going to last for three hours . . ." Mark hissed, during a performance at The Band On The Wall, towards the close of 1977.

REPETITION

Right noise.
We're gonna get real speedy
You gotta wear black all the time
You're gonna make it on your own.

Cos we dig
Cos we dig
We dig
We dig repetition
We dig repetition
We've repetition in the music
And we're never going to lose it.

All you daughters and sons
who are sick of fancy music
We dig repetition
Repetition on the drums
and we're never going to lose it.

This is the three R's
The three R's:
Repetition, Repetition, Repetition

Oh mental hospitals
Oh mental hospitals
They put electrodes in your brain
And you're never the same
You don't dig repetition
You don't love repetition

Repetition in the music and we're never going to lose it

President Carter loves repetition
Chairman Mao he dug repetition

Repetition in China
Repetition in America
Repetition in West Germany
Simultaneous suicides

We dig it, we dig it,
we dig it, we dig it

Repetition, repetition, repetition
Repetition, repetition, Regal Zonophone

There is no hesitation
This is your situation
Continue a blank generation
Blank generation
Same old blank generation
Groovy blank generation
Swinging blank generation

Repetition, repetition, repetition . . .

BINGO-MASTER'S BREAK-OUT!

Two swans in front of his eyes
Coloured balls in front of his eyes
It's number one for his Kelly's eye
Treble-six right over his eye

A big shot's voice in his ears
Worlds of silence in his ears
All the numbers account for years
Checks the cards through eyes of tears

Bingo-Master's Break-Out!

All he sees is the back of chairs
In the mirror, a lack of hairs
A light room, which he fills out
Hear the players all shout

Bingo-Master's Break-Out!

A glass of lager in his hand
Silver microphone in his hand
Wasting time in numbers and rhyme
One hundred blank faces buy

Bingo-Master's Break-Out!

Came the time he flipped his lid
Came the time he flipped his lid
Holiday in Spain fell through
Players put it down to

Bingo-Master's Break-Out!

A hall full of cards left unfilled
Ended his life with wine and pills
There's a grave somewhere only partly filled
A sign in a graveyard on a hill reads

Bingo-Master's Break-Out!

The Fall at the Band On The Wall became something of an institution. Ironic too, that the often superior musicianship in the Manchester Musicians Collective couldn't drum up anything to compete with this swiftly unfolding band . . . and unfold they did, with the prodigious Smith showing early signs of his solid work ethic by throwing more and more lyrics into the pot . . . not that the set changed fast enough, for Mark, who had already harboured a vision of The Fall as a band on shifting esoteric sands, never allowing a trace of staleness, forever fresh, occasionally bewildering, always challenging. This was not necessarily a dream shared by Bramah, Baines, Friel and Burns.

Friel was undoubtedly affected by the Smith/Carroll axis. Elsewhere, in various organs and even in a couple of books, he has stated that he felt that The Fall had been as much his band at the start . . .

but saw that particular dream snatched away as Mark and Kay increasingly gained control.

One fact remains firm. If The Fall began life as a ragged collective, willing to take on board the problems of such a collective, it soon became obvious that this wasn't to be the case. And the surprising factor here is not that Mark E. Smith, aided and abetted by Kay Carroll, wished to start a 'dictatorship', as has, again, been stated elsewhere. It was simply that all had underestimated Smith's talent at the beginning . . . and when Mark started to lead by sheer force of talent, ideas and charisma, it was too late, not just for Friel, but Bramah and Baines as well, who all needed a slower pace, a steadier line of musical progress. They would later find just that as The Blue Orchids, a far more conservative outfit altogether, not without moments of inspiration, not without turning a few heads either, but not The Fall. Bramah, to his credit, would be the last to leave, hanging in until 1979.

Mark: "It was the same in America, in Cleveland and Seattle. I remember thinking about that so-called Seattle scene. When Nirvana were supporting us. You could see it . . . but you can't say that at the time. Whenever we supported the Buzzcocks . . . they were very supportive, I have got to say that about Buzzcocks. They were always good in that way. Richard Boon, the manager, was particularly good. They paid for the first Fall single. Richard did not manage the group. We went down to London, eventually with Miles Copeland . . . It was Danny Baker, actually, who got us that deal. With Step Forward. He had seen us at that Huddersfield gig. He was the one who went in and told Miles Copeland that he should release this record by The Fall. You see that was typical Manchester in a way. Buzzcocks paid for our single but wouldn't release it. So we waited like a year and a half for some kind of release . . . but they didn't. It wasn't going to be released on New Hormones. Richard Boon just paid for it. That's why I always liked him . . . and them really. 'Cos, when they realised that they couldn't do anything with it, they just gave us the masters. You don't get that anymore, I can tell you.

"It's strange. That attitude has gone. Richard paid for it because he thought we were good. I mean, can you imagine that, now? He was pissed off with the Buzzcocks because they were going really poppy and I don't really think Richard was like that. So he might have recorded us to piss them off a bit. I found myself talking to him, years later, at Rough Trade.

"The master take was then ours. It was a good year and a half after we recorded it until Miles Copeland. It was Miles paying for Mark Perry's label. It was great for us to get them. They suited us perfectly. It was great to get to London. To get something out on a London label rather than a Manchester one. That really suited us.

" 'Step Forward' just seemed to be Mark Perry. Danny Baker . . . the Sniffin Glue stuff. They were really sick of stuff like The Police. They wanted control and Copeland was good to them. He was dead American in attitude. He got things done. That American attitude, which was fucking cool, to be honest. So refreshing. 'Cos that Manchester thing was so fucking claustrophobic.

" 'Cos I always train my group. How to play and how to stop. How to not be a musician. That goes right back to the band at the start, because they started to become musicians and I realised then that I didn't get on with musicians. Before the band we used to go out together and that but it stopped. I'd be in the pub with some fucking plumber because I thought he was more intelligent than them. That's the problem with all musicians. Once they get a camera in front of their face, they change completely.

"The advantage I always had was, and is, that I am not a musician. My attitude towards music is totally different than any other musician that I have ever met. I have never really related to them. Still don't. They live in a different time.

"I have worked with classically trained musicians and it's still the same. It doesn't change. They still think, because they play an instrument, that they are cleverer than you. But I have got like a layman's ear you know. I know what I like. To me, it's still like going to a show. If it sounds crap, I will walk out. And that's what musicians can't stand. Does that make sense? A lot of people say that that is the battle of The Fall but I have never lost any sleep over it and I still don't. I have no disrespect to musicians. Because, like me, they have their ups and downs. It's not really part of the dynamic of the band. I know what you are saying . . . maybe it was for a time. No, no . . . there was tension in the band at that early time . . . but like, I kicked them all out after the first LP. And people told me I was crazy. But I knew what I was doing. I didn't want to put an ad in the fucking *Melody Maker.* I have dragged people off council estates, me, who have just been strumming away on their own and told them that they are fucking playing in The Fall. It's about time they started earning a living. We never have had any auditions, so to speak, in The Fall. Never auditioned. Just knew. We had to get people at the right stage of learning. Yes. Yes. Right up to this day.

"I don't want to sit round listening to a drummer going through his fucking routine. I held about two auditions in the history of The Fall and I will never do it again. It was years before we got that many people wanting to join. They would turn up and be bigger shits that . . . you know the amount of record company people who, down the line, tried to get me to be a solo artist with a bunch of musicians. You know, fucking professional punks on £400 a day and they would be shit. You would get some cunt who doesn't care. They could play what you want, technically but it's not what I want. You can't knock them because it's their trade but it's not The Fall.

"Yeah but if you are in a group and you are getting paid £250 a week . . . I have to pay fucking proper rates. I believe in that. I believe in paying everybody fair and square, not like some of them fucking Manchester bands. But then they talk to some fucking idiot from one of them bands who tells them about getting £15,000 from some publishing deal and the lads start wondering why they can't have that. And I have no respect for people like that. They don't see what is really happening. Because I pay it out of me own money sometimes. I've had to go and fucking borrow to pay the lads at times. Sometimes they complain because there is nothing happening. But, fucking hell, I wish someone would do that to me . . . pay me £300 a week to sit on me fucking arse.

"I always thought that the other Manchester bands were just scrambling to get on the Manchester ladder. We had a deliberate policy not to get involved with the Manchester scene at all. My attitude then, and it's the same now, is to not get involved in scenes. How many fucking scenes have you seen just blow up. Just like everyone gets five years . . . then you open a paper and there is some other fucking scene and the old one just fades away. That was always so obvious that I couldn't understand why the other bands couldn't see it. I really thought they were stupid to go along with that . . . it was the same, later, with all that Manchester shite. Well . . . remember the Glasgow scene and all that? I always thought it was very important that The Fall stay away from all that.

"Listening to our stuff in the early days, when John Peel started playing our stuff . . . to be honest . . . I wasn't sure about the Peel connection *at that time*. I thought that Peel was going the wrong way. I wasn't particularly happy about getting the exposure at first. People don't believe this about me but, you know, when we were getting on the front cover of the *NME* and all that, I thought it was wrong. I thought we were doing something wrong, here. That was the way my mind was working, that I wasn't so sure of it. Of whether The Fall fitted in with any of that at all. And everyone was turning around saying how great it was that we were getting exposure. But I was seeing a bigger picture and I do think I was right. I used to think that, well, what is the big deal? Every fucker was on the front of the *NME*. I could see that there was danger coming with all that. I could see that that was when the trouble fucking starts. Because they suddenly think they are special, or something and that's not what The Fall are about. Like that thing with Parsons and Burchill. I nearly kicked his head in that day . . . in fact, I nearly kicked both of their fucking heads in. Kay was with us. To be honest about it though . . . stuff like Kay, who would crack on that it was her who turned that down. It wasn't Kay at all, it was me. Kay was quite happy to sit with Julie Burchill and tell her how she used to be a nurse and chat away, smoking pot together and I was like, 'We are out of here . . .' And they were saying how they could make us the biggest band in the world. The Fall against the National Front . . . you're the only hope for the northern people. That was the most patronising load of shit I have ever come across . . . I was saying, stick it up your fuckin' arse. I mean, c'mon, these people were fucking ludicrous. And they had the audacity to tell me that I wasn't doing it right, like The Clash or someone. They were telling us how we should fit in their little slot. But I was just telling them that they couldn't pigeonhole us like that. It was hard to do for me in them days, because I was on the fucking dole at that point. So we turned down the *NME* front cover. But I knew that, as soon as the musicians saw that, they would be expecting the Rolls Royces to start turning up. I used to like *Sounds* a lot more than the *NME* to be honest. It had honesty about it. I thought so, anyway. I knew that it was better to be on the front cover of *Sounds* than the *NME* for all kinds of reasons. Our fucking followers never read the *NME* anyway. Some of them were just out of Wakefield jail and all that . . . and they got into The Fall by reading *Sounds*. And those guys are still fanatics. I did actually think about this in a business kind of way though. I knew that the *NME* would connect us with a student audience who would only be there for about three years. The kind of people who read *Sounds*, generally speaking, were more your ordinary, everyday people who were also a bit odd. Like those guys from Wakefield jail . . . from all over. I knew that if The Fall could connect with them they would be there for life. It would mean something a bit more special, rather than some passing fancy for Parsons and Fucking Burchill. "So I wasn't being stupid about this and, if you think about it in those terms, it was quite astute. Because if we had gone down that *NME* route, those life-long fans . . . and they are real fanatics too . . . would never have come to us. Those guys could see through *NME* shit. They would just laugh at people like Paul Morley and all that. Because . . . well, because they are actually more intelligent. I knew I was right. Damn right. But, anyway, *Sounds* was just great. You'd get a heavy metal band on one page, a black band on another, a punk band. I used to love reading it. The *NME* was more jumped up *Daily Mail* or whatever. Meant fuck all to me. Children of the *Daily Mail* reader. I have given up reading any music press today. Just fucking horrible, isn't it?

"But this is the way I am, Mick. I have got these two Jewish friends. One is 19 and one 24. I go round to their house and they see this thing in the *NME* about the most influential groups in history.

And it has got The Fall at 21 and they are amazed. They are all 20 years younger than me . . . I mean, Bob Marley at 22 . . . how did that happen? Mark is more influential than Bob Marley! You go to Greece or Turkey and there is some pub band doing Bob Marley . . . they don't do fucking Fall songs, do they! Marley should have been number five. Fucking disgusting. You go to some very nice club in Portugal and some guy will be doing Bob Marley songs. No. It's just bad journalism, that. The Fall shouldn't be up there with Bob Marley in those terms. I just find that really stupid.

"I mean the fucking Wailers in the Sixties . . . the way they generated that music . . . the massive and real political influence they had. You can't pitch The Fall above that in terms of influence. That scares me a bit and, once again, I am relieved that I never went fully down that *NME* route. Just imagine what would have happened. We would certainly have never released all those albums. And I am very proud of that. But The Fall are influential, don't get me wrong, I am proud of it . . . but good journalists would have some sense of perspective."

4

The *Only* Band In The World

Two gigs

Blackburn, Lancashire. Sunday, September 22, 2002, 7.30 pm

Mansion/2 Librans/Cyber Insekt/And Therein/Mere Pseud Mag. Ed./Behind The Counter/Telephone Thing/Touch Sensitive/Hey! Luciani/ Free Range/Roadie reading football poem concerning the trials of supporting Blackpool FC/Enigrammatic Dream/The Classical/Ghost In My House/The Chiselers/New Big Prinz/Jerusalem/Mr Pharmacist/ Bourgeois Town/Victoria/I Wake Up In The City/My Ex-Classmates Kids/Victoria (second attempt)/White Lightning/Hit The North

We chose the pub badly.

Blackburn had succumbed to the mist that arrives on Sunday afternoons, and had greyed into evening, with traffic eventually thinning from roar to purr, with streets emptying to eeriness, leaving a malcontent air hanging over the shopping precinct.

Seven black Mariahs – if we can still refer to them as such – now lay tired, dormant and, no doubt, overworked, outside the police station. Leeds United had been in town. You didn't need to know this or, indeed, know anything about football, to be able to tell . . . something powerful had been here although, in footballing terms, they had gained nothing from a match with a stalwart and resurgent Rovers. The *Lancashire Evening Post* would overtly champion the victory, casting a nod back to the club's weird championship years while noting, albeit buried deep on page 16, that small pockets of violence darkened the city centre on late Sunday afternoon, as Leeds United fans drained from the area, leaving small clusters of mainly jovial but increasingly inebriated Blackburn fans to cling territorially to their chosen pubs, including the one we had chosen, which sat in innocuous shadows directly opposite the King George's Hall.

The signs were not good as we opened the door. Sham 69's 'If The Kids Are United' flowed into the street. We pushed through, ignoring the ageing familiarity of a song that, though it raged from an era when watching The Fall was almost a nightly occasion, was markedly the antithesis of anything that was fired from Fall speakers. Dumb bonhomie, artlessly anthemic. Stepping into the pub, and through time – and on the other side of the street from a Fall gig – seemed achingly symbolic, especially as men, mostly men, red faced and leery, with baseball caps – another bad sign – and punching the air with glee turned to flash suspicious eyes at the invasion of us three which, including yours truly – who had been beaten up by football pond life a month or two earlier – attempted to slide surreptitiously into the comparative peace of the back room. This peace that was soon to be shattered as trousers – not ours, one might add – were dropped to a circle of guffaws, when a bottle smashed and pushed the atmosphere right to the edge and when one man stood firing finger pistol signs in our direction, as if to note our intrusion. We were never, we told ourselves, in any danger. For a start, nobody could look less like Leeds United supporters intent on breaching this undesirable fortress than we three, as we sat, attempting to recall 'Fall' moments from distant eras.

On reflection, I think that it was probably the vomit that did it; the vomit onto the carpet directly in front of us. More guffaws. A landlady attempting to physically hold in her anger. More Sham 69 . . . and, again with surreptitious stealth, we exited the pub.

(There was a Fall song in that. Had Mark been with us. Had he noted the Blackburn Rovers pictures on the walls. Had he sensed the lingering of northern football legacy, a favoured Fall subject matter –

and the way it clashed so violently, almost literally, with contemporary blind idiocy – he might well have been tempted to pull the notebook from his pocket.)

As we left, three more like us entered, another foray from our rather curious invasion of Blackburn. We were not football fans, although signs of allegiance were worn with equal vigour. Tonight was to be a very special night: the return, of sorts, of The Fall.

A film crew would circulate, capturing segments of the evening on DVD, capturing a slice of the atmosphere . . . but only a slice. I mean, I couldn't have known, as we rather nervously left that pub and strode briskly into the King George's Hall, just what was about to take place. To be honest, given Mark's apparent lack of recent enthusiasm for home country, let alone home county gigs, I wasn't expecting the mightiest of performances. There would be a certain Fallish frisson, of course, poignancy even . . . as there always did appear to be . . . but surely the edges would be blurred, the attack softened, the point blunted. Surely it would provide, at best, glimpses of greatness, enhanced by memories, encouraged by nostalgia. But then again, The Fall, more than any other band, had resolutely forced any trace of nostalgia into squealing submission. So maybe . . . maybe a spark would remain. I didn't know, to be honest. As it came at the precise point, almost to the day, when this book would be kick-started in some kind of earnest, I really had no idea quite how the evening would affect me. Whatever it was that I might have been expecting . . . it certainly wasn't the finest Fall performance I had seen in 25 years. Which, much to my pained astonishment, is exactly what was about to happen.

It was a hall bustling with ghosts.

That was a good start. Before a single face had entered the bar . . . the ghosts were blatantly obvious. Buzzcocks, firing pop bullets to a crowd who, one hour earlier, had rioted in unified objection to the jazz tones of the legendary Ludus. That was, I sadly calculated, in 1979. Not too long after that, a further riot had occurred during a typically sullen non-performance by Public Image Limited. You see, I couldn't help it. I was 46 years old. My companions, Liz, a colleague from the Warrington newspaper where I stare blankly into computer screens for eight hours a day, and her brother, Dave, were considerably younger. It is relevant, I sense, to mention them because, ardent gig goers though they both have been, they initially seemed out of sorts as this fascinating crowd began to assemble.

And it was as if a painting. We sat at the end of the bar . . . and watched . . . for my part, in a state of astonished awe. It is true, the word had gone out. In stark contrast to Mark's claim that 'old saddoes' no longer attended Fall concerts, this bar slowly filled with ghostly hints of past Fall gigs. Face after face, hints of recognition, familiar features now etched into ageing faces, fuller figures . . . at times rather disturbing as – a number of times – I noticed advancing pain in the eyes. I wondered about myself, too, especially as, time after time, flashes of recognition hurtled straight back at me. I am thinner, arguably sadder, certainly carrying some dark weight of experience. To the casual eye, this could, and probably did, seem like some wearying revival evening, both too far removed from those horrendous Eighties jumble of synth pop acts, or unwise comebacks of The Sex Pistols perhaps. But it wasn't like that at all, of course. This was The Fall . . . and The Fall roll on. The Fall audience roll on, accepting change as a way of keeping alive, staying fresh, keeping aloof.

Mark's inevitable entry into the bar was preceded by Elena whose extraordinary beauty sliced the room in two, as she stopped to chat to the raucous assembly who surrounded Fall manager Ed Blaney and assorted faces from The Fall's label, Action Records, local to the town.

It was an audience worth pondering. How to be 48 years old and still wear a 'Prole Art Threat' T-shirt with absolutely no sense of irony. How to look like you were still playing bass guitar in a raggedly assembled band from the grubbier edge at the Band On The Wall. How to look as if you have just stepped straight out of the old Manchester, a place with dense black pockets, where food came via a lukewarm pie machine in The Peveril Of The Peak, or old-style burger and egg scoffed from laminated tables in the local Wimpy Bar . . . an audience who had stepped out of classic Fall territory . . . steeped from a Fall song, perhaps, where magic could be found in artless mundanity. These were the people who inhabited Fall songs and they knew it. This band was special, mainly because Mark E. Smith had lassoed their lives and filtered them into a 25-year span of songwriting. The world, perhaps, would never know it . . . and a few will surely be suspicious of reading it here. But this audience attained a remarkable significance to me . . . partly because they were all – seemingly – close to Mark, they were all caught in that emotional net. Ed's little gang, looking like Kerouacian 'beats' from a northern town . . . out of time, out of place but never . . . ever . . . out of date. Unique indeed.

"Hello and welcome to the *only* band in the world . . ."

A whistle hurled its way from the speakers, lodged in the ears . . . to be mercifully replaced by the amplified and disembodied mumble of Mark E. Smith: "DEAD BEAT DESCENDANT . . . DEAD BEAT DESCENDANT . . . DEAD BEAT DESCENDANT . . . DEAD BEAT DESCENDANT . . ."

Curiously, I had never spent time scrutinising this most Fallish of Fall phrases. Right now it held a detached, faintly sinister air . . . the, by now, sizeable crowd, edged closer to the stage . . . and then two steps back as the sheer force of sound hit them. In a rather ironic contrast to Fall gigs of old, a rather perfect sound, too, given the cubic nature of the King George's Hall, with bassist, guitarist and drummer dutifully jamming into a delicious groove, funk with wobble . . . and Mark, entering from the left, hanging his coat on a symbol stand, fiddling inconceivably with the microphone, staring into space, staring straight into our eyes, mouthing the words, sauntering to the back, humping to an arch, striding to the left and – I swear – twice punching the air, safe in the knowledge – which was gradually dawning on this crowd – that he was the epicentre of the finest band that had ever flowed around him in the name of The Fall. This was going to be a show. The Fall in a show? How did this happen? And how did this band, on this mundane night in Blackburn, manage to punch across a greatest hits package and yet still sound like the most avant-garde unit still in circulation on the otherwise staid college circuit. When The

Velvet Underground reformed, in 1993, we had to forgive them their flab, but no flab here. A young band, true . . . but Mark, however old you might mention that he looked, still looked as sharp, as distinctive and thoroughly vital as the gloriously winning music that swept through this hall, inviting dozens of aged feet back into an ungainly juvenile dance. And even they didn't seem sad, as they grasped the joy and bounced together in a harmless huddle at the front of the stage, whooping it up as each and every intro sparked a ripple of familiarity – not at all a Fall thing – and, for once perhaps, it seemed difficult not to smile. It didn't seem like nostalgia, not at all. As the songs tripped by – 'Telephone Thing', 'Hey! Luciani', 'Victoria' (twice, once as a tempting instrumental), 'Mr Pharmacist', 'Free Range', 'Behind The Counter' . . . bizarrely, bizarrely, the band played on . . . through the hour . . . through the hour and a half . . . falling in with the groove . . . breaking only for an acting roadie and north west poet to spit out an absurdly lovable rant that, through the haze of crackle and feedback, reared nostalgic nods to the history of Blackpool Football Club. Could be wrong, but I was prepared to go with that. Nothing could seem more poignantly apt, anyway. Through the right-hand side of my eye I could see Ed Blaney and the boys tumbling into more raucous bonhomie, soon they too, would be up on stage, rapping with glee, allowing Mark moments backstage. These were strange moments, with Ed spitting into the microphone. Suddenly it didn't seem like The Fall at all. Well, it wasn't, was it? Although deft and not unlovable, and not without talent either, Ed Blaney couldn't quite capture that same charisma. And it was then that it really hit me. The power really did lie with Mark. And no one knew why . . . indefinable power, really, that simply took the stage and meant something . . . something that no other band could ever get near . . . the something that John Peel understood all those years ago . . .

I WAKE UP IN THE CITY

Turn the music up . . .

When I wake up in the city
I look around to see who's with me
And all the thoughts that pollute me
Canal and the gallery

How many of you are stable?
And the boxer with thief
The Deputy Collector is the Command in Chief-uh

I wake up in the city
I look around to see who's with me
A lonely cloud descended
The Bill and the bushes haven't grown

Don't keep laughing
Can you give a dog a bone?

Cough

Cough

When they give me breakfast
Politburo KGB
Maybe a Flight-Commander
Is curled up in a tree

And even Jesus had a tail
And General Custer was the same
That old dollar bill
Came out backwards in the machine

When I wake up in the city
I find I'm not around
I look at who's with me
All the thoughts that pollute me

The Only *Band In The World*

I got glasses under my skin
I don't know how thin I been
I don't want Jesus to keep laughin'
I don't need no reason to keep laughin'

Even Jesus had a tail
And General Custer was the same
Now I'm the enemy of the city
And the dollar bill came out backwards
And you know it came out backwards
And the new euro it came out backwards
And the new euro it came out backwards
And the euro it came out backwards

Tatton Community Centre, Chorley. September 27, 1980

The N.W.R.A./That Man/Totally Wired/Your Heart Out/Pay Your Rates/A Figure Walks Behind You/Container Drivers/In The Park/ English Scheme/How I Wrote 'Elastic Man'/New Puritan

We arrived en masse. The postman was there. Everywhere. It was in Chorley, too, deep deep in the heart of Lancashire, where I most liked to see The Fall. It was a spiritual home. Of sorts. There was always an added poignancy here. As at Bolton Technical College, when a universally speeding crowd gyrated onto the stage . . . as at Rochdale Tech, too . . . it was just home turf and, to some extent, this bizarre community centre in the heart of Chorley, a less than handsome town that huddles grimly beneath Winter Hill and is forever soothed by the swish of the M6.

Kay greeted us with an enormous, suffocating hug. "C'mon, fuckin' 'ell maan, come on in . . . we've gotta fuckin' sort these fuckers out, man . . . we've got to fuckin' do a show here. Maan . . . jeez this is a typical fuckin' Fall show . . . jeeeez maaan."

It was, indeed, a typical *fucking* Fall show. Fifty per cent of the audience had trundled up the motorway, as they would trundle anywhere, into the deepest and most unlikely venues in the country. Kay reckoned it was just her, just Kay being sussed, that managed to squeeze this band into the most unfortunate, and often unwelcoming places. As captured, and rather superbly, by the *Totale's Turns* album – see review . . . on how it changed everyone's life . . . The Fall would work best when preaching to the unconverted, when the dynamic of the crowd would be torn by those who adored every wayward chord, and believe the band to be the manifestation of a surreal magic that swirled around their everyday lives . . . a mixture of those weird people . . . and those who would arrive, in full innocence, wholly expecting to see a genuine 'turn', be it a cabaret run-through of Sixties light chart material or some duo, locked in an endless circle of soulless one nighters. This is The Fall. They take you to the strangest places . . . they make even Chorley seem wildly exotic.

It was an exaggeration, though, to suggest that the audience at the Tatton Community Centre were transformed into a riotous assembly via exposure to The Fall. Nevertheless, the atmosphere sharpened noticeably as the band courageously plodded their way through the opening chords to 'The N.W.R.A.' ('The North Will Rise Again'). A hugely ironic choice, given the nature of the event.

Mark: "It is sometimes difficult to explain to people quite what The Fall are about, especially to people like broadsheet journalists. They pretend to understand, and some of them are very bright . . . much brighter than me, if the truth be told. But they still often have a false idea of quite what we are about. When I think of some of those gigs, what we were trying to do then . . . at some of those strange venues. When I think of that I knew, completely fucking knew that we were the only band in the world doing that. The thing is that it was never a big deal. It was just real. Still is. The Fall are for real . . . and that is precisely what nobody can ever grasp. It's not some scam . . . some career move dragged up in the pub. It's just how it is. How The Fall are. Every minute of every day. Do you see what I am tryin' to say?"

At Chorley, perhaps more than anywhere else, the above seemed blatantly obvious. For a start, the set was back to front. Arse about tit. 'The N.W.R.A.' should have been an atmospheric crawl to a climax, preceded by the daft and snappy 'That Man'. OK, fair enough, one can shuffle much of the remainder of the set about like a pack of cards and it wouldn't make a great deal of difference. But song by song there, following the disorientating rant of 'The N.W.R.A.' and its musical antithesis, 'That Man', most of the Chorley crowd had been thoroughly unhinged. It was the simple absurdity of it. The ferocious desire to make that fucking audience work. The opposing view, of course, would suggest that The Fall owed every single paying adult £1.50 worth of entertainment, but Mark never bought into that concept. He would deliver, given time, but only if and when it suited.

"The north will rise again . . . not in 10,000 years . . ." Unlikely that it would rise in Chorley, to be honest . . . or so it seemed in 1980. Twenty years later, one couldn't be so sure.

And, that night, at the precise moment that 'Container Drivers' burst into flight, Kay Carroll grabbed yours truly, dragged me over to the mixing desk and screamed at me.

"Tell that fucking cunt behind the desk to fix the fucking sound."

Funny, but it had sounded perfect, to me. How, given the fragmented, occasionally cacophonous noise deliberately punched across by the band that night, could one so precisely tell that the bass sound was in a slight wobble?

I didn't know. Two knobs were touched; Kay's eyes burned into the 'sound guy's' neck, before the said manager, thus satisfied, took me to the corner of the room, and plied me with lager. It was a classic evening.

5

Locations

There is one Fall song, above all others, that seems to perfectly symbolise the true talent of Mark E. Smith; the ability to scratch at the surreal edges of a mundane day. It is not largely regarded as a Fall classic, nor does it surface often on John Peel broadcasts, at least not to my knowledge. The song is 'M5'. With typical Fall perversity, a second-rate version of this sits irritatingly proud on the *Middle Class Revolt* album – and this appears to be the version that most people acknowledge, while a full-blooded, spine grabbing run-through sits on one of the lower-selling Fall singles.

No matter. 'M5' is carved direct from tedium . . . from the tedium of being trapped, on tour, surging down another godforsaken motorway or, more often than not, standing in hideous coned gridlock.

"But ahm city born and bred, too many car fumes in my head," sings Mark, as we noted in Chapter One. And the song punches into the rhythmic plod of a motorway drive.

The simplicity of Mark's vocal attack is absolute Fall perfection.

"M5 . . . six seven pm," he shouts, and somehow manages to make poetic force from the tedium. One imagines him sitting, notebook in hand, pencilling jagged thoughts before, later perhaps . . . in some hotel room, fuelled on single malt . . . pulling them from the notepad and moulding to fit the latest ferocious jamming from Hanley and Scanlon.

It is a great song because, I strongly sense, no other band would even think of producing it. Mark's lyrics dismiss the possibility that drabness is nothing more than an accident.

"This is not an Autobahn . . . it's an evil roundabout," he notes, as

well as offering a throwaway slice of unlikely self-effacement.

"The man who thinks he knows it all . . . is destined for a mighty fall . . ."

It's throwaway, for sure and one wonders if Mark simply slotted it into place, perhaps pilfered it from different notes, but the whole thing swirls around in the backbeat and hurtles out these odd lines that say nothing specific, but tend to snag onto the imagination and stir the creativity a little. I am not suggesting that 'M5' is any kind of conspiracy theory melted into a succinct lyric. But it does state, as so many of the great Fall songs do, that nothing is quite what it seems, that it is possible to see beyond the obvious, even in the dullest moments.

"Yeah . . . 'M5' . . . go with it, Mick. I liked that song . . . something clicked with that one . . . you know what I mean? You know what I am getting at? Use it in the film, if you like. Be good that . . . yeah, yeah . . . like it."

This little, and unforgivably insignificant, statement has been snatched from some lost context and placed on this page for a reason. The statement, the song and, indeed, the moment, though perhaps not being a landmark in the history of The Fall – far from it – will be forever embedded in my memory as the opening remark of a rather grim three-month mess of work, intended to produce some kind of film about The Fall. What transpired, at the death of this scenario of ineptitude, was a pile of video cassettes containing about 36 hours of disjointed and virtually unwatchable Fall footage, interspliced with a few rather telling interviews (which, indeed, I will get into later), all of which is preceded by a half hour demo film which, despite being ruined by the appalling, stumbling and cringeworthy narration from yours truly – fronted by 30 seconds of brilliance from John Peel – proved rather endearing and has been known to fetch curious amounts of money within The Fall's increasingly bizarre fan market.

The germ of an idea came, I think, from an artistic, fun-loving couple named Ro and John Barrett. Ro, a one-time *Old Grey Whistle Test* presenter and Radio One DJ, has also spent time as producer of Pete Waterman's flagship cheap nightclub show, *The Hit Man And Her*, which also plucked Michaela Strachan from the shadows of one Timmy Mallet, and hurtled her into some kind of mini-skirted downbeat glamour celebrity. All of which is relevant here for two reasons. Firstly, it would establish a tentative link between Mark and Pete Waterman – and a most unlikely respect exists to this very day, swinging both ways it seems; and, secondly, it would lead to a musical liaison between Mark and Waterman's PWL empire, such as it is, that would settle into a musical outlet with Dose's 'Plug Myself In', more of which later.

It was difficult, to begin with. As already mentioned, Mark had dragged me tentatively into Granada's blackly Levi'd complex on one occasion and, through that and a hundred other cul-de-sacs I had encountered around the very bottom rung of the television industry, I had little reason to believe that this could run any further. (And, as it turned out of course, it didn't.)

Nevertheless, it was to be a fascinating process, not least because it would slice through the ever-curious dynamic of this ever-curious band, clearly showing all manner of contrasting passions . . . and personal difficulties . . . and emotional jealousies . . . and of sex, of loyalty . . . and of disloyalty, too. All the things one might normally associate with a band . . . all pulled a little more towards the extreme. Simply because this particular Fall, arguably more than any other version in their history, seemed a precarious balance between the old and the new. For even Karl Burns had returned, if only for a short and rather bad-tempered period. Hanley and Scanlon were still in charge of creating that savage rhythmic pull, of course . . . but back had come Brix, as an emotional wild card to be sure . . . and as a musical wild card as well, tugging the band this way and that . . . and settling behind Brix, quietly, tentatively . . . Julia Nagle. It was to prove a heady mix.

Moving towards the filming wasn't a distasteful process as it involved the ebullient John Barratt, whose legendarily volatile state would amplify considerably in direct proportion to the daily alcohol intake.* The first time John and Mark met was simple

*John is a sweet character, really . . . once a *Coronation Street* child prodigy, latterly a forceful band manager who, in stark contrast to both Mark and the author of this book, no longer partakes of even the occasional drop.

enough although, knowing that two singular volatile states could easily have clashed and rather horribly, I lingered nervously in the shadows, and allowed them to talk. We wandered, naturally, from Mark's house to the pub on the fringe of Heaton Park, with John and Mark volleying anecdotes at each other while I enjoyed sitting in the shadows. At the end of that first meeting, Mark turned to me and asked, "Where the fuck do you get them from?" although I noted that this question wasn't laced with any kind of complaint, in fact a certain fondness had started to develop. (I wasn't to know it, but the relationship between Mark and John would eventually crash on the rocks of Waterman's empire, some time later . . . but that was way into the future.)

Weeks passed, punctuated by various meetings, more often than not preceded by a gathering at the Cog Sinister office at 24 Mount Street, a shambling cube presided over by Jon The Postman. The Postman – Smith axis of Cog Sinister wasn't entirely harmonious. By day, Jon would be fending off calls from Fall devotees, from local journalists, from local bands hoping to procure a support spot – including an utterly ignored, revamped and hopelessly out of time latter-day version of The Distractions – and, quite often as it happens, independent film-makers with no finance, no ideas either, pushing their brief inebriated ideas a stage further. Everyone, I noted, wanted to make a film about The Fall. It wasn't difficult to see why. For they were, and remain, one of the few bands blessed with both a cultish legacy and comparable accessibility, despite Mark's belligerence. Cog Sinister, while being a well-intended operation, was not, strictly speaking, a successful operation. Although fighting hard against the hideous tag, it still survived as little more than an official fan club, at least in the day-to-day running of the label.

But the split was occurring. The loyalty of The Postman, who was attempting to push towards a politics and history degree, was floundering despite his years of devotion. "I'm gonna fookin' twat Mark if he treats me like thaaat," he screamed at me during one of our first nights of filming. I found this quite difficult to understand. The Postman, perhaps more than anyone, was accustomed to Mark's volatile nature. What's more, and again more than most, he knew both how to deflect and how to ignore it. He had been there, a thousand times . . . in a thousand dressing rooms. He'd surfed the trauma and often enjoyed it. Surely . . . surely a big part of the thrill.

But Jon The Postman, travelling into town from his twelfth-floor flat in Collyhurst, travelling to his studies at Salford University, sitting at the door, counting the takings from the first of two Fall gigs at The Roadhouse, had seemingly fallen out of love. I liked Jon The Postman, found him good company (even when embedded in the tiresome old Mancunian punk camaraderie that surrounds the brief '20 years since punk' celebration in July 1996, or the appalling micro celeb bashes that flowed in the wake of the travesty called *24 Hour Party People*), Jon always remained the proverbial reasonable if faintly inebriated egg. But during this period, something soured. His bounce and wit dulled. Couldn't quite work out why.

The filming began effortlessly with Mark sitting naturally behind a pint of Boddingtons in the Crown pub, Heaton Mersey, with sound and vision men fluttering about in a mix of stout professionalism, and barely concealed awe. I sat opposite, appallingly bearded and corduroyed at the time, finding my questions deflected with arrogant ease . . . with John Barratt jostling in the shadows and insults flying thick'n'fast.

Mark: "Nirvana's tried to get on the bus in the States . . . ha . . . can you believe that? Fuckin' Kurt Cobain and his girlfriend . . . that fucking Courtney Pine [*sic*] . . . trying to hitch a ride. We fuckin' just threw 'em off. Wouldn't put up with it . . . I mean, someone said they were big fans of ours . . . a lot of those Seattle people are. All those fuckin' grunge bands. Scruffy fuckin' bastards. Can't fuckin' be doin' with 'em meself."

"You lived in LA, though Mark, didn't you? A lot of writers . . . pop stars go to LA because they say it is near the edge."

"What, like Billy Idol an' all that?"

"No . . . no . . . I meant more kind of Tom Waits . . . Leonard Cohen . . ."

"It's not near the fuckin' edge at all . . . it's the most boring place in the fuckin' world, maan. And yes, I lived there for months at a time . . . and in the best bits. Hollywood . . . Santa Monica . . . fuckin' terrible. You can't go out. If you have a beer you are a tramp. Fuckin' horrible . . . wouldn't live there for all the money in the fuckin' world . . . guns goin' off all over the place . . . bit like Manchester . . . ha!

"You see, what you have to remember is that America is like 50 countries. You can't generalise at all. Chicago is a completely different world to LA . . . so, I mean, there are bits that I really like . . . there are places that really understand what The Fall is about . . . and then there are places that have no grasp of subtlety or irony at all. They are just not capable of that level of thought . . . or even that level of honesty . . . mind you, there are fuckin' places in England like that, as well. Manchester during all that Manchester shit, for one."

"Top man," said the sound engineer, as he reeled in his various strings of wire. "Always loved The Fall . . . more than any other band, I think."

This was a common reaction . . . and I still encounter it today . . . on practically a daily basis while writing this book.

Roadhouse, Manchester. September 1, 1994

M5/Behind the Counter/Free Range/15 Ways/ Reckoning/Glam Racket/Hey! Student/City Dweller/ Dead Beat Descendant/Big New Prinz

Newton Street. Set dark and dotted with neon, backdropped with bill posters, damp glistening pavements, angular leering buildings . . . by day one of the streets that besuited office types hurry past . . . but by night, and particularly when trapped on video tape, attained a romantic edge. Hints of traffic sweeping through LA . . . of dark Chicago streets, straight, windblown and threatening. But this was Manchester, a Manchester perched on the fringe of intensive rejuvenation, before the rebirth, still a city with nasty black pockets, with the faint omnipresent fear of violence.

They came in dribs and mainly drabs! Hunched shoulders, whiskery chins, edging through their thirties, one presumes.

We stopped them on the pavement. Watched them flinch under the glare. Shunted a microphone in front of them and asked a singular question.

"Why do you think The Fall are different from other bands?"

These were hardened Fall gig-goers, schooled in bad beer and dank clubs, in arduous journeys and bad sound systems. Happy to soak in whatever it took, happy to support the cause. But not pop fans. Not rock fans. An ageing audience, at this point. Soon they would peel away. Leaving space for a younger pack. But this was, for many, a last stab of studenthood, perhaps.

One guy, long straggly white hair, bristling with enthusiasm . . . and dressed in some kind of flag.

"I've been all over to see them . . . I have been to America . . . followed them over there . . ."

"But why?"

". . . er . . . because . . . er because they make you think. It's not just delivered on a plate for you. You have to work with The Fall. But it's always worth it in the end. I mean, the band know us anyway."

"Oh yeah, the band know us," said the guy who was seemingly dressed in the Stars and Stripes. "We go everywhere with them. Meet with them. Drink with them. We are part of the whole thing."

"Who the fuck are these guys?" said Mark. "Look at him, dressed in a flag . . . never seen 'im in me fucking life, man."

The roadhouse spins back in time. Just drifting down the steps is enough to tease out memories of a thousand lost gigs . . . many of them featuring The Fall and, once inside, this nostalgic vision is further spiced by blackness, by sweat, denim and noise. By raucous little huddles to the stage front and, on this occasion, by faces from the past. Faces that would loom out of nowhere. Dave Bent(ley), fresh from lengthy spells driving buses in Australia, affecting the unlikely look of a redneck . . . mingling oikishly with Jon The Postman . . . Inspiral Carpets man Clint Boon, long since emerged from the shadows. But in the old days . . . right back to The Electric Circus, Clint would be lost in Oldhamite obscurity, watching The Fall, dreaming of some kind of pop stardom for himself, dreaming of sharing the same stage with Mark E. Smith. It was hopeless, back then, in Oldham. Still is. I suppose, if one is to remain truthful here, I must count myself among the ex-punk also-rans, "The old fucking saddoes we have to get rid of," as Mark would unflatteringly note.

But whether Mark liked it or not, the audience at the Manchester Roadhouse was brimming with old fucking saddoes like me. I don't know . . . a bit younger now. I guess, during the filming, I was rather weightier and, alas I now think, rather bearded too. What was I thinking?

But, then again, that was partly the point of The Fall crowd. With more than a nod back to the *Grotesque* peasants, The Fall crowd would by and large have little in common with the fickle run of fashion. Well, this was one fucking weird crowd, and no mistake. The unusual figures cast by myself, The Postman and Dave Bentley – I'm much thinner now . . . and younger I feel, for what it's worth – were by no means alone. Although, down at the front, down where the drunkards roll, the entire thing rolled like a breaking sea of denim as the grunge fringe of Mancunia reacted in a way that would never have occurred to The Fall fans of old . . . they dived, surged and staged mock fights even as Mark was sullenly sauntering on stage to the sinister repetitive line: "THE FALL THE FALL THE FALL THE FALL THE FALL." Then the stage-front urchins erupted, lost in music . . . in some kind of strange music, with Steven Hanley and Craig Scanlon ripping into an unlikely funk wobble and with Mark, black-suited and leery, spitting into the darkness . . . spitting out words and phrases and half phrases and chinks of jagged edge vocabulary: "EEEEMMMMMM FIIIiiveeeeaaaah . . . sixxxxxseve peeeee eemmmmmmmm!!!!"

It was like being home again, and at gigs end, I caught sight of Manchester United full back Denis Irwin, dancing in the shadows.

Filming The Fall. Part Two

Vector studios and editing suite, Heaton Mersey, Stockport

Heaton Mersey has always seemed to me to be more an escape route – from Stockport – rather than an entity in its own right. And so it is . . . strung along a rather dull and uneven main road, peppered with large pubs and off-licences, skirting the unlikely Bohemia of Heaton Moor and landing on the fringe of the more obvious Bohemia of Didsbury.

"Fuckin' hate Stockport, sometimes," said Mark, as he strode purposefully through Heaton Mersey's dour leafiness. "Like those bastards in the pub. Fucking deerstalkers, wearing deerstalkers, typical Stockport thing, that."

It was a curious statement, especially when delivered to myself . . . who had spent the previous 38 years floating about Stockport's deadening streets, searching for some kind of magic. However, I couldn't recall ever seeing a single deerstalker in Stockport. Nor, indeed, had I seen any in the pub in which we had just sunk two swift pints of Boddingtons, before Mark was due to amble into camera shot, flanked by the edgy and fractious personnel who hovered in the dynamic of that particularly intriguing version of The Fall.

The studio was duly cavernous, hanger-like: a cold, deadening, concrete shell. Vector Television. A corridor to the rear led to stark dressing rooms . . . tables lavishly bulging with food. Technicians stalked the corridors carrying wires. Scruffed in the manner one has come to expect, lost in techno gossip, dreaming of locations, spilling many beans, wholly unaffected by The Fall.

9 am

Even as they entered Vector, even then, the signs were showing. Karl Burns, back from the dead, or from a Mancunian obscurity, seemed brimming with precocity, as ever, hurtling insults in every direction . . . true to drummer caricature . . . Hanley and Scanlon, rather dutiful, workmanlike, organising the equipment like two seasoned plumbers tackling a particularly tricky central-heating system. Brix, overwhelmingly brash as ever, anxious to wash over of any trace of English reserve, which she found in bucket loads from me.

"Hi maaan, heey, you have changed, maan. Hey, are you really the same Mick Middles? Jeez, you look like you have been away to university and have got an accountancy degree since I last saw you . . . hahahhhhaaaa . . . hey, don't worry, coming from my warped state of mind, that is almost a compliment."

"Well thank you Brix, I am very touched," I offered meekly and, if only momentarily, she backed away, as if to inspect my statement for any trace of sarcasm and then, bizarrely deciding that it had been a harmless rebuff, she countered in the way she seemed to know best. By thrusting into rather fetching American style vulgarity. I kid you not. This is what Brix said next . . . to me . . . a virtual (and unrecognisable, apparently) stranger.

"This is my boyfriend's lumberjack shirt . . . it's my favourite shirt . . . it's still got his come stains on it . . . see!"

"Oh, very nice, Brix . . . yes . . . erm . . ."

"Is Julia here? Oh yes, she has arrived and has set up . . . knew she would . . . eager beaver."

It was a put-down. No mistake about that. Tension crowded around Brix like a swarm of flies. Julia Nagle was unsettled. Karl Burns too: "Fucking Brix wanders back in and thinks she runs the fucking show . . ."

And Julia, quietly setting up her keyboards, sliding in computer disc, gazing forlornly into the monitors, losing herself in her slice of technology . . . and, as yet to gain official Fall status, hidden behind a curtain, wiped from the stage, allowed to fill the sound, but not crowd the cameras. A pity, too. I had vaguely known Julia Nagle from the time we flitted around the hostelries of Heaton Moor, from the time she almost joined a band I managed, and I recalled her fleetingly, driving me to Out Of The Blue studios in Manchester, talking of the heavy rock band she managed and, years before that, I recalled her as the keyboardist in Heaton Moor band Illustration, momentarily the brightest sparks on a burgeoning Some Bizarre roster that also included Soft Cell. Psuedo whacko Some Bizarre boss Stevo had taken such a shine to Julia's not inconsiderable charms that he proposed marriage during the Some Bizarre tour. Duly spurned, he seemed to lose interest in Illustration's fading star. It was a forgotten moment when tightly knit local rock had clashed with something about to break on a national scale. Just a moment . . . but I recalled it, as I watched Julia Nagle donning headphones, running through her musical role. I knew then that she would soon grow in stature within the band. I knew, too, that Brix, whom I genuinely liked, wouldn't be hanging around for too long. This band was about to crack and Julia Nagle, I guessed, would be an instrumental feature in that split . . . in the pivotal moment when the old Fall would peel away, and something younger, fresher would emerge.

It was strange in the dressing room.

"What's going on? Who's in charge? How many songs do you want? What the fuck are we doing here?"

Mark looked at the food, scowled and picked up a camera balance and slammed it against the inside of the door, trapping himself, Brix and me inside the dressing room and, perhaps rather more worryingly, trapping the band out in the corridor, in the cold.

It wasn't a big deal, apparently. Tentatively, I asked Mark why. "Will just keep 'em on the edge a bit," he stated. "Will just get them ready to play."

And so they did. As we relaxed next to the table laden with untouched food, with Mark and Brix seemingly at ease in each other's company, and accepting yours truly into the tight triangle, the strains of 'Behind The Counter' cranked along, murkily, in the distance. Like an absurd spoof spy, Mark pulled a cassette recorder from his coat, opened the door, wandered into the studio, placed it on the floor and wandered back into the dressing room. He would listen later . . . much later, as he relaxed in his house, sipping whisky, mulling over the next direction.

"Can tell much more from a taped rehearsal than an actual gig," he stated knowingly. "I'm not fucking joking. You can hear it here. When these guys relax and just start messing around, just start playing. That's when they become The Fall. And you have to search for that. That spark. I've said it before. You can't learn it. They have to not become fucking pub rocky . . . like that, right now. That is exactly what they are sounding like, right now. Some dumb fucking pub rock unit. And I won't have it."

Five days in Vector. Five days lavishly punctuated by trips to The Railway and Crown pubs. Not, one swiftly adds, that trips to The Railway and Crown pubs were undertaken in any kind of feverish need of alcohol. It was neatly beyond that . . . in a different place. Mark E. Smith, cold and dry of a morning, watching his band setting up, needing to soften into shape, needing to trip to The Railway or The Crown, to loosen into shape. It really was that simple.

"Is that fucking Derbyshire over there," he asked me bluntly, indicating the Peak District rising in the distance. "Is that where you go hiking?"

It was an affectionate sneer . . . Mark, as ever rather scathing of my natural slide toward the country.

"I don't know, Mick . . . it's not something I've ever wanted to do. I kind of like to have the people and the cars around me. 'Cos, you are from Stockport and I've never been that comfortable with Stockport . . . lots of blokes in deerstalkers. Look at those cunts in the pub. They have Jaguars and they are as empty and as miserable as sin. It's probably really unfair of me . . . but it's like that South Manchester vibe. And everyone knows that the best art comes from North Manchester. Everyone knows that. Not sure what Stockport has ever produced."

Three times . . . four times . . . perhaps five, our pub was invaded by film producer Rosemary Barrett, forcing a smile while, ever so politely, as is the endearing Ro Barrett manner, pleading with Mark to return to the television studio, where a wearying band, and several equally wearying and somewhat highly paid technicians awaited, and where Brix stood stage left, practising an overtly sexual rock pose, where Julia Nagle peered from behind her screen wondering about how to climb into the band on a full-time basis, where Karl Burns glowered from behind an unlikely guitar, where he devoured the food, slobbered in the corner, asked to be interviewed then feigned absolute disinterest, and skulked like a trooper or journeyman from the old Mancunian musicianly stable, glowering knowingly.

"I've fucking seen it all, man," he would say. "I mean there's nothing fucking Mark can do to intimidate me 'cos I've been there since the beginning." I cast a nod back to the vision of Burns and the late New Order manager Rob Gretton engaged in a mock fight on The Hacienda dance floor in 1982 . . . and I remember him, also, scowling in the corner of a hundred dressing rooms, scribbling juvenilia on the wall, falling into the field of a roadie, with Mark laughing in the background.

And the stalwart omnipresence of Scanlon and Hanley, propping up The Fall scene. If it all fell in a lovely shambles . . . only to be resurrected in the 60 minute glare of the gig, and then fall away again . . . if it did that, night after night, then Mark E. Smith would be doing his job, The Fall would be doing their job and fans would wander home happy, wallowing in the glow.

Bit different in a television studio though, where it wasn't The Fall's money draining away . . . it wasn't my money, either, though it was the possibility of future money draining away before my eyes . . . and then.

"Oh, Mick," asks Mark, rather too politely, "I forgot to tell you . . . this is Lisa Verrico, the journalist . . . she's just come up from London on the train. I invited her here. Thought it would be good. You don't mind, do you?"

I didn't.

"So I will just go to the pub with Lisa here and we will have a few drinks . . . OK."

It was. It was even fun, in a way, watching the astonished faces of the cameramen as Mark and Lisa slipped out into the greying Stockport air, leaving the band to slap around the mock stage, with Brix hurling her guitar into the corner, casting vicious eyes at Julia Nagle, and stomping into the dressing room.

For us, it provided a simple opportunity to grab Brix, install her in the control room, where she would be suitably soothed by sexual dim lights, gently touch her ego, flick on the camera and ask her questions about The Fall. She was, it must be noted, more than complimentary about Mark.

"I think Mark is the greatest poet of his generation," she pronounced. "I think his work will outlive everyone and everything else. One of the few true geniuses in rock. No doubt about that . . ."

And on Manchester.

"Hey, well, you know, it's how you eat. I mean I ate a pineapple fritter and drank a few Bloody Marys and felt really sick, maan, you know. I meaan . . . how do you guys eat that stuff . . . I mean, it's delicious but seriously unhealthy."

"We don't," we universally informed her . . . myself, Ro Barrett, her husband and co-producer John Barrett, two cameramen, one sound technician and, beyond, 98 per cent of the northwest of England would have said the same . . . having never eaten a pineapple fritter as well as being at odds to understand just what it was about Bloody Marys that might be considered English, let alone Northern.

"Why have you rejoined The Fall, Brix?"

"Because they are the greatest English band. Because I feel part of The Fall . . . and actually was for a long time. Because I genuinely think I have something to add . . . it won't . . . er . . . it won't be forever. I am enjoying the bit of freedom I get in the band at the moment. It's quite a loose arrangement. I don't know what the other guys think . . . well, maybe I do, but I don't really bother about that. But no, it's not long term and I have a boyfriend and I have a life . . . and my boyfriend is a really talented guy . . . and I want to work with him anyway but I'm here because . . ."

It wasn't often that Brix allowed her thoughts to trail off but she did there, right there and then, when the cameras clicked to off and her endearing smile dropped, her eyes saddened a touch and . . . just for a few seconds . . . just fleetingly, Brix Smith no longer seemed like the sheer embodiment of American precocity, bright, beautiful, go-getting and ultimately successful. I thought she seemed lost, in Stockport. I thought she seemed as if she suddenly realised that she didn't know the answer to that question. Didn't get that in film. Perhaps as well.

"You are not fucking filming me now . . . the moment has gone. I'm no longer interested."

That was Karl Burns, five cans into the afternoon, sinking fast . . . but then he returned. "I mean I could tell you some shit about this band. You'd be fucking surprised, Mick. We hold this band together, we, the musicians. Mark is great . . . don't get me wrong. But the suggestion that he is wholly the dominant force is no longer apparent here, believe me. The musicians are The Fall and Mark, well, he just flits around the edges."

"I wouldn't say that was true," countered Steven Hanley, perhaps six cans into the afternoon.

Six months later, following a run of farcical negotiations, and huge amounts of patience on behalf of everyone concerned, including Mark it must be noted, filming continued, this time in Manchester city centre, in The Grinch café bar – a forerunner of the lavish and wearying peppering of similar establishments in latter years and well known for serving upmarket beans on toast. Here we found Mark, grimacing amid the cosmopolitan edge of studenthood.

"Who are these people and what are they doing here?" he asked mockingly, before continuing. "The weird thing is that they are looking and . . . and your film is looking at me and making me out to be the freak! I am not the freak . . . I am the Mancunian . . . well, Salfordian actually but I sense you catch my drift. Tell me where there is another Mancunian in this place."

I try . . . and then point towards the corner of the room where the strikingly stringy figure of Durutti Column man Vini Reilly sat scribbling lyrics, or something, into a notebook.

"Take Vini over there," I offered meekly.

"Vini . . ." He laughed. "Vini is cool but he's hardly a good example or your archetypal Mancunian, is he?" countered Mark . . . and I was somewhat forced to agree.

Filming eventually staggered to an inelegant halt when the team became knee-deep in a mud block of editing that stretched forward for months . . . with little prospect of any kind of financial carrot hovering on any noticeable horizon. Mark informed me that he had been involved in numerous similar projects, ideas that, although well meaning, had not been thought through on a commercial level.

"The thing is," he explained, "that The Fall have fanatical followers around the world and, whereas the band can reach them via the simple media of gigs and albums . . . when it comes to a film, backers need solid assurance of big hit sales. And we are not that type of band . . . deliberately so. People should realise this before they come to us with all manner of projects. I mean . . . this doesn't bother me, partly because the film was a good rehearsal on many levels for the band, partly because I enjoyed it and actually wanted to do it, partly because I know you and that's cool . . . but also because things like this, even if they don't come to fruition, and I never thought that this would, often lead to something else worthwhile. That is how this business works and I find that quite exciting. It's a constantly evolving situation which is very Fall in concept."

Who knows where the leads will go? In The Fall as in life. And The Fall film, in establishing a link between Mark and John Barrett – two of my closest friends, finally slotting together – also forced an unlikely connection between Mark and celebrity star maker Pete Waterman. John Barrett, being studio manager, ensconced in a dust encrusted Gothic church at the fag end of Manchester's Deansgate, proved instrumental in ushering Mark into sessions that resulted in the DOSE dance track, 'Plug Myself In', released on Pete Waterman's Coliseum label, overseen at the time by John Barrett, a crazed, acidic dance fest of a single, fittingly several steps beyond the measured techno that resulted from a liaison between a Gallagher brother and The Chemical Brothers. 'Plug Myself In' was a perfect exercise in the power of Smith's vocal delivery being able to stride across all manner of genres. It had happened once before, with that Inspiral Carpets' venture, where Smith's sardonic attack just seemed to crash the boundaries with effortless ease.

Mark: "This whole thing . . . the period of the film . . . was . . . to me, part of having Brix back after five years. It provided us with a chance to do things together. That was the other reason for doing the film that was not to do the film, but to gel; to many people it seemed absurd. Brix coming back, and I can understand why. A few weeks prior to that, if someone had asked us to have Brix back I would just have fucking laughed. No fucking chance mate . . . it was something that had sunk into history. She was with us for seven years and then out for five, and we hadn't even spoken for three full years. I had no interest in getting Brix back in the band at all. To be honest, I had no idea where she was, nor did I particularly care.

"Then . . . must have been in the summer of 1994, she suddenly called me up. She told me that she had been rehearsing with Hole and had grown really pissed off with it all. It was funny because, at the time, I was on the lookout for a guitarist and for someone to come in and act as musical arranger. I had decided that I wanted either a really young kid or an older person, a producer or someone like that. Someone who could kick the fuckers up the arse a bit, because I think it was getting a bit stale at one point. I think that I was starting to lose it a bit, too and I wanted to change all that. I remember mentioning this to Brix and she immediately perked up . . . in fact she said she wanted to do it and got straight on the plane. I wasn't completely convinced but I knew that I preferred to take a chance with someone I know rather than get some kid who really wanted to be in Oasis. Brix is actually a really great musician. She revitalised The Fall . . . she had a massive and positive impact on the new album. I was actually really flattered that she decided to leave Hole and come and work with The Fall again. I don't know how long she will stay . . . that's not really the point of this. The point is that Hole could have paid her about £1,000 a week and, in The Fall, in time-honoured fashion, she gets about fucking £50, but she actually likes that, she understands that, she really does. She knows that she is in The Fall for exactly the right reasons. I think she understands that it will never be a career in terms of the money . . . although being in The Fall will help her in so many other ways . . . she's not that daft.

"When I first saw Brix again, it was just like meeting an old mate, you know. Just like bumping into someone in the supermarket, really. She just looked so different, too. I thought that she would look like Nigel Kennedy's ex-girlfriend. But she *didn't.* She had changed her image. I admired her for keeping up and keeping things together, really. When she was in The Fall, last time, she looked like a rock guitarist. I really have no idea what Brix thinks of me, now. But I do know one thing . . . I know what people think of her. She certainly stirs people up, she puts the wind up a lot of people. I really love that. I love seeing how she deals with people, especially if they are arseholes . . . there is just no shit, you know. She just won't wear it. She never would. She is a great weapon for The Fall. If some guy is giving us hassle . . . and a lot of guys do . . . she just fucking scares them off. Says, 'Listen buddy, I am from LA . . . don't fucking mess with me,' and they just run off. It's really corny sometimes, but great for all that. She tells them that she is a black belt in karate and they instantly believe her. It can be really funny when Brix is around . . . yes, she can be a bit much, sometimes . . . she knows that and plays it to her advantage. But the thing about her is that she has a fantastic sense of humour. I do miss that.

"When me and Brix split, it was actually very amicable, despite what the newspapers said. Well, despite what a lot of people said . . . they all reckoned that Brix was on the make, but she never was. If you think about it, she wouldn't have stayed in The Fall for seven years if that had been the case, would she? Brix never demanded money, not after the split. She did ask me politely, and I respected that. The thing is, I didn't mind seeing her with Nigel Kennedy, or whoever. In fact I thought it hilarious when I found out who she was with . . . I just knew him as that punk violinist. I am not the jealous type, strangely enough. I didn't want us to fall out. It was the bastard lawyers who made it all seem bad, as is usually the case. When I tried to contact Brix, they called it harassment, but we both knew that was crap. But it's good that we are pals again. It is very mature. If I see any other ex-girlfriend, or wife . . . or even old band member and, let's be honest, there is a lot of them around, there's a lot of mutual tension. With Brix, there isn't, because she has got her head screwed on. She is a very solid person, even though she seems a bit mad sometimes. She is very LA and into working out and all of that . . . all the therapy stuff, but . . . even though she is very LA on the surface, she is not as transient as they can sometimes be. She is actually very solid as a person, which is why the suede Yanks don't like her a bit. One thing that is great . . . all those fucking grunge bastards who followed Courtney Love around, they all really hated Brix because they thought she was too LA and therefore too false. Irony is that she is more real than any of that fucking lot.

"The rest of the band are like my children, but Brix isn't like them. I actually do not get off on them being afraid of me. They think I am Oliver Cromwell. When it comes to Brix, we are a lot more honest with each other. We can tell each other when something is crap, and we often do. She was fantastic when we toured in the States last year. The press were very prurient. Brix told them that we split but she then knew how good The Fall were. I respected that a lot. Not many ex's would say something like that.

"I am not still in love with Brix. I have actually been married, twice, since. She's got her boyfriend and I have got a girlfriend. But I suppose it depends on your definition of love. I just think that Brix is great. Just like one of the lads. There are no songs on the LP that are about Brix, not even 'Don't Call Me Darling'. It's really funny. I write about ex-girlfriends all the time, about roadies, friends, the milkman, but never Brix. You would think I would, but I don't feel that I need to."

Brix: "I left Mark because I needed to find my own identity outside The Fall. I was only 20 when I married. I moved from my mum's to Mark Smith. I had never been on my own. I was socially retarded. I didn't even know how to sign a cheque. I was just this weird cult pop princess and a really arrogant bitch. You know the bit in *Spinal Tap* where the guy goes, 'This bread is too small for this meat?' That was me. I was really unhappy except when I was playing.

"For a couple of years Mark and I had no contact at all. I wouldn't say that we fell out. I just wanted a completely fresh start. After I left, I didn't try to keep up with what The Fall were doing. I did manage to hear *The Infotainment Scan* and I thought it was awesome. It really hurt me . . . it was like a punch in my gut because I wasn't on it. I never wanted to go and see them play live, though. I mean, I just couldn't. It would have been like seeing a child I had abandoned. Friends kept on telling me what Mark was doing . . . saying that he had written songs about what a bitch I was. To this day, I do not know if that was true. I always thought that 'Bad News Girl' on *Kurious Oranj* was about me. He wrote it when we were going through our break-up and I used to really hate playing it. It drove me crazy.

"The reason I contacted Mark again was very simple. It was because of the American singer, Freddie Johnson. He's a massive Fall fan. He just couldn't believe that I didn't own any of our own records. He actually went out and bought them for me and made me play them. For the first time, really, I was really, really proud of what we had done. I just phoned Mark up and told him that he was brilliant. He was really shocked, I know he was. I don't think he trusted my motives. Then he just called me and said that he wanted me to come back. He said he would give me anything I wanted. I had been doing that Hole thing. When their bass player died, Courtney invited me up and I ended up by staying at her house. She's so fucking smart . . . it's really scary. In the end though, it didn't work out and she got someone else. I was already committed to The Fall by then but I think that Courtney was pretty freaked out by me. She is very much the star in that band.

"Mark is less angry these days. He is definitely calmer. I think that he is a happier person. It's easier working with him now because I have grown up . . . and we are not married any more. We had our house and our cats. He is still the dictator of The Fall. That's probably why the band has lasted for 18 years. I stand up to him, though. He respects me because he knows that I can kick ass.

"I never compare myself to Mark's girlfriends. I know I am special and he knows he will never find another me. My current boyfriend is Mark Hudson, who was in The Hudson Brothers in the Seventies. He is now a really successful songwriter and producer. He wrote 'Living On The Edge' for Aerosmith and stuff for Ozzy Osbourne. Mark met him and asked why he hadn't bought me a house. I do miss Mark, in some ways. It is hard to let go when you are with someone 24 hours a day. I just filled up my hole with other things."

Lisa Verrico was laughing, giddily. Skipping back from the pub, dancing around Mark and Brix who were standing, in a considerable chill, outside in the featureless Stockport industrial estate . . . a photographer flitting around. "Smile Mark . . . yeah . . . yeah . . . smile . . . that's it. Ta."

15 WAYS

No need to be down-hearted,
There must be 10 ways to leave your man.
Don't be broken-hearted,
There are many ways to leave your man,
Leave your man. ×3

You gotta be cheerful-hearted,
There's at least 15 ways to leave your man.
Get a flat and a magazine,
Get your body ahead and out of that scene.

Don't be disconcerted,
There must be 15 ways to leave your man.
Soon you will discover you are no longer undercover.

Break! Now! Fly direct! Post Office box!

You'll get a dallying notion,
But you will soon recover.
No longer undercover,
Branch out into complete disorder.
You gotta be cheerful-hearted,
There's at least 15 ways to leave your man.
Get a flat and a magazine,
Get your body ahead and out of that scene.

But don't be disconcerted,
There are 8 ways to keep your man.
Don't be down-hearted,
There are 15 ways to leave your man.
Don't be too disconcerted,
Use all 15 ways to leave your man,
Leave your man.
16 ways to leave your man,
Leave your man,
Leave your man.

RECKONING

I phoned you up from Dallas
But your heart was still in marble
And your head
Was reckoning

Your friends are dis-compos-mentis
And like most in leather jackets are
Coveting
Reckoning
Reckoning

And you're sleeping with some hippie half-wit
Who thinks he's Mr. Mark Smith
Reckoning
Beckoning
Reckoning

I'm left alone in Europe
Consulting an atlas
Wandering
Wandering

And it's evil that you spark off
In disguise as basic truth
Listening
Listening
Listening
Reckoning
Reckoning
Beckoning
Reckoning

BEHIND THE COUNTER

They're always hitting on me
But I'm getting thin
From waiting on
They just want me to be

Behind the counter

The hen centre
Was always picking on me
There they are tucking in all over the shop
Got no time
For dinner or tea

Behind the counter

Every car I see
Is always picking on me
They take a left turn when I cross, guaranteed
They park on the pavement
Some have paid parks on the pavement
Here

I say "Wait sir, wait sir,
You'd better wait sir"
Guaranteed

I'm getting thin
From idiots who write rock books
Disparate
Ex-groups cold would've played this
"For Nose Pin and the Punk Piggies
Didn't quite make it," they say
Get behind the counter
The other side of the counter

Chill it, boy

The other side of the counter

M5 #1

You'll never see me trying to raise Cain
You'll never see me wear a suit of green
There's a slip-road up right ahead
leading to the agragarian
But I'm city born and bred
Too many car-fumes in my head
Just a well-read punk peasant.

But you'd think a country man would understand
the devil makes work for idle hands.
M5 6–7 pm

And the man who pretends he knows it all
is destined to a Mighty Fall.
Gets into your house with cheer,
then proceeds to take all you've got to offer.
This is not an autobahn
It's an evil roundabout
That leads to the Haywain
And you'll never see good trains again.

In late Sixties, my daddy said to me,
you'll never see trams and clogs again.
Now they roam the city.

Can these people not understand
The devil makes work for idle hands
M5 6–7 pm
The devil makes work for idle hands.

M5 to the country straight ahead
It's stuffed to the gills with crusty brown bread
Can they not understand
there's nothing worse than a bored man?

M5 6–7 pm

6

The Whole World Is A John Peel Session

It might well be that The Fall are 25 years wrapped in a John Peel session. Or 23 John Peel Sessions to be precise. Everything that happens with The Fall, everything that has ever happened, every album, every band member, every gig, every bust-up, absolutely everything, is all punctuated by a John Peel Session.

By sliding down to Maida Vale Studios, by performing 'almost' live songs selected by the whim of Mark; Falling in . . . quick fire . . . fast Fall . . . free Fall; the perfect Fall format.

The first time that Mark E. Smith asked me to attend a John Peel Session, I was 46, a *young* 46, but I still liked to think that I could dust down and look cool in black Levis, still felt like a Fall fan, how a Fall fan should feel and look.

I had waited a long time for this, seemed a big deal to me.

Wasn't really.

Mark: "Why not come down to London on Wednesday, Mick? We doing a Peel Session . . . our twenty-first."

"It's your twenty-third, I think, Mark."

Mark: "You see. That's what I can't stand. It's always happening to me, and in lots of trivial ways. People are always correcting me about my own life. It really fucking gets to me, sometimes. I wouldn't mind so much if I was some big, dumb rock-star idiot Liam Gallagher or something. But I get it at ground level. Stood at the bar, and someone will say, 'Actually Mark, you played the ICA in 1986 not 1985 . . .' That is just a pain, sometimes, because it's such a waste of time. That's why I am never keen on retrospectives . . . you know, articles that trawl through the past with evil and meticulous intent. That's why I don't want this book to be like that, scrutinising every twist and turn. You told me that you are putting stuff about Deeply Vale in it. Well that's fine, maybe people want to read that, but I don't. I'm sure it will be very good and very interesting to some . . . but not me. You have to realise that this is a very weird year for me. They are calling it our twenty-fifth anniversary year, although it's not, really. I regard the twenty-fifth year as 25 years after our first record, not 25 years since we got together in some bedroom, somewhere. Who cares about that? Anyway, The Fall roll on. There is nothing backwards about this fucking band and there never will be."

"Yes . . . I will come!"

The occasion of The Fall's 21st or 23rd John Peel Session, BBC Maida Vale Studios, London. February 19, 2003

The weak obliging sun softened the chill on a day when Maida Vale attained a surreal sheen, where colours had faded to pastel, and the expected array of idiosyncratic city dwellers strode purposefully to and fro, bellowing into handsets, casting anxious glances across busy streets, bargaining for exotic vegetables, ogling a designer furniture showroom, dropping into a Pret a Manger for coffee. I felt suitably at home, sitting in some pseudo Parisian coffee house, nibbling away at something containing goats cheese, failing to resist casting a vaguely sexual glance at the head-numbing waitress . . . me, a middle-aged northern goat, leering over the coffee.

At this precise moment, Mark and the lads and Elena were sitting pubside, homing in on the bitching of various BBC managers, the namc John Peel being banded around openly, all seemingly unaware of The Fall's presence. All, equally, unaware of the contemporary institution that is the John Peel Fall Session.

I sat ruminating this, in the French café. Peel Sessions are curious phenomena, a timely kickback at the encroaching trend of artless overproduction; a live-in-studio blast – give or take the odd cosmetic overdub – that would, more often than not, simply shimmer with freshness. And no other band, surely, could be more suited to John Peel Sessions than The Fall, who have always been guided by Mark's belligerent refusal to allow any trace of staleness, be it production-wise or musical, to soften the proceedings; and yes, Peel Sessions had become the stuff of legend. One recalls many supreme moments, a surging 'Australians In Europe', a pulsating 'M5', among the many highlights, with huddles of 'Peel Sesh' compilations peppered through The Fall's extensive discography, offering a second glimpse at favourite songs; offering, too, the chance for Mark and whoever was flickering in the band at any given time, to inject a touch of humour, have a little fun, shake off the po-faced purists. John Peel Sessions are all about taking the odd risk. Sometimes it works . . . sometimes not.

And Maida Vale seemed locked in respectful loveliness, as the band made their way back to the studios, and as I duly wandered in, suddenly struck by the realisation that, despite devouring several hundred of the things, often from bedside radios in numerous bedrooms across the north west, I had never really paused to wonder what actually happened at these recordings and, more pertinently, whether the atmosphere was really any different to any given studio session. It would be intriguing, to say the least. The young band, though obviously highly gifted in the art of striking an instant groove – see Blackburn show – were hardly schooled in the art of studio recording. Their time spent recently at the Lisa Stansfield/Ian Devaney complex in Rochdale for the recording of *Country On The Click* being their first lengthy spell in a quality subterranean environment.

And Maida Vale Studios sprawled, fat and white, shimmering beneath the sun, on this stunning February afternoon and, once inside, once past the steely gaze of reception, once the pass had been pinned, the nod given and your guide in this meandering biography . . . meandering himself, through myriad catacombs of BBC Maida Vale Studios, where direction signs hold no grip on reality and where scruffy engineers dart to and fro, and sullen violinists lurk in the toilets, lost in musicianly reverie. Past and, indeed, through various studios I trooped, pausing to sneak a listen to cacophonous warm-ups and kettle drums . . . and through ghostly expanses before, some way in the distance, a piercing, sliding guitar intro instigated a rush snare drum and the unmistakable sound of a band that could only be The Fall.

A bearded, corduroy-clad gent, heavily into his silvered years, stood before me, twisting his neck at the unlikely sounds.

"Oh I forgot. . . ."

He appeared to be talking to me.

"Is Mark in today? I will drop in and say 'Hello' later . . . haven't seen Mark in ages . . . hah . . ."

And with that he trundled deeper into the catacombs, fumbling in jumbo cords, another in the seemingly endless procession of unlikely Fall acquaintances.

Mark stood with his back to the control room . . . face contorted, deep in mock grimace. By the time drums had pounded to a halt, he had formulated his criticism.

"You were too lazy there, I don't know . . . just do your stuff, as in rehearsal . . . but it was too slow and you" – indicating in the vague direction of guitarists – "start it off with that great da daaa dada dah dah dahh that you do, clever dick . . . go on, do it now . . . practise it now . . . dad dah dah that's it . . . only do it higher."

"I can't do it higher . . . I just can't play it higher, Mark . . ."

"Yes, course you can . . . it needs that edge . . . come on practise it . . . come on get it right . . . now! . . . Oh hi Mick . . . Mick, go and sit in the control room, cocker . . . go on . . . this is serious business here."

And so it was. A hexagonal studio area in light wood, with off-shoot bays, and the usual studio nubbins with Elena pitching in, hitting into the instant and infectious groove of 'Theme From Sparta FC' – unknown at the time of this visit, though within two months, famously opening *Country On The Click* – hammering through a neatly angled take on Euro soccer hooliganism . . . of more in a little while. And so from the adjacent control room I watched, intrigued to be aware that, despite attending one or two Fall rehearsals over the years, I had never really witnessed Mark in full studio flow and, indeed, in full, if sometimes rather unfathomable, control.

"Hold your bass higher, Jim."

"I can't, it doesn't make any difference how high I hold it."

"It does . . . do it now."

"Mark, this is daft. It doesn't work."

"It does."

It *did*, actually, strangely, I noted, before exiting to a control room, ably if loosely manned by producer Mike Walter and engineer Ralph Jordan, both quite the epitome of aged studio chic, chain-smoking and amiable, locked in a tumble of musicians' in-jokes and sheer bonhomie. As Elena's organ pitched in with two familiar opening notes, both instantaneously started to sing The Stranglers' 'Peaches' and both accepted my intrusion with an agreeable nod, presuming me, I sensed, to be the new manager or some floating agent. They didn't care. Seen it all, I sensed, watching Ralph Jordan, bean thin, with greying locks flowing down his shoulders on which hung a Tindersticks T-shirt and Walter, hunched over the deck, entertainingly cynical. Between them there's 60 years of solid BBC studio experience all stacked into a tumble of endearing anecdotes, and within minutes both would be talking about their pensions.

"Don't mock," pleaded Walter. "It's a very good pension."

It was unfair of me to mock, even gently. Wouldn't turn down a BBC pension myself and can think of worse occupations than training it in from Sussex each day, lumping it with the latest bunch of ragamuffin oiks down from Nottingham or Darlington, fading gently from a career spent in the shadows of celebrity, be it here or at Broadcasting House, a place both would openly refer to as 'BH', which made me think how it would have been to drive the shows of Simon Bates or even Tony Blackburn during Radio 1's surreal golden years . . . although both would claim loftier allegiance with Radio Three and both – I am guessing here – once featured in provincial late Seventies prog rock outfits and still, again I guess, turn out, now and again, for a pub night run-through of the old songs. Nothing particularly wrong with any of these things but I recognised these two . . . recognised them from a thousand of Mark's descriptions. The battle of Fall against studio. An eternal battle, I sensed.

Walter: "Is this The Fall's 19th Peel Session?"

Me: "Oh God, I think it's the 23rd. I don't know. How many have you produced?"

Walter: "The Fall? I have never produced The Fall before. Not here, anyway. I did do a Reading Festival thing once. And neither has Ralph. Have you Ralph?"

Jordan: "No . . . never worked with Mark. But absolutely everybody else in this building seems to have worked with Mark. When I mentioned The Fall, all over this building, people would come out with some story of how they were involved in this session or that session. A Fall John Peel Session genuinely is an institution here, you know. A lot of famous things have happened here, but The Fall have made a huge contribution to these studios . . . and this is great. The band are here and they just kick into gear . . . they know exactly what they are doing. It's all very professional. Great to witness and great to work with."

Walter: "With Peel Sessions, we often are faced with very young bands who are a bit unsure, a bit nervous, so we generally use a more 'hands on' approach. The whole point is to get a 'live' feel, but sometimes they don't quite appreciate the difference between being here and, say, recording a few tracks for a CD or something. It really is a different approach, but The Fall seem perfect, because Mark is out there making sure that the raw edges remain. That's just great for us. We will just sit back and basically record this and, let's face it, it is sounding fantastic, isn't it? I mean we've had them all in here. Bands coming in with a couple of fire extinguishers as their only instruments. One band, from Brighton I think . . . God, what were they called? Anyway, their hi-hat was a shopping trolley. I mean, exactly how do you mike up a shopping trolley? That's the kind of thing we are used to dealing with. As it turned out, the trolley proved to be one of the best hi-hats I have ever heard. Amazing."

And so it was. 'Theme From Sparta FC', an unholy tale of Euro thuggery, spitting blood and verve, took two takes . . . at least, once past Mark's initial belligerence.

"Play it with feeling, for a change."

"I am playing it with feeling."

"Not enough . . . it needs to hurt!"

"It hurts . . . it fucking hurts Mark . . . honestly."

The 'play through' proved conclusive. With the band anxiously gathering in the control room, the thrill of hearing something fresh and unpolished was slightly lost in their critical eyes.

Guitarist: "Think there was a bum note, there . . ."

Drummer Dave Milner: "I wouldn't worry too much about that. The whole point of a Peel Session is to capture a live feel, not to lay something perfect down. I think this will do."

Mike Walter: "Well, you can add overdubs if you like, but I don't think there is much wrong with that. I've done a thousand Peel Sessions and there aren't many bands that can hit the spot like that . . . sounds wonderful. Will be good too, with the backing vocals."

Song two, 'Contraflow' , which contained clear lyrical echoes of 'M5', proved equally effortless, once that groove had been established. And here flowed the expected camaraderie, with Mark rising to waggish mode, looning with the band, closing the control room curtains, turning down the lights to effect atmosphere . . . and general mess around.

Walter: "What's he doing? He's closing the curtains so we can't see what he's up to . . . he's not daft, is he? You have to watch him . . . he messes with things, all in good fun . . . but you have to watch him."

Mark: "Haven't you got any microphones that aren't dented?"

Walter: "All our microphones are dented. This is the BBC."

Mark: "Well, can I have one that isn't? It won't record properly if it is dented . . . obviously."

Walter, to Jordan, wearily: "Go and see if you can find him a mike that isn't dented."

Both producer and engineer affected a mock shrug, casting seen-it-all eyes to the ceiling, inferring that an outbreak of mild rock star affectation had transpired although, frankly, one could understand Mark's point. Why dented mikes at the Beeb?

Mark: "I've been paying me telly licence for 30 fucking years and they give me a dented mike! That's no fucking good for me, not for a live session. You have got to be bloody professional about these things. Many people perhaps would have said nothing. They would

Door stepping in Notting Hill Gate. (*Paul Slattery*)

Making a point at the LSE, January 7, 1979. (*Paul Slattery*)

Grimace in Gorton. At the 'Stuff the Superstars Festival' in the ramshackle Mayflower Club, July 28, 1979. (*Paul Slattery*)

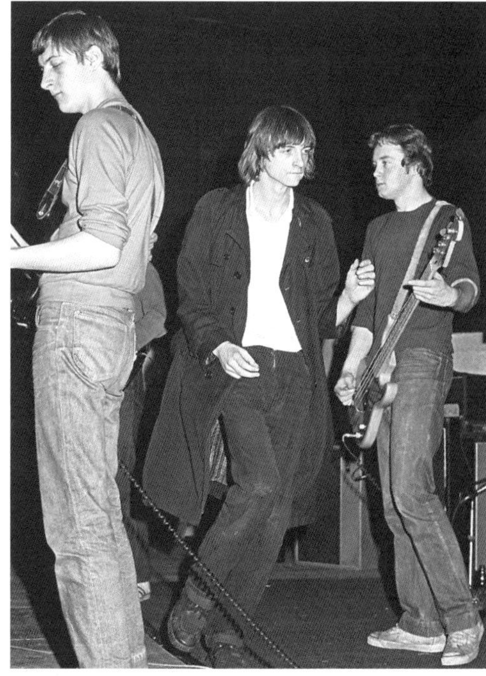

Flanked by Marc Riley and Steve Hanley at 'Stuff the Superstars'. The Fall played with Joy Division, The Distractions and Ludus, staking a claim for Manchester. (*Paul Slattery*)

Kings College, London, March 7 1980. Hanley, Scanlon, Riley, Paul Hanley (Steve's brother) and MES. (*Paul Slattery*)

Early 1980 shot, immediately prior to another of Karl Burns' departures. (*Marcia Resnick/Retna*)

Mystery train, Manchester, May 28 1980.
(*Paul Slattery*)

Relaxing at Faulty Products. February 12 1980.
(*Paul Slattery*)

Smith and Hanley, ignoring New Romantics upsurge at The Venue, Victoria, December 7 1982.
(*Paul Slattery*)

"Fancy a pint, Dad?" Quality time for Jack and Mark, April 1985. (*Courtesy of Smith family*)

Mark and Brix. Good times with guitar. (*Peter Anderson/SIN*)

Mark and Brix as Lord Nelson and Lady Hamilton on video set for 'Victoria'. (*LFI*)

F-4921-1 Oslo. Gateparti ved natt.
Norway Street view by night.

Dear Mam & Dad,
We have had an interesting time here. We went out to the beach by boat twice. Food v. good + weather is to. Everything a bit expensive, but people v. nice. Went to pictures last night, everything v. late here. Love Mark + Brix

HUSK POSTNUMMER

NORGE 300

ENERETT: KNUT AUNE KUNSTFORLAG A/S

Mr & Mrs. J. E. Smith
6, Dorchester
Avenue
Sedgley Pk.
Prestwich
Manchester
England
U.K.

Postcards from the edge. "Mark always found time to write home," said Irene.
(*Courtesy of Smith family*)

BERIC TEMPEST
COLOURCARD
GREAT BRITAIN · TR26 3HT
Tel 0736 752500 Fax 752515

ST. MARYS ISLES OF SCILLY
4 -PM
21 AUG
1995

Be properly addressed
ADDRESS
POSTCODE IT

2ND

Dear Mam & C.
Me & Lucy down here in Cornwall + having a great time. On a boat now to Scilly Is. - which sez a lot!!
Hope you are well eating pasties, sunburnt etc.
LUV - Mark XX

MRS. IRENE SMITH.
6, DORCHESTER AVE.
SEDGLEY PARK.
PRESTWICH.
MANCHESTER / U.K.
M25 8LJ.

The Eastern Isles flanked by St. Martin's with Tresco in the distance, Isles of Scilly.
F. E. Gibson, St. Mary's, Isles of Scilly.

FREE "Distort to find the grotto of thought"

THE FALL

the 'yeh' ning pandered

Riverside Programme

HEY! LUCIANI

PART 3

Tuesday-Saturday 5th-20th December 1986

Hideous Noise Group Write 'St' Pope Biog

Ohio, Sweden: A group has written a character portrayal of a Pope J.P. One — rumoured to become a 'SAINT' which will be presented at the 'Riverside Studios' near some river where 'Rule Brittania' was written. The Vatican commented "We have been waiting for a sign for 7 years".

Today 7.5103 *Years ago "I could have been a journalist. I could've been head of Rueters" Albino Luciani 1978.*

"It's nonsense" claimed their manager from a St John's Wood face lift surgery. "I was promoting big time heavy metal/Top 20 groups when they concocted this scheme in Hull, almost 497 miles away from Albert Side Studios, Croydon".

'Wild Bill Hicock Relative traced in U.K.

Boston, Lincs — a descendant of the legendary Wild West Hero, Wild Bill Cody, has been traced in Boston, Lincs, England. Known locally as 'Big Dave' Cody he bears a striking resemblence

STOP PRESS
BORMANN FOUND
CHIL
VICTORY FOR ROBSON
AGAINST FIST 1 — 0

Program for *Hey! Luciani*. December 1986.

"Well, she makes a change from Marc Riley." Brix and Mark on the set of *Hey! Luciani*. (*Tim Bauer/Retna*)

I Am *Kurious Oranj*. Surreal times captured by Kevin Cummins. (*Kevin Cummins/Idols*)

MICHAEL CLARK & COMPANY
V
THE FALL
20th September – 8th October
I AM CURIOUS, ORANGE
Sadler's Wells Theatre

Cup Final frolics.
Note traditional spelling!

Meaning business, 1989. (*Fotex/Rex Features*)

have held a certain reverence for the BBC. Well, I do, in a way, but you have got to take control to some extent. These guys were fine, as it happens, but we so often come up against in-studio laziness. Guys who think they know it all and are so used to bossing young bands around . . . well, they often can't handle it when they come across someone who knows what they are doing."

'Green-Eyed Loco Man' began with a surreal flashback! A tune burst from the studio, with Elena's organ surging over the chop start . . . what was that tune . . . what the hell was that tune?

The question was bouncing around my head throughout the recording, what was that intro tune? Flashback to a school playground in the mid-Sixties . . . flashback to airhead bullies in ill-fitting blazers, to impromptu smoke sessions behind the garages, to a Dansette and a stack of singles . . . to 'Groovin' With Mr Bloe', a gimmick instrumental early Seventies pop hit, the product of some darkly obscure studio session. What a bizarre notion . . . to pick up on 'Groovin' With Mr Bloe'.

Mark: "I often take bits from the past, you know. It stirs people's memories. I mean I didn't have much music in my life when I was a kid, but certain pop hits were always in evidence and they are often not the things that are remembered. You know, you get all this Sixties nostalgia stuff these days that might go on and on about the Grateful Dead or something. Most of us at school never had any contact with any of that stuff. All we heard was stuff on Tony Blackburn's show. Just pop hits. Those are the things that take me back in time. Not Dylan. Not Traffic!"

Mike Walter: "That 'Groovin' With Mr Bloe' was a great idea . . . man, that takes me back a bit."

Dave Milner: "I had never heard it or had heard of it. But Mark brought the single round for me to listen to. As soon as I heard it I knew that we could do something with it."

Mad enough for The Fall, 'Groovin' With Mr Bloe' never held any kudos when it was released in 1970, attaining neither pompous recognition from prog rockers nor cult status from the reggae-hunting skinhead as most novelty reggae hits did. It was just a naff song that floated in the air, constantly pumped from the all-powerful

Radio 1 playlist, pumping from buses, in clothes shops or undermined by bass-less transistors. 'Groovin' With Mr Bloe', asexual and jaunty, the perfect transistor pop hit.

And now it was in the hands of The Fall, if only briefly, and only to lead into the main body of 'Green-Eyed Loco Man'. Driven, repetitive, belligerent, with Mark off on one, and Milner pounding for dear life, and Elena sliding melodies neatly into place . . . and a lovely steadying moment . . . a moment of silence as the music splintered to a halt, leaving Mark's lone disembodied voice, eerily talking through the words, "Say goodbye to Glastonbury!!!!"

"To be honest," exclaimed Milner during the brief intermission, "it doesn't really matter what Elena plays in that song. I mean absolutely everything will do, it just all fits together or rather none of it fits. That's the point, if you get my drift!"

It was a Fall thing, and it was ever thus. If the song had started to feel too wholesome, too rounded, too perfect, too much, in the immortal words of Mark, ". . . like fucking pub rock . . ." then it would need to be dismantled. Time after time after time . . . it would all have to settle in some lovely unholy pool.

Dave Milner: "There are times when the stuff Mark tells us doesn't seem to make any sense and it's easy to start thinking, 'Oh, maybe Mark doesn't understand, 'cos he's not the musician, in that sense.' But when you work with him a bit you realise that he does know. Even his most bizarre requests are done for a purpose, and nearly always, it works. We come away all the better for it."

And this session, this 21st or 23rd John Peel Session was already becoming a prime example – an example of a band settling into a groove and being pulled swiftly out of complacency by the ruse of Mark E. Smith. The looning, the belligerence, even the arrival of yours truly, all seemed designed to unsettle the band slightly, to keep them on edge, to inject uncertainty. You could hear it in the three songs, you could sense it, and so strongly.

Mike Walter: "It's quite an unusual process this. Even Mark telling us off about the dented microphones. It added an edge there . . . just a little, stopped us from just wandering in and going through the motions, another day at the office."

Of course. Because you are never quite sure what is going to happen next.

And then Mark disappeared.

Walter: "So what is the fourth track, lads?"

Bassist Jim Watts: "I don't know. I think Mark wanted to do 'Mountain XXXX'. That's what he said this morning."

Dave Milner: "Yeah, that's what he said this morning but he has since gone off that idea. I don't know. Could be anything, what is it? 'Mere Pseud'? 'Mere Pseud'? What the hell is going on in Mark's head, now? Surely not. [To me.] Do you know it?"

Of course . . . Of course. 'Mere Pseud Mag. Ed.' Seemed hopelessly out of context here . . . which, of course, is the point. A Beefheartian ramble from the days of *Hex Enduction Hour*, with Mark bursting into life, and the stop-start chop funk driving through the song, tumbling through two short takes, and an instant overview from Mike Walter.

MERE PSEUD MAG. ED.

His heart organ was where it should be
His brain was in his arse
His hand was well out of his pocket
His psyche's in the hearth

Had a beard which was weird
Some time ago heard Ramones in '81
Has a Spanish guitar

Real ale, curry as well – sophisticate!
Spanish guitar doesn't get far
In computer teaching job
His dreamgirl sings adverts for the Weetabix
A fancied wit that's imitation of Rumpole of Bailey

Whose causes and rags were phoenix-like
They were do-do like
They were comfort blanket type

Pho-do in fact
Pho-do in fact
Pho-do in fact

He had a weak pisser
And one night at darts match
Decadent sandwich quaff

He showed he was a big fan of double-entendre
Saw *Not The Nine O'Clock News History of the World Part One*
Twice each at least
Twice each at least
Twice each at least

"Well, there's not much wrong with that!"

Mark: "Naaaah. I think what we want to do is use that take but add an organ and a tom-tom. Can we do that? Can't be too difficult for the BBC, can it?"

Feeling surplus to requirements, as The Fall moved seemingly backwards through the process, from perfect 'live' takes, through . . . well, not so much dismantling as a process of chipping away at the edges, keeping the sharpness intact . . . curiously, quite the antithesis of the very point of the overdubbing process which has always been, in my experience at any rate, a method of actively polishing those edges, buffing that vibrancy, often wholly necessary, of course . . . at times, quite astoundingly pompous, but, nevertheless, the mainstay of the recording art for the past 40 years has been based around the development of the overdub. That is recording at its simplistic.

Mark: "Sometimes, you just know. You just know that something is right, or something is wrong. I have always been the boss of The Fall and, as such, have trusted my instinct, you know. And that's what it has always been about. Many, many clever people have failed to grasp this simple fact. This is the essence of The Fall and it is why there is no other band on earth like us. I may not always be right . . . and technically I am often completely wrong. And I have been inconsistent. There are times when I say something that might seem to contradict something I said a month earlier. But it doesn't matter because what I do is ride with the instinct. Always have done, since day one. Since 1977, it has been guided by instinct, for better or worse. And I have never compromised that, even during the spells when I have lost my way. It has been a wholly honest process . . . and it's true, you know. That's the point, isn't it? That's why all those fucking wankers from the music press, including you at some point, Mick, that's why they couldn't actually get close because they wrote themselves away from The Fall. As soon as they tried to grasp it, the point was lost."

This last statement wasn't actually taken from the Maida Vale session, but from an evening spent annoying waiters in Manchester's Midland Hotel back in 1986. Nevertheless, it started to swish around my mind as I sat in the artists' relaxation room, or green room, or recreation room, as ever, a blackened shell blessed with a television – eternally tuned to starkly dubious daytime television – and a coffee machine that more often than not refuses to accept whatever coinage you proffer. All studios in all countries have this identical room, and most of them, at any given time of day or night, are inhabited by a sprawling gaggle of badly dressed musicians who, when not conspiring to sneakily sack the bass player, are voicing their opinions about Harold Bishop from *Neighbours* and how, at one time, he seemingly died, after being swept off a rock on the Gold Coast and then miraculously returned to the series, blessed with a conveniently unhinged memory, several years later. It will be ever thus. In Brazil, one senses, as in Rochdale and, indeed, in Maida Vale.

For the moment, I ignore the banter and begin to wonder if this strange book – and please allow me the courage to proclaim it strange – is doing likewise, writing away from The Fall, rather than grasping the essence of Mark E. Smith.

"It's a possibility," I muse . . . and shrug . . . and realise that it doesn't really matter. It has to be this way . . . it just has to be.

"I mean, it must be really, really weird to be Harold Bishop," states Jim Watts. "I mean, what else can you do in life after that? Absolutely nothing. You can't bloody well act, you can't do anything. You are just Harold Bishop and everyone knows you can't act."

"Kylie could act," I countered . . . and immediately regretted it.

Mercifully, the conversation moved on, to a variety of other, equally unholy matters related to television, with Elena pitching in with thoughts on the validity of Germanic variations of a *Kilroy* theme. Surreal would, perhaps, be too strong a word here . . . the afternoon was settling nicely, settling down from the tensions of the recording. Even Mark, fresh from berating the producer, seemed happy enough to comment on the whereabouts of The Crossroads Motel, remarking quite correctly that it was located on the fringe of Birmingham. I did attempt to prise further revelations from him by temptingly placed reminisces of Amy Turtle and Shuee McPhee, but at the very mention of the name of that idiosyncratic Scottish chef, Mark just stared at me in, I strongly sensed, a state of pity if not sheer disbelief.

"You don't remember Shuee McPhee," I countered.

Ten minutes later, a sweet little bombshell.

"Yeah, yeah, we need some backing vocals for 'Sparta'. Mick . . . come on, you are in on this one . . . come on . . . earn yer fucking keep for a change, give us some backing vocals."

I am, I swiftly informed all and sundry, blessed with a voice that is, at best, fevered and reptilian . . . well, that's how it always sounded to me. Quite the worst voice in Stockport County's Cheadle End in the late Sixties . . . quite the worst . . . and that is saying something.

Ironically, this proved to be the very quality that Mark had been seeking . . . as Rimmer – who would be my vocal conductor for the afternoon – stood opposite me, sharing my angst, pouring a terrace chant into the wonderful BBC microphones . . . egging . . . goading . . . egging me into the heart of this crazy football song.

Not that it was difficult.

"OK, let's take one . . ."

And so it went.

Like this, with yours truly suitably affecting the role of Euro thug on the hunt for blood. No Grammies, one instantly sensed . . . nevertheless, deep down . . . very deep down, a little fan inside me seemed to be stirred. I had actually appeared on a Fall record . . . could life get any better? I mock, but it was a lovely little moment, enjoyed by myself, if nobody else. Mark's cheekiness had been endearing. And this is how it went!

YOU HAVE TO PAY FOR EVERYTHING
BUT SOMETHINGS ARE FOR FREE
WE LIVE ON BLOOD
WE ARE SPARTA FC

ENGLISH CHELSEA FAN
THIS IS YOUR LAST GAME
WE ARE NOT GALATASARAY
WE ARE SPARTA FC

Walter: "I think it needs to be more German-ish . . . try it."

YOOOO AVVV TOOOO PAH VOR EVRFIN
BUT SUMFINS ARE VOORR VREEE
WE LIVVVV ON BLOOOD
VEEE ARRRR SPARRRTAH EFFF CEEEE

EEEENGLEEESH CHELSEEEE FAANN
THEEESE EEEES YOOOOR LAAASSST GAAAAME
VEE ARE NOOOOT GALATASEEEEERAAAY
VEEEEE RRRRRR SPARRRRRTAHHH EFFFF CEEEEEE

Walter: "Yeah . . . thanks . . . great that."

Of course it wasn't.

It wasn't even barely adequate and, I sensed at the end, rather too German-ish. Still . . . Dave Milner seemed content enough, as did the remainder of the band, by this time locked in the warmth of blessed post-session trivialities.

Postscript to Peel Session: the band looked tight and tight-knit. There were tensions, undoubted tensions, but none that could compare to one or two of the first-hand instances to be found later in this book. There was, as I hinted, the typical Fall undertone, where Mark would impose a benevolent despotism, although even this was delivered in a fairly light-hearted manner; in fact, rarely had I seen him so ebullient, content, or so it seemed to me, to allow this particularly young Fall to flourish around him. And, in particular, Jim Watts, three years in the heart of the action, contributing greatly, both in terms of general musicianship, at the very heart of the songwriting too, seemingly coming into the band, three years previously, blessed with the good heart and determination to play rock'n'roll, stripped and pared in The Fall tradition . . . a perfect fit.

And yet . . . typical Fall . . . typical Fall . . . on March 3, 2003, as the band settled for a pubside gathering preceding a short shunt to Turkey – a rather unwise sojourn, considering the proximity to the impending war – Mark would stride purposefully into the pub, ordering drinks for everyone, apart from Jim Watts.

As Watts told *playlouder.com*: "It was the night before Turkey and Mark came to the pub to meet us. Bought the others a drink and purposefully didn't get me one, then came out with some nonsense saying I was off in London spending The Fall's money." At this point he laughs: "Playing with a heavy metal band and his contacts at MI5 had intercepted my calls to book rehearsal rooms. And [he said] I could play the gig in Turkey then leave the band, and obviously I opted not to go to Turkey and just walked out."

He added, "Have to give him that though – he can be extremely funny. It's a pity as I feel short-changed. We didn't have a blazing row as I was laughing too much."

Which is how Jim Watts was sacked just prior to the gig in Turkey on March 5. Steve Evets stood in on bass in Turkey at very short notice (same way Jim started). Evets is an old mate of Mark E. Smith who did vocals on Mark's spoken word album, *The Post Nearly Man*, and some backing vocals on *The Unutterable*. His band, Dr Freak's Padded Cell, supported The Fall at the Camden Electric Ballroom in November 2002.

Eight days before the 23rd John Peel Session. February 11, 2003, 8 pm

Cold. Foggy, very foggy. Prestwich, Salford. Mark's living room.

I sat at the table, in a submarine grey room; a well-pinned, heavily daubed map of the world to my right, a space on the wall that used to be decorated by a vivid Pascal painting. Through the connecting double doors a television blares to no effect. Light stacks of CDs littered the floor, and I sat rather dutifully at the table, watching Mark crack down a packet of cigarettes, expressing sympathy over the recent and sudden demise of my mother six months previously, when I had informed him that I was taking her for a holiday in a Lake District cottage, an idea to which he had instantly warmed at that time.

"Nice one, Mick . . . good one, yes," he had enthused. "I have been thinking about that, myself. About taking my mother away, somewhere, somewhere and having no distractions. No business at all, just a week . . . probably in Blackpool, to be honest. I've said it before, but I like it there . . . we would get one although I'm not sure she would want to go there. Should do it some day, though . . . yes . . . think it would be a good idea."

And this time.

"I am so sorry about that. Always difficult. Always difficult, isn't it?"

Genuinely, I sensed, he shrugged himself into a sympathetic frame of mind, struck a match, cracked a beer can, stared at the lonely grey wall.

"I'm relaxing a bit at the moment. We have just finished the new album, you see this is always a time where there is a bit of a lull. I mean, not too much. We have this Peel Session next week, which will be good. They always are. To be honest, it's a bit fucking pointless at the moment . . . I mean, we recorded the album at Lisa Stansfield's place, up in Rochdale. A studio in the garden. I don't know, it was the first time that the lads had ever been in a posh studio. And it was great. Perfect for us . . . can't think of any reason why we should have to go to London to do it. Even our record company are up in Blackburn, so you know . . . it was great. It felt great and that's the main thing, really. Feeling at home. But, you know, the usual thing then happened. They had to take the stuff away and mix it in fucking London. To this day I can't see any reason for that . . . and the inevitable happened, it really did. They actually lost some of the tracks in transit. Completely gone. All that work . . . absolutely fucking mental. But then they found them again. It was just so inevitable, really. Has happened over and over again . . . I don't know . . . shall we go to the pub? How do you fancy The Ostrich?"

"Er . . ."

"I mean, I've been in The Woodthorpe with the record company this afternoon and I am a bit talked out, to be honest. I actually did a lot of business, a lot of talking, sorted all kinds of stuff out and then this guy from the record company, well, his missus came in and seemed really upset. Could tell it was a dubious situation . . . will be all right but I fear that he will now have forgotten everything that I have said. These are the problems we face . . . and increasingly, as we get older. Let's go to The Ostrich."

A lengthy walk, sinking deeper and deeper into freezing fog, with Salford fading into silence all around, shuffling through rows of ghostly semi-detached homes . . . the enveloping night given an added power, it seemed . . . dreamlike . . . cinematic . . . a cheap horror flick in Prestwich, swirled about by increasing mist, with the fat slug of blackness – Heaton Park – screaming from across the road . . . and a ghostly travelling fairground emerging from the gloom . . . white-faced clowns dawbed onto stationary waltzers . . . posters proclaiming the 'Return to Belle Vue', stirring memories from the deep.

"Strange night, isn't it, really strange atmosphere," observed Mark. And so it was. Really strange indeed, and as he shuffled on, I told him about that Blackburn gig and about that Blackburn pub.

"Oh no, not that pub opposite . . . oh nooooh, you went in there?" he exclaimed and, considering the standard of a good many of the hostelries featured in this book, his reaction did seem extraordinary.

"You see, oh yes, that is a really dodgy pub. Funny, because it looks like some kind of annexe to the King George's Hall, doesn't it . . . that's what we thought. In fact, that was the first English pub that Elena went into. She thought she was going in to some quiet little place and it was full of football thugs. She thought the whole of England was like that. Oh that's really funny, you going in there."

Naturally, and resting on the verge of sycophancy, I informed him that the Blackburn show was my favourite Fall gig for at least 20 years, even stooping to acknowledge the part played by Ed Blaney in the scheme of the evening.

"Yeah well, funny you should say that," countered Mark and – typical Fall, typical Mark – preceded to explain just why.

". . . funny because Ed quit the very next day. Oh yeah, it even made it into the *Manchester Evening News* . . . How Fall guru had had his eyes set on greater things. And he told me at the time that I had been making his life hell, and all of that. But I kind of knew that it had run its course. I led him to the position of quitting, if the truth be told, and it was the right thing to do. I don't know, he was saying that he wanted to move on with a younger band, all that kind of stuff. But it was after he had gone that I kind of learned a few things, things that he had never told me about. I'm not saying that he did me any wrong, it's just the way managers tend to work. They do things for whatever reasons and they avoid telling you some of the important things. That's their job, to some extent. But there have been a number who have fallen from The Fall."

Indeed. One thought, most obviously, of Kay Carroll, or of middle-years managers such as the remarkable Welshman Richard Thomas – seen performing the role of downbeat sports reporter on the 'Kicker Conspiracy' video – who was booted free because, in Mark's words, ". . . his bonhomie was becoming a danger . . ." now to be found sitting on the 'other' side of a bar, running his own pub, nudged close to the A5, I believe, where occasional drifting rock stars nip in for a touch of that old bonhomie. For my part, I will never forget an evening spent with Richard at The Hacienda, circa '85. There simply weren't enough spirits in the Kim Philby bar to support our watery habits, on that most blurry of nights. Then there was Trevor Bold, later to be immortalised on 'The Birmingham School of Business School'.

"Yeah, well, there is a right business Mafioso from the Midlands and we got caught up in all of that for a while."

It was always a strained relationship between The Fall and whatever manager took on the challenge at any given time. If not a poisoned chalice, then it was certainly always difficult, taking hold of the burden, wriggling into the power dynamic, whichever way you approach it, difficult to operate when the band is so pointedly the creation of Mark E. Smith and nothing could ever escape that fact. The role of Fall manager has been kicking around Manchester for several years, flickering from acquaintances of the band, in the Kay Carroll mould, to agents who hustle too far into the band's heart, to, as was the case with Ed Blaney, linked to The Fall via regular slots with a support band.

Mark: "Nobody is the manager at the moment. Well, nobody and everybody. The band all think they are taking on managerial roles and I do, and, yes, our bass player acts like he's manager, which is great of him, actually, but the truth is that no one is really fulfilling the role and that suits me at the moment."

Managing The Fall

Kay Carroll once told me, while managing The Fall: "It is impossible to manage The Fall. They are an unmanageable band. You have to sit on top and tug the reins a bit, this way or that, and hope they respond but, mostly, they will all tug in different directions and then me and Mark will shout and get our own way after a lot of arguing. But it's not always that easy. One of the problems is that we have had women in the band. You should never have women in a band. Completely screw things up, they do. Bloody women in bands."

It was an odd statement . . . emanating, as it did, from someone who declared herself to be an ardent feminist.

I didn't argue, though. You didn't argue with Kay. I mean. I loved her. But I didn't argue with her!

Nor did I ask to which particular women she was referring. (There were only two possibilities and, frankly, I don't wish to go there right now. Partly because Una Baines once threw a glass at me at the Romiley Forum, after I had announced that her band, whatever they were called, would not be taking top prize in some dreaded band contest, and partly because the other one, to which Kay might have been referring, was Yvonne Pawlette, who once threatened me with violence if I didn't send a Sex Pistols album to her Doncaster abode after Mark had surreptitiously lent it to me. There weren't any other Fall women around at the time.)

Shift-Work. April 1991

So What About It?/Idiot Joy Showland/Edinburgh Man/
Pittsville Direkt/The Book Of Lies/The War Against Intelligence/
Shift-Work/You Haven't Found It Yet/The Mixer/A Lot Of Wind/
Rose/Sinister Waltz.

There was a time when I wondered what it would be like to actually 'manage' The Fall. What kind of teases and torments such a role might bring, particularly, as seemed to be increasingly the case, an element of artistic whim had entered into the day-to-day running of the band, where even Mark's famous work ethic became subservient to the notion of keeping an edge on proceedings. At the time, the band were effectively managed by Trevor Bold, although this liaison was beginning to stagger into a strangely muddied area. It was the occasion of the launch of *Shift-Work*, back in 1991, where a Fall trimmed to a quartet of Mark, Craig Scanlon, Steve Hanley and Simon Wolsencroft had decided to dispense with the fringe band members, Marsha Schofield and Martin Bramah (who had fluttered about the band in the vacuum left by the departing Brix), and had pinned back down to basics – aside from Kenny Brady's innovative violin – and had seemingly fallen into a solid live unit less at the mercy of multi-member logistics. By comparison to larger Falls before and after, it was an almost manageable unit, locked solid by the Scanlon/Hanley axis and, one presumed, comparatively easy to manage.

It is here that I declare an interest. Not that I ever had any designs on managing The Fall – I am, indeed, the world's worst manager of *anything* – but friends of mine were beginning to encircle the band with vulture-like intent. I had tried to warn them off and, as it turned out, they fell from Mark's orbit fairly meekly during an oncoming spell of music business angst. Nevertheless, the band occupied, and still occupies, a unique position in the scheme of things. As such, prospective managers knew that although they would not make a killing with such a labour-intensive task as managing The Fall, the band would nevertheless add kudos to a burgeoning manager's artist roster. This was a fairly cold and merciless quest on their part. While claiming to be fired as a result of Mark's artistic integrity on the one hand, their attempts to gain some kind of foothold were based on nothing more than self-advancement. To be a manager of The Fall, albeit for a short spell, would shine brightly from any CV. I wondered, therefore – and I still wonder – how Mark copes with the surrounding shimmer of sycophancy; everyone is a fan, everyone is on the make.

I recall meeting Mark one evening, at an unlikely trendy nightclub just off Manchester's Deansgate, for the occasion of the launch of *Shift-Work*. It was a slightly irritating evening. The DJ of the hour had decided, true to the unchallenged wisdom of club DJs, that the kind of people who would be likely to attend a Fall launch party would be the kind of people who would enjoy their conversations swamped by ancient Mission tracks, pumped through at the kind of volume that would challenge any wartime assault. Through the murk of this reverberating cacophony, however, it was intriguing to observe Mark switching from host – a role he performed with a higher degree of charm than might be expected, circulating through the club like a groom at a wedding party – to a sudden switch of persona, as two London-based agents came to the bar.

"I'm sorry," he said, utilising a phrase not generally uttered by Mark E., "I've just got to go and buy these agents a drink . . . be nice to them . . . it's business, you see."

And off he went, full of charm and poise, happy to sweet-talk, if only for a short while. I remember this striking me as being rather at odds with the Mark I had grown to know.

Mark: "You've just got to work harder than other bands. I mean there have been times when I have just totally ignored agents and people like that, or left it all to some manager or other, but sometimes you have just got to take hold of the reins. That agent was quite important. He was also a good guy, a hard worker, which is a rarity in the fucking music business, so there is no point in upsetting people for the sake of it, although I have done that as well, once or twice!"

Through that, you may glimpse that work ethic again, which also intrigued me, as the title track and prevailing theme, if one discounts the disarmingly touching 'Edinburgh Man', in which an unusually wistful Mark, no doubt fuelled in some deadening hotel room, is heard pining for the bars and charm of Scotland's drama capital, seeming to take a cold and deliberate view of the nine-to-five life, a life endured by many of Mark's friends, but lost to a parallel universe as far as this life is concerned.

Mark: "Yes, I was a bit wistful in regard to Edinburgh. I've often said that I have always felt at home in Scotland, in Edinburgh as in Glasgow. It's probably just down to my granddad, that. But it is true and that's possibly the reason I like Blackpool too, because there is simply no trace of Southern affectation. It just doesn't exist. I have always felt at home there. Had a flat in Edinburgh. It was amazing. The women in the next flat would knock on the door and offer me a full beaker of Scotch. Before I went there, I really thought I had a drink problem but I was a mere beginner compared to what they put away . . . and before lunchtime as well. I couldn't keep up. Fantastic place, Edinburgh."

At the time of *Shift-Work*, Manchester, although still shivering from the insanity of the mess that was Madchester, and certainly slumped into the void of backlash, had yet to begin the astonishing period of regeneration, a period that would pull a cosmopolitan air into the heart of the city, for better or worse. *Shift-Work*, with its nod to Edinburgh, and statement of unpretentious domesticity, seemed to be predicting the end of the Mancunian, or Salfordian norm, the end of a proletariat wisdom, where genuine values would rise above social affectation. Within a handful of years, finding a Mancunian, or at least finding someone who admits to being such a thing in the traditional sense, would be impossible in this city centre.

The Ostrich, Heaton Park, Salford. February 11, 2003, 8.30 pm

The stillness of the night flowed into the pub, the same pub where, six months previously, we had enjoyed a strange encounter with the man whose dad liked cockroaches. No such local colour tonight, no curious glances, or nods of half recognition. An empty bar, where brickwork meets beams and where, curiously, above a fireplace, the brickwork actually appears to have been framed, as if a painting.

"Why? Do you think the landlord was a brickie, or something?" quizzed Mark, cracking open the first lager of the evening, politely failing to wince at my red wine . . . doesn't like red wine, Mark. Makes him feel . . . paranoid.

Mark: "Used to. Used to send me mental, red wine. Had a very weird effect on me. But I've been drinking a lot of it, lately. It has been helping me, actually . . . helping me get a bit healthier . . . when I met you, when we went to the Lake District, I was in a bit of trouble, to be honest. Couldn't put my finger on what the problem was, but I was in a state where I just couldn't get any sleep. It was really, really worrying, you know. I wasn't sure what to do. That was why I went out walking at night, looking for cigarettes. It was to give me something to do. It's terrible when you just can't sleep. It creeps up on you . . . puts you in a state of semi-trance. I really was a bit worried back there. It was like that film . . . have you seen it . . . *Fight Club*? It's about that kind of neurosis. A lot of people didn't get that aspect of the film, but I thought it was obvious. The state where you can't sleep . . . like speeding, only worse than speeding, actually. It starts to play tricks on you. But I'm better. Red wine, yes, it has helped a lot. So has Elena."

The quietness remained that night, despite the trickle of customers, and I noticed that, red wine or not, a colour had flushed back into his cheeks. There were even moments in The Ostrich that night when he seemed to have regained the colour of his youth, and I couldn't help but flash back to days when he would be fired by the spirit and glow of youth, fired too by an intelligence that seemed beyond his years, and yet seemingly trapped in the mannerisms of a

20-year-old chain-smoking in that old Kingswood Road flat, with Kay, with the K-Tel Record stack, and Patti Smith's voice soaking into the walls and Colin Wilson books on the floor. The journey, the 24-year journey through the most gloriously Hellish maze of rock'n' roll – and a thousand ego clashes – suddenly didn't seem so arduous. There was a great moment, too, when a tubby to cherubic car mechanic, face reddened by 30 years of intense bitter drinking and cragged by the accompanying hits of tobacco, turned to his wife and exclaimed that he would be "39 next week".

Don't know if Mark heard that, but it was rather warming. The persona of Mark, famously living through 25 years of rock'n'roll excess, suddenly slammed back into perspective. The cherubic mechanic, living a normal, if not quiet life, had managed to edge far deeper into the ageing process than either Mark – fags, bitter and all – or myself, no fags, good food, plenty of running but still too much wine. It reminded me strongly of one of those 'know all, done nowt' types, who sat regularly barside in the heart of Stockport, swilling and chain-smoking for a stack of years yet berating me for fraternising with those 'rock'n'roll people' presumably because they felt that their excesses were rather more dangerous to life and limb than their own. I remember it and I remember it well, because Mark and Kay were sitting directly in front of him, barely able to comprehend the moronic jibes he was unleashing. I could even tell you the date, time and place. It was The Blue Waterfall disco, a Seventies kick-back disco – still there, I believe – down in darkened Stockport. It was May 24, 1980 and a disparate blend of acquaintances had bizarrely assembled, unlikely, unfulfilled, and a wedding, my wedding, as it happens, my first wedding, an inebriated maelstrom preserved now on photographs where ageing aunties from Whittle le Woods are captured on film talking to Mark and Kay and . . . God knows who else . . . but I can't forget the fat man at the bar, who thought the entire affair debauched, presumably because members of local glam band V2 had arrived wearing purple spandex and pink earrings. The best argument of the evening was between Mark E. Smith and Mark from V2, about the wisdom, or lack of, that goes with the wearing of such gear. Mark and Kay were, intriguingly enough, the two most soberly garbed people of the entire affair. And in two letters later, Mark would refer to the downbeat event. "Why do people dress like that? They outlaw themselves. Could never do it myself," he said.

More bewilderingly, in a letter he sent to photographer Kevin Cummins, he offered, "Mick's do? Best night of me fucking life."

I never enquired if a touch of sarcasm darkened this astonishing statement.

Needless to say it was not the best night of my life.

And the cherubic mechanic didn't recognise Mark in The Ostrich. Mind you, I doubt if he would have recognised Kylie's bum if it had wiggled past, such was the extent of the day's inebriation.

Age was in the air . . . talk of age. How it feels, indeed, to be with such a young band.

Mark: "Well, that's funny. Sometimes I forget that they are so young and I have to remind myself. I feel sorry for them, in some ways, because they are just not as equipped for life as we were. Well, I don't think they are, they certainly expect more on a plate than I ever did and I wonder why I always have to push them so hard. Well, actually I don't push them hard at all, just a little, but I shouldn't even be doing that, should I? They should be pushing me. I should have my feet up. I don't know. The thing is that I introduce them to a lot of music that they would otherwise not hear, but often it is me pushing newer stuff at them rather than the other way around. It's funny that. And also, like everyone else of their generation, they are massively into *Lord Of The Rings*. Like everyone is into these fucking . . . I mean I won't watch them. Never could stand that stuff at school . . . and, as you well know, it was responsible for so much hippy shite, wasn't it? All those fucking terrible bands, man. And I wonder how this fucking stuff can come back and be on people's minds again. The band knows my opinion on it and they talk about it behind my back. They even had an evening at one of their houses where they showed the film and they didn't dare tell me about it . . . hahahaha . . . a secret *Lord Of The Rings* evening. But I found out their little scheme. They can't get away with that kind of thing. It's dangerous."

Indeed. They might ask Mark if they can do a concept album next (which made me wonder . . . could *I Am Kurious Oranj* be considered a concept album?).

I didn't ask.

Perhaps people are able to accept Tolkien these days without it affecting them so badly. Without feeling the need to form a prog rock band . . . no need to take things so seriously anymore. I don't know . . . I asked Mark, do people take The Fall too seriously?

"Depends what you mean by seriously. I have always wanted my work to be taken seriously, because it deserves to be . . . but no, I can't stand it when people go too far. Like all those fucking web sites about The Fall. I've shut a load of them down, to be honest. People chatting away, discussing the meaning of lyrics. There's some fucking professor in America who teaches about the meaning of Fall songs. I mean, can you believe that?"

Well, yes, frankly.

"Really upsets me, that . . . well, maybe not, but I just think it's pathetic. The whole point is to understand and move on . . . not hold seminars or open fucking web pages. I mean, I'm not against the official one, though I never, ever look at it. As a way of conveying info, that's OK, but all that stuff beyond that. Really hate it. The only reason I agreed to be part of this book is because . . . I know I've said this before, but I know you won't trawl from release to release in that trainspotter fashion. That would be so dull . . . can't stand dullness . . . can't stand being taken too seriously and I can't stand bad writing . . . oh God . . . yes, you are right. It's not good when someone takes you too seriously. I remember going to the launch of Dave Haslem's book about Manchester. I don't know why I went . . . I should have known. I mean, I'm sorry, but I don't like that book at all. Like a school essay. But I knew Dave and I thought it would be OK. Then, I was there and there was this slide projector thing and it had an image of me on it. It was the first I fucking knew of it. It was just so embarrassing. I wanted to get out of there but that would have made a scene, so I was trapped and it was dreadful. And Dave got up and said that it was all my fault. I get that a lot, you know. People coming up and saying that it was all my fault. Got it from Fatboy Slim. Fucking hell . . . I am responsible for Fatboy Slim! 'Cos he said that he started The Housemartins because of The Fall. And the same thing was said by Paul Heaton. I mean, I like Paul, he's OK. I don't listen to the fucking Beautiful South of course, but I like the honest way he is about it all. But he was saying that it was all my fault and saying how awful things were. It was bizarre, he was pouring his heart out to me and I was completely skint at the time. And I mean, really, really skint. I just thought, 'Fucking hell, I wish I had your problems, mate.' People have no idea. Even people like that, who have been in the business for years and have been really successful. They still seem to have this naivety thing that if you are in the music business for a long time and if people know your work, then you must necessarily be rich. And it's rather ironic that half these people portray me as some kind of money-grabbing tyrant. The truth is rather opposite to that, if you think of the number of people I have taken off the dole and have put in the band. Considerably overpaid some of them, as well. People don't seem to mention that. God, yes . . . DJs? How did they become superstars? What is that all about? Yes . . . I know, Dave Haslem has written about it in his second book. Forgive me if I don't go legging it down to Waterstone's. Can you imagine anything duller than that?"

The ambience soft, the pub darkly lit, the clientele unusually sparse, generally sombre, something hanging in the air, could have been the threat of impending war with Iraq, which had intensified this very day. By the time this book reaches the shelves, hopefully the war will have been averted, or will have swiftly passed, with minimum casualties. These seemed like vain hopes, on this paranoiac day, with the Americans out for the kill and Tony Blair clinging to their coat-tails.

But although paranoia might be a bad sign for humanity, it always appears to suit Mark's muse superbly well. Mark's perception suddenly appears finely tuned, not that he is always correct. I recall him predicting a Labour landslide on the day that Maggie Thatcher achieved a stranglehold victory. That was a curious one, partly because Mark E. Smith's vision had seemed so clear and perhaps rather too early, as he also spoke of a new Labour – seven years before that became a reality – where the protagonists were no longer scruffy, aged socialists garbed in unwise corduroy, reddened faces topped by the kind of uncut hair worn only by those who would balance university degrees with days slumped in tap rooms. All a thing of the past, he had stated. No, no, the new Labour men would be young, handsome and dressed in designer suits and ties. They would be groomed and smart, they would be attuned to contemporary spin. I remember it vividly, sitting in Mark's living room, with Britain voting Thatcher massively back into power, and Mark envisaging New Labour. He wasn't smiling, either.

Neither was he smiling in The Ostrich.

"I don't read the newspapers any more. Not at all. Absolutely no point in them now. It is really sad how they toady. They are unbelievably reverential towards Tony Blair. It's just so fucking embarrassing. What I really can't understand is how they get away with it unchallenged. I mean it is just so obvious. Any idiot can see through it. I wouldn't waste my time reading that stuff anymore, celebrity journalism, all of it, even the so-called hard journalism. Nothing in it. It's the same in America now, which is even sadder because it used to be the best press in the world. I don't read that, either. At least, not the political stuff. Have you ever read American sports journalism? That is where the really clever stuff lies. A lot of it almost seems coded. It's like, the best journalists know they will not be allowed to say what they think on the political pages, and so they enter into sports journalism, and you read it, and it's so intelligent. There are times when they are hardly talking about sports at all. I always try to read that stuff . . . absolutely brilliant. But I don't think the British writers have that kind of intelligence any more. It's really amazing to see how it has happened. People who used to be radicals, all softened. People like Andrew Marr . . . can't believe it. It used to be full of fire . . . now you see him stood outside 10 Downing Street talking in hushed reverential tones. It's totally fucking mad.

"That kind of softening so obviously goes on in the political end as well. I will never forget, a few years ago, when Jack Straw and Robin Cook came into the public eye, when they got to the top and they were scurrying around, pushing their careers. I remember looking at them really hard because something flashed before me. I didn't know what it was at first, and then it hit me. I had seen these guys before. God yes . . . it was incredible. I remember them when I was at St John's College and these guys came down and they were the ultimate radicals, really, really focused. I fucking hated them, to be honest. I remember the NUS screwing up everything they touched. But at least, I thought, these guys were committed. And look at them now. Total, complete and utter tow-the-line yes men. It's just so pathetic it's hardly worth thinking about any more. Maybe I am stating the obvious here . . ."

And in the same pub, in The Ostrich, on a Saturday afternoon, some six months previously, it was a day of stark contrast, with sunshine streaming through the window, with Saturday afternoon hustle and bustle, with chatter and smoke swilling in the air, while we were trying to divert our attention away from the black stare of the heavy-set guy opposite swinging into his fifth pint, chasing it with vodka and Red Bull, burning eyes at us.

At that moment, Mark exclaimed: "I tell you what, Mick . . . you know . . . part of me was fucking glad about the twin towers."

Huh!

"Not the people . . . obviously! What do you think I am? Not that fucking insensitive, but that stuff about the second tower not being insured was so perfect and so fucking typical. Those useless bastards who think they rule the financial world, and it had to happen, really, it had to come crashing down . . . and actually a fucking whole lot of debt got wiped clean away . . . this hit home with me, you know. It really did because I had just been through a really terrible time with a New York company that was based in the twin towers. It was a typical situation, you know. I had been really skint and I mean really skint. Almost down and out, you know, Mick. I'm fine now, things are moving, but this was a really terrible period. I was on my own before I met Elena. I wasn't sure what was happening. I will admit this now, but I wouldn't at the time. And I was struggling to pay stuff. I was giving the band their wages out of my personal money and I was going seriously into debt, to be honest . . . that's something that a lot of people don't realise, when they say I am a dictator. There have been a number of times, during the past 20 years, when I have had to pay the wages of the band and I haven't had a bean. This was probably the worst time. And I was asked to write some stories for an Internet thing in America. So much per story. It was a number of stories and I thought, 'Why not?' I wasn't writing Fall stuff at the time. So I really put a huge amount of effort in and got this stuff done, and just sent it off. I know you freelanced for 20 years . . . how did you get money out of these people? God knows, I couldn't. I kept ringing them and ringing them, and I can be fucking tenacious as well. I was like a terrier, not all nice, like you Mick. But they kept fobbing me off. They would say, 'Oh, who are you?' I'd have to explain who I was and that I had already fucking spoken to them 15 fucking times and they had lied to me 15 times. Honestly, the publishing industry is fucking evil. They never had any intention of paying me. They were just people who have no ideas of their own so they steal somebody else's. Fucking unbelievable. I mean it happens in the music business all the time, but it's not so bad. But a novel could. So, yes, I haven't forgotten that and there are always ways and means of getting your own back . . . ha . . . haaaa!!!!"

And then came another Mark, almost a persona change, a Mark whose smile split his face, whose eyes glistened with malicious intent, a Mark who slapped an arm over my shoulder and pulled himself within six inches . . . and smiling . . . smiling still and joking, I think.

"I think it's getting time to launch Cell 4. [I have disguised the actual words here . . . just in case there was a touch of reality about this.] Yeah . . . Cell 4. It's going to be the only way. We will take out [name of prominent irritating politico . . . insert the name of your choice]. It's going to start running next January. Do you want to be involved . . . hahhhaaa!!"

I wasn't entirely comfortable with this, joke or otherwise, so I attempted to shunt the conversation forward and this was the precise moment when the man with the intensive stare strode briskly towards us.

"Oi, you two . . . cheer up, fer fucks' sake. It might never happen."

The tight huddle of Mark and myself loosened simultaneously, and we pulled back, placing our drinks before us, attempting to gauge the true intent of our new companion. As it turned out, he seemed to be beyond the violent stage. I sensed he had entered into the surreal hole that exists beyond the Salford Saturday scrap. I sensed this when he offered the words: "There's cheap drink on offer here . . . well you have to, don't you. God . . . my head is killing me . . . do you know that I am barred from every pub in Prestwich? I was barred from here, but not any more. Are you two from round here? I am. Oh God, my missus hates me. Oh, and my dad. Do you know that he used to really encourage the cockroaches in our house? He would say, 'Don't hurt the little black guys.' He really liked them. I don't though . . . I don't like them so much."

And with that he staggered out, no doubt in search of another pub whose threshold he was permitted to cross. Mark was staring at him, curiosity crossing his features.

People watching, Mark.

Mark. "Yes . . . yes, I see what you are thinking. Songwriting . . . and that's what I am . . . a songwriter . . . songwriting is easy when your local is full of characters like that. I mean he was clearly mad, wasn't he? You could tell that before he even opened his mouth. And what was that . . . cockroaches?"

Which is, of course, a major aspect of The Fall . . . the characters that crowd Fall songs. Many are culled from television, from life on the road, from partners, friends and adversaries, occasionally all three. But also, perhaps even more intriguingly – given that Mark's objectivity cannot be tainted by emotional pulls – from fleeting acquaintances, a postman, the chap who serves him in the local off-licence, the kids in the street, ex-teachers, even Fred the Weatherman, that cheerful mixture of camp and middle-aged comfort who stood astride his weather map at Liverpool's Albert Dock, even Fred the Weatherman made an appearance (on the legendary 'Lot Of Wind', from *Shift-Work*, which sat at the rear end of 'White Lightning' and appeared to be about nothing other than lounging around one afternoon and watching daytime television).

Mark: "Yeah, correct! But really, if you live a life where you are travelling a lot and spending time recording, playing gigs, if you are doing that then day-to-day normality becomes kind of surreal in itself. Because suddenly you may land back in your house. It may be

10 am or midnight, it doesn't really matter. You tend to land straight back into a normal life."

This, one presumes, is the most surreal aspect of all. There is a life that Mark E. Smith leaves behind when he ventures into The Fall. And you can see him living it, too. Venturing into Manchester on the bus each morning, shifting files around some office, somewhere, writing off-the-cuff sci-fi in his lunch hour, observing his fellow commuters, returning home to fish fingers and *Neighbours* . . . still the same Mark, still exploding with opinion, just as intelligent, as entertaining, as belligerent. Still Mark, in the same house, in Salford. Still the same Mark, albeit unknown by the rock intelligentsia ". . . and considerably more wealthy."

Songs such as 'A Lot Of Wind' or 'Bad News Girl' from *I Am Kurious Oranj*, or 'An Older Lover' from *Slates* or pick one, say 'The League Of Bald-Headed Men', about how ageing rockers grabbed garish T-shirts and began to dance appallingly during Madchester's unholy and artless explosion, beg to be expanded into prose. Would it be nice, Mark, to see your songs expanding into fiction?

Mark: "They often are fiction."

Into stories? Into books?

Flashback: Kay Carroll, clearly affronted at the very same suggestion, sometime in 1979, after the author had listened to a demo tape of *Dragnet* and, in particular, 'Flat Of Angle' and 'Muzorewi's Daughter' . . . two songs . . . two novels waiting to be written . . . I had meekly opined. "They don't need to be expanded into prose," she countered. "They are perfect as they are. The mere fact that you suggest they should be expanded means that they have affected you. That's the whole point. Rock'n'roll is a great medium, you know. It's instant. It has a great deal of power, often more powerful than books . . . I mean, not always, but it is wrong to suggest that, because something arrives in novel form, it is somehow more important, or has more aesthetic value than a song. That's the kind of thing that some of the poncy papers seem to suggest and it just serves to make decent, intelligent rock'n'roll all the more valuable. And why shouldn't it be taken seriously?"

But wouldn't the time come, I asked, when Mark would lose the hunger for rock'n'roll performance, perhaps even for performance of any kind, and simply write? Mark: "I don't really separate the two. I do spoken-word performances and they are very, very interesting because I get a different kind of audience. But I still regard it as the same thing. I certainly wouldn't say that a book has more value. I've done quite a lot . . . those things for America . . ."

"Do you," I asked him – now back in The Ostrich – "want to write some original prose for this book?"

Pondering this, he cracked open another can, grimaced, glanced down at the table, slapped down his cigarette packet, and shrugged, offering me an open palm and offered: "No, I don't, Mick. I want you to do it . . . I mean, it's something that I have struggled with a bit, partly because I feel a bit ripped off with prose. The one thing I did like was that little bit I did for the *City Life Book Of Short Stories*, although even there I had to fight to get a couple of lousy copies of the bloody book. But if you want an example of how my writing can stretch into straight prose, then put that in the book. In fact I want you to . . . I've retained copyright on that, as with a lot of stuff."

It was a strange little piece, I recalled. And I also recalled how the books editor, the esteemed Ra Page, had badgered me to review it in the *Manchester Evening News*. And I did although, alas, I wasn't granted the amount of space such a book merited. "Isn't Manchester literature to be encouraged?"

Mark: "I don't know, there is too much bad writing around."

I wasn't, if I recalled correctly, overtly enamoured with Mark's contribution at the time, rather ironically suggesting that the hollows and shadows between his words work better in spoken format, Mark being such a distinctive voice, which perhaps answers my query. But there are still qualities here that could be expanded upon, surely, should The Fall actually cease to exist as any kind of unit.

Judge for yourself . . .

No Place Like It by Mark E. Smith

PONDERING at half step on the gross arrogance, blatant incompetence and thievery of the white trash in their late twenties, and their shaven-

headed, middle-class imitators, Frank circumnavigated what seemed like endless sand holes, foxholes, spastic-convenient kerb stones punctuated by upright, kicked over, reddy, orange and white fences on his way through the Manchester Victoria post-bomb development.

It had been a muggy, slow-coach taxi ride, due to the incompetent driver, who, in his porn-stupefied brain, had not turned left before the Cathedral, where Frank had made an early exit.

The only thing he remembered was the three healthy kids who'd thrown two rocks at passing vehicles near the Rialto in Higher Broughton.

He was getting the black illuminations again. I.e. All is substance – You Have Contact With None, or There's Been Nothing on Granada for at Least Ten Minutes, Never Mind the Digital Testing.

Delivering leaflets 22 hours a week was just about manageable, thought Joe, if it wasn't for those big overpowered cars making him jump every time he crossed the road – they made him remember the small metal splint in his upper right thigh from that time he had ventured into Rusholme, pissed, and got half knocked over. He had agreed with most of the shit on that political leaflet that the other bloke he'd bumped into was giving out, apart from that repeated phrase, 'It all makes sense, doesn't it QUESTION MARK.*'*

The men in the yellow hats sniggered as he limped by, and it seemed that they had deliberately sanded near him, sending vicious particles coupled with lime flowing through the muggy, close damp Cheetham Hill mid-afternoon onto his forehead and into his eyes.

Stewart Mayerling sat down in the Low Rat Head pub near the bottom end of Oxford Road, trying to work out how his plans to distract and confuse his English drama lecturer hadn't quite worked out. Mother was a teacher, and the attention/distraction games had always worked on her. The pager going off, mid-lesson, the showbiz titbit asides in the middle of 'Hamlet', my vegetarianism – how the jumped-up prole sneered at that, of course, not understanding my code of internal hygiene, well advanced beyond that of mere travellers and their ilk, or polytechnic balding lecturers. For that matter – I think I'll head up to Victoria, skip the lecture.

The Mitre Arms, adjacent to the Cathedral and next to The Shambles, was empty this afternoon. Frank walks in, having well given up on getting past Marks & Spencer, and bleaching the apostrophe on the Finnegan's Wake pub sign, towards the station. Picking a table was fairly hard even though – only one large eight-seater occupied by Joe.

In walks Stewart.

"Is it OK to sit here?" he asks the seated two.

"Sure."

"It's crap out there, isn't it?" says Joe.

"Damn right it is."

"Let's form a party," says Frank.

THE END

(The author – of this book rather than the above piece – heartily recommends a dip into the *City Life Book Of Short Stories* which sees such idiosyncratic talents as Val McDermid, Jeff Noon and Tim Willocks step out of their normal lives to add a bit of fun. Dave Haslem is in there, too, although Mark, one strongly senses, will not have spent too long devouring that. Nor, indeed, the work of Michael Bracewell, who Mark famously left floundering, after quitting in the centre of a public interview at the Barbican.)

The Bracewell incident

Mark: "That Michael Bracewell . . . you don't hear much about him now, do you?"

Mick: "He is still there . . . somewhere . . . still writes books . . . still reviews stuff."

Mark: "Does he? I wouldn't know. I don't read newspapers."

Mick: "You read books though."

Mark: "Yeah, course . . . you daft cunt. But not books by Michael Bracewell . . . have you read any books by him?"

Mick: "Yeah . . . one . . . a novel."

Mark: "What was it called?"

Mick: "I can't remember."

Mark: "What was it about?"

Mick: "Er . . . can't remember."

Mark: "Why did you read it?"

Mick: "Because of you. Because he had done that thing with you."

Mark E. Smith with Michael Bracewell at the ICA, The Mall, London. March 8, 1994

The ironies began to stack up; the atmosphere is uncertain. Novelist and media face Michael Bracewell would meet Mark E. Smith before an audience at the ICA in Pall Mall, a theatre, a small, tight, dark theatre, where rock shows occasionally rumbled. An outside bar area was populated by the Sheffield band, Pulp, Cocker and all who, having spent 15 years in the shadows of bands like The Fall, were in London to celebrate the release of 'Do You Remember The First Time?', a turning point that would see them suddenly grasp the fickle public imagination. Of course, they had no way of knowing that, after so many years trawling the murky indie backwaters, the bright lights of Brit Pop now lay beckoning.

This fact would, no doubt, have depressed Mark further, and he wasn't in the best of moods to begin with . . . and it would go downhill from there.

Michael Bracewell, besuited, *Arena* reader. Mark E. Smith. Smoking. Hunched. Scowling. Likes Can and Colin Wilson.

An audience. One hundred or so . . . mainly pulled from the *Guardian*'s readership, intent on learning something about the 'self-taught artist'. At least this, one senses, was a theme worthy of exploration. The beauty of the extra curriculum. Why students are incapable of looking outside their own career path. Why the biggest lie in the world is that examinations passed are the only measure of ability. Why does someone like Mark E. Smith continue to successfully defy such gravity? Is it difficult to take that one step beyond? Could Mark ever retire? Is that even possible?

These are the questions that Michael Bracewell should have asked. To be fair, it wasn't entirely his fault . . . an intelligent man, an artist himself perhaps and, I am sure, a perfectly acceptable writer . . . and indeed, a good wearer of suits which appears to be the most important aesthetic skill these days.

However, these were not the questions that surfaced.

Michael Bracewell informed the audience that they were "privy to an event". A sentence that made Mark E. Smith squirm a little, as it does me . . . here, now. And that was another phrase: "In the here and now."

The point of the event was to be in the 'here and now'. (Though one finds it difficult to be anywhere else . . . actually, since you ask, the 'here and now' as I write, is the final day of March, 2003, and I have spent much of the day in the unlikely Warrington sunshine watching a terrible local rugby team lose profoundly . . . just thought I would let you know . . . also, I have just remembered. Bracewell's book was called *Saint Rachel*, and it wasn't too bad either, though hardly a toe tapper!)

However . . . what transpired there and then was something that could only loosely be described as 'entertainment' or, indeed, as 'art'. No change for the ICA then. It is recorded that Jim Morrison once sat inside a giant egg on the ICA stage while punters, who had paid a pound, filed past. Their quid entitled them to ask and receive an answer from the guru. No documentation of these transcendental murmurings exists. Would this 'talk' with Mark Smith produce anything worth reporting?

The audience sat patiently. An ashtray. Six bottles of beer . . . and Mark E. Smith, about to sink into the dullest interview of his career. Mark didn't quite appear to grasp the gravity of the occasion and Bracewell, to his credit, tried everything to kick the conversation along.

"Those original lyric sheets you do with all the corrections on them are real works of art. Will you publish them?"

"No."

I had some sympathy for Bracewell. Mark does use the monosyllabic as a defence at times; and at other times complete silence. It always works, too. I have been on the receiving end a number of times. I recall that film. I recall also one or two false starts with this book. He has to move at his own pace. He has to find his own theme. Planned interviews are utterly pointless; such was the case at the ICA.

Bracewell was embarrassed and drowning.

"Were there any musicians in your family?"

"Who is Roman Totale?"

"What was your favourite lesson at school?"

"Me uncle Joe used to play the saw. Beautiful sound."

"Favourite lesson, ah, yeah, I was always in that music class."

Clearly, there was not going to be much discussion of the concept of the self-taught artist. At one point, Bracewell reminded Mark how he was once arrested by a SWAT team for smoking on an American internal air flight.

"How did you know that?"

"You told me when we had lunch together."

So there was a sense of relief for Bracewell and the audience at moments like this when his 'talk' degenerated into little bits of anecdotes and the Mark E. Smith sound bites which have been finding their way into the music press for a decade and a half.

Mark did the Nirvana and Courtney 'Pine' bit – the mistake, deliberate and deliberately irritating.

Mark: "I don't care if we've done 20 albums or if we do 30."

But there will never be mainstream acceptance, it seems. When Mark crossed a generation gap to team up with the Inspiral Carpets to do *Top Of The Pops*, they were given the worst of all the dressing rooms. Then there was the recently sacked Radio 1 DJ, who wouldn't play a Fall record if it was the last on earth.

"We're identified with John Peel."

When will Mark write his novel?

"The book world is an evil world."

Will there be another *Hey! Luciani* or *Kurious Oranj*?

"No."

When Michael Bracewell's best efforts had been spent, questions were invited from the audience.

"The words of the track 'A Lot Of Wind' send up daytime TV. What do you appreciate in modern popular culture?"

"What do they think of The Fall in Europe?"

"Who are your favourite lyricists?"

"Do you like Sebadoh?"

It was an elastic 40 minutes. Mercifully, Mark finished it with a cursory, "Mind if I split?"

Mick: "Did you enjoy that experience, Mark?"

Mark: "Enjoy it? Of course not? It was an insult . . . just middle-class crap."

Indeed.

Mick: "Do you enjoy spoken-word events? Is that what you will be doing . . . after The Fall? Mark at Hay-on-Wye Festival, perhaps."

Mark: "They are alright, yeah. Makes a change and I am quite happy to do them. But it's not rock'n'roll. It's not what I am really about. And I meant that about the publishing world, too. A profession of evil. They pin you down with contracts. I went along that route once. Had the contract in my hand and was almost ready to commit. Then I realised what I was doing, the enormous amount of work for such little return and I realised what was going on. No. I don't think I will write novels. That *City Life* thing was bad enough. What did you think of that?"

Not sure that I answered that question at the time. There is a mumble on the Dictaphone, but it is smothered by a whole mass of rustling which sounds, for all the world, like two people relentlessly plunging their hands into crisp packets . . . and subsequent crunching. Not Mark and I. Neither of us would, I sense, waste energy on a packet of crisps. Perhaps I had departed to the bar? Doesn't really make sense. Doesn't matter. Gave me time to think about Mark's curious prose.

A number of things immediately struck me on reading that particular piece of writing. Firstly, and most importantly, the geographic base. The pub at the end of the piece is within yards of the place where Mark's father and granddad went immediately prior to that savage bombing raid. It is also set in that part of Manchester one crosses if travelling in from the Prestwich edge of Salford and, as such, always seemed a stubborn, contrary area, darkly at odds with the glamour of Market Street until, that is, Manchester's huge regeneration programme transformed this very area into the epicentre of the city's cosmopolitan heart, transforming the dusty Corn Exchange – always a haven for short-contract, loan-shark companies and traders one step beyond the market stage – into a fashion multi-mall, The Triangle. Marks & Spencer is, of course, a further shining example of the new Manchester, especially as it is now partnered by Selfridges. It's interesting to note that Mark's character, Frank, fails to make it past . . . as if failing to make it into the new Manchester. Other than that, there are varying references to the decaying literacy of Britain in the new millennium . . . but mostly, one strongly senses Mark's disenchantment with the loss of a Manchester he used to love to inhabit.

One other powerful feeling struck me, when I first read this piece. It is a Fall song . . . not necessarily stretched too much, either. One could feasibly place a backbeat behind this, on top of which could come Mark's recital. Bang! An instant classic, filled with North Manchester reference, filled also with Mark's perceptive venom. Maybe he was right all along. No need to transpose his writing into book form. What you hear is what you get.

There was time for a break. The cherubic mechanic and his wife had left the building. We both drifted for a while, myself with the old red wine, staring at the framed bricks on the wall. It was sinking deep into the night, by now. For whatever reasons, the populace on the fringe of Heaton Park had decided not to join us this Tuesday evening . . . too much fog . . . too much war on their minds . . . too much anxiety and speculation . . . surely the perfect environment for Mark's turbulent muse? It was a good time to meet, as Mark was enjoying the post-album void, and was immersing himself in the complexities of everyday life and world events and how the two would be shaping the way we were all thinking. And, of course, the concept of Mark's lyrics providing an off-kilter reportage, where perception became the guiding light and no agenda, no sense of journalistic duty would be allowed to prevail; the prerogative of the artist, to see things his way, beyond the facts. But how, psychic intuition aside, could a Fall album ever be bang on the button, given the expanse of time that would elapse between the recording and the release, between the words scribbled in Mark's notebook and the words floating into the listeners head . . . in some bedroom, in Grimsby or the Ukraine! It's happened many times before, of course. 'Marquis Cha-Cha' on 1982's *Room To Live*, being the rush of blood to the nation's head that became known as The Falklands War, rather beautifully collapsed into a Mark E. Smith lyric . . . and very timely too. ('Marquis Cha-Cha' story coming up . . . in a few paragraphs time . . . wait for it.)

And so to *Country On The Click.* Falling together back in Lisa Stansfield's studio, produced, mixed and muddled effectively by Grant Showbiz. Would it, I asked, be in tune with the times? One of *those* Fall albums that seem to capture the spirit.

Country On The Click Mark? What the hell is that? What does it mean? Is it relevant? I had thought it might have something to do with the countryside. Apparently not.

Mark: "*Country On The Click* . . . don't you get it?" He was clicking his fingers.

"*Country On The Click* . . . when you see news footage of dignitaries attending the White House, it is always the same. You see these solemn-faced individuals from, I don't know, Germany or somewhere, England for that matter, they all arrive with the world on their shoulders. They greet and wander into The White House. It's always the same. And then you see them leaving, and they always, always have this beaming smile on their faces. And it's obvious. The Americans – the CIA – are really good at it. They spike the drinks. It's very clever. I know it sounds absurd, but that's how they get away with it. This is what is going on in this world. It's a mixture of criminal incompetence and criminal cleverness. I don't know which is worst but together it's very dangerous. That's how they like it. You know the millennium-eve story about Salford, don't you? About the phone call to the Irish pub at midnight . . . to the landlord. It was Bill Clinton on the phone . . . no one could believe it . . . but it was. Talking about Manchester. Talking about the Manchester bomb . . . saying it was a shame . . . saying we will get them next time! Are you with me? Are you? I'm telling you, even some of the IRA guys around here were saying that this was out of order. That Manchester bombing was sheer fluke that a lot of people weren't killed . . . and I don't think anyone really supported that. Not even the IRA people in Manchester. But Americans are really fucking stupid when it comes to Ireland. I mean, I can see the big picture, I certainly don't just see it from the English perspective . . . but the Americans don't get that. They just think they should win over the terrible English . . . which is rather ironic when you think of what is going on now."

Perception, you see, is a dangerous thing. But great songs can be carved from the scenario above, be it truth or wild speculation. In a sense, it matters not. If the fear is there. If the paranoia is in place, then it is quite correct for the artists to paint the full picture, or stretch the reality into a song . . . and it hit me, actually, while pondering this, just how far we have regressed since The Fall's inception. Back then, many of the fringe punk bands might have been devoid of talent, but at least the ideas, the ethos, the passion, the political awareness . . . at least all of that was thrown in the pot and, however naive it might have seemed at the time, at least it was healthy to see it surfacing in the music culture. But no more. Isolated dots of Mickey Mouse polemic . . . whole bucket loads of sexual attitude, ladies stating their case, gangster rappers and rock screamers opting for machismo and, beyond it all, nothing? Who, exactly, are The Fall's peers . . . as we speak?

Not a problem for Mark. Perhaps it's better now! Better even, than in 1995, when every young Fall musician secretly wanted to be in Oasis. But one struggles to even find *that* comparison now. As for hidden CIA references in *Country On The Click*, intriguing though they may be, there are actually two CIAs – one which operates in the present, under a blanket of respectful conservative honesty. The other operates in the past – the retrospective CIA – which is the organisation that is revealed when the astonishing extent of their absurdity comes to light. By this time, of course, the world's media is focused on something else entirely and the unholy tractor of American intelligence trundles grimly onwards. In such circumstances, the art of perception is to peer into the present.

I suggested, perhaps glibly, that Mark should have employed such tactics with previous members of The Fall. I was only half joking . . . perhaps he has. (And, as I write these words, in March 2003, a further tumble in the fluid history of their membership transpires, as The Fall's increasingly on-the-spot web page reports the sacking of Jim Watts as well as the increasing and welcome influence of Elena –

mock puppetry dancing onstage, apparently – and, indeed, the weirdness of playing a gig in a Turkey that was squirming beneath the dark clouds of war, a terrifying gathering on the horizon.)

For the paranoiac Fall band musician, all of that could be another example of Mark's unsettling mind games. Mark denies this, naturally, but the anecdotes are sitting by the side of this book in sack-loads.

All of which, rather untidily brings me, as promised, to the 'Marquis Cha-Cha' tale.

Room To Live. November 1982

Joker Hysterical Face/Marquis Cha-Cha/Hard Life In Country/ Room To Live/Detective Instinct/Solicitor In Studio/Papal Visit

Sifting through The Fall's unholy, disparate and absurdly fluctuating band membership is a curiously unrewarding exercise. Once past the major players, from Hanley to Dave Bush, Yvonne Pawlett to Julia Nagle, Mark Riley to Ed Blaney, and *already*, having mentioned six Fall members in one sentence – or five with one manager-cum-part-time band member – it is possible to sense a tangle of jealousies and conflicting interests. There are many who believe the constantly crumbling dynamic of the band to be an essential element of its unique and continuing 'edge' although, earlier in this book, Mark has hotly disputed this, stating that such tensions are largely irrelevant and can be found simmering away in many staid pub-rock outfits, if not, if the truth be told, in every band that ever existed.

A rock band, a band of musicians of any kind, is not a natural settling, not an easy marriage. A harmonious camaraderie can be little more than a bland masking of a swirl of emotion. With The Fall, and with any band, it was ever thus.

If The Fall really are different to every other band, then one always sensed that the true core of that uniqueness lay not wholly with the centrepiece of Mark E. Smith, but with the way the maverick spirit fans out through those on the fringe of band membership, onwards and outwards, through the ungainly blend of Fall fans. Sandwiched between those fans and those who have contributed largely to The Fall's barrelling linear path, however, are the curiosities who ever so nearly gained a foothold, edging within a whisker of band membership, only to be unceremoniously shunted into the shadows. This is a large group. No other band, certainly in Manchester, almost certainly beyond, could possibly have left behind such a lengthy wake of bewildered also-rans who drifted into the shadows of less successful projects.

They comprise guitarists, bass players, drummers, keyboard players and, of course, managers.

Take Andy Zero. Immensely likeable, intelligent, somewhat spaced by substances of the day, rider of small motorbikes, spike-haired writer and peddler of *City Fun* magazine, ligger and lugger. Often to be seen bundling boxes of *City Fun* into cars – more often than not cars owned by me – and it was me who would whisk them across the city to curious liaisons in darkened corners of North Manchester where I would deflect the intense hatred from some savage female of rad fem persuasion who objected to my unfortunate South Manchester middle-class appearance. Apologies. I digress. It was Andy Zero who so often seemed to be hammering on the door of The Fall, for a long while, almost endlessly balanced on the brink of membership, as a drummer and as anything else he could grab. Andy was an important, and latterly ignored, force in Manchester's musical history. *City Fun* was the 'zine with attitude and the only magazine that effectively captured the rolling spirit of, in particular, perennial outsiders The Fall.

Kay Carroll: "Andy was always around, and great fun and blessed with a fantastic sense of enthusiasm. The problem was that he wasn't really a drummer. It was one of those situations where we thought he might blend well within the group as a personality, but didn't quite have the musical qualities. And The Fall needed a strong drummer at all times. He nearly came in around the time of *Room To Live* but things were changing fast then, anyway."

Andy Zero had a curious glue-like effect on the disparate blend of misfits involved with *City Life* and this even appeared to be the case with The Fall. Andy could be seen scurrying backstage, unofficially lugging things this way and that, urging involvement, adding a spark.

But not as a band member.

A new member comes into the band when Mark E. Smith desires one.

Sometimes, Mark would make his mind up before the musician himself would even know.

Sometimes Mark would then change his mind, leaving a musician confused, having been asked to become a member and then unceremoniously dumped before even being given a chance.

Sometimes, though Mark hotly disputes this, the whole affair would be set up to keep the band on their toes, to remind them that replacement musicians and non-musicians were waiting in the wings.

Such was the case, I strongly sensed, with the long-lost Arthur Kadmon, a man about whom Pete Wylie once remarked: "Arthur Kadmon . . . massive talent . . . eats babies though, doesn't he?"

Arthur Kadmon didn't, to the best of my knowledge, eat any babies although it might be noted that, despite being one of the most intelligent men I have ever met, and one of the finest songwriters, he wasn't always fully in control of his senses. He was the founder of the legendary Ludus, a band famously championed by Morrissey and fronted by the artist Linder Sterling. They now appear to have been wiped from history, but the intriguing jazz offshoot fumblings of Kadmon's Ludus attracted a great deal of attention as the Seventies drew to a close and Kadmon, following his departure, continued to make a series of bizarre solo appearances where his avant-garde music would lift him beyond the attention of any serious record companies.

But not beyond the attention of Mark E. Smith, who locked into Kadmon's peculiar genius before Kadmon eventually opted to join a latter-day version of The Distractions.

"Mick, you know that Arthur, don't you?" Mark asked me, following a Fall gig at Manchester Polytechnic. On hearing my affirmative reply – I was courted by Ludus and Buzzcocks manager Richard Boon for a while – Mark suddenly looked serious, and wandered off to chat with Kay Carroll. Ten minutes later Kay approached me, drink in hand, also looking intense and stated: "Mark thinks that Kadmon guy is a genius, thinks he can bring something to The Fall.

And the more I think about it, the more I agree. Can we set up some kind of a meeting?"

"What, with Arthur Kadmon?"

"Yes."

"An audition?"

"Sort of."

And 'sort of' it surely was. A venue was set for the occasion, a pub, not surprisingly, the Gorton Brook in . . . well, in Gorton, which was seen as neutral territory between Stockport, the home of Arthur Kadmon and myself, and Prestwich. I would duly chaperone Arthur and we were summoned to appear at the bar at 12 noon on a Saturday. This was no hardship, nor indeed was it a break from the usual routine, so along we trundled, linking up with Andy Zero, who assumed a 'Master of Ceremonies' rôle. After all, he was a veteran of a number of Fall auditions himself, albeit a number of failures, and, for no apparent reason at all, Mike Finney, rotund 'anti-star' of The Distractions. It may have dawned on you that some dubious pub in Gorton is a curious venue for an audition, particularly if there didn't appear to be any need to bring an instrument along . . . well, yes . . . it was rather unorthodox but, hey, this was The Fall. What do you expect?

Arthur was unusually nervous which surprised me a little since, although I had attended a good few Fall gigs in his company, I was never entirely convinced that he liked the band at all, or if he was merely going along to hang out at the bar with all the other musicians who went along for precisely the same reason, to bitch about the band and perhaps pick up a few pointers and to be seen 'hanging out at Fall gigs'. Step out of the shadows, Ian McCulloch, Julian Cope, Pete Shelley, Bill Drummond, Morrissey . . . you know you were there!

The afternoon proceeded in inevitable fashion, beginning with cheerful bonhomie and sinking steadily into alcoholic ramblings. Mostly, I think, the talk was of the government and the *NME*, which was just about par for the course. Curiously however, no mention was made of The Fall or their music or Arthur Kadmon's possible involvement. No questions were asked of Kadmon and, as far as anyone could tell, no actual audition was taking place. Exiting the pub, I couldn't help sensing that Kadmon was a mite deflated, although, during the sobering bus ride back to the safer confines of Stockport, he had already started to plot a course for certain superstardom via the piecing together of his own group.

The very next day, however, Kadmon was surprised to be told by Mark that he should henceforth present himself at a Bury studio to commence the recording of The Fall's next LP, which would eventually surface as *Room To Live*. Excited beyond belief, and yet cool enough to keep it duly contained, Arthur Kadmon picked up his guitar, his essential Albert Camus paperback – such was the prevailing hipness of the day – and set forth, clearly under the impression that he had joined The Fall.

The session began badly for Arthur. He wandered cheerily into the studio, proffering a hand of comradeship to the assembled band members, although he didn't know their names, or indeed what they played. Presumably it was Mark Riley, Craig Scanlon, Steve and Paul Hanley and Karl Burns, who had returned to the fold, and not for the last time. Although wise enough to realise that cool musicians were unlikely to slap him on the back, offer him a joint and organise a welcoming dinner for him, he was slightly affronted by the general air of "Who the fuck are you?" that appeared to prevail. Only one of them, Karl Burns by the sound of it, recognised Kadmon from his Ludus days and remarked that he had always found that band "completely unlistenable, though that Linder's a bit tasty, ain't she?" (Apologies to Karl Burns. It probably wasn't you.)

"Oh yeah, forgot to tell you lads, this is Arthur . . . he's the new guitarist," announced Mark when he eventually arrived.

Blank looks met this announcement.

"Look, if this is a bit awkward, I'll just go," pleaded Kadmon, strongly sensing that the band weren't too enamoured by the fact that they hadn't actually been told of his impending arrival.

After enduring the seemingly eternal set-up that precedes any new recording session, he was duly told to go and tune-up and play a few test samples, which indeed he did: four chords, a tune-up and a finger loosening solo. It took just sixteen seconds.

"Thanks Arthur. That's superb. That's just what we wanted. You can go home now."

"What? That's it?"

"Yeah, thanks cocker."

To this day, Arthur Kadmon never knew whether he had upset Mark with his short soloing, or if one of his remarks had increased the tension, or whether he was ever really a possibility for a Fall guitarist . . . or whatever! He was never contacted again although, to his credit, he continued to listen to The Fall for a handful of years, until finally succumbing to a semblance of reality. He now works in an office in Macclesfield and has a big house.

For what it's worth, *Room To Live* remains this writer's least favourite Fall album, despite the intrigue of 'Marquis Cha-Cha'. There was a disunity within the band at the time which would soon result in the infamous walkout of Kay Carroll and, equally infamously, the departure of Marc Riley. Whether this disunity filtered into *Room To Live* is a matter of opinion. Mark, naturally, disagrees.

"I don't think there is anything wrong with it at all. I think, at the time, it was one of those albums that tended to stretch beyond the expectations of The Fall fans, but that has always been a Fall thing. It probably isn't the easiest Fall record to listen to, but that's partly its strength . . . there's a lot of good stuff in there. It was one of those albums that started as a single, really. I had forgotten all about Kadmon, but he was great, wasn't he. I remember seeing him, years later . . . I was with you, I think and Arthur was dressed in this ridiculous clothing, covered in card symbols, clubs, spades, stuff like that. And he must have been in his late twenties then. Ha. He is one of the great people of Manchester who never really got anywhere. There are a lot of people like that. I mean, he's probably done very well in other areas, I have no idea. I am sure his two minutes in a studio with The Fall isn't the highlight of his life. Hope not, anyway. That is something I hate, right down the line which brings me back to that Baines and Friel thing. It's just very sad."

Room To Live, although released some time after the Falklands War, was nevertheless a record that shimmered with the disinformation of life during wartime, where nothing you read can be trusted, and the sleeve simply exploded with information.

Mark: "My idea was just to get people's heads going, because they don't fucking read. But also, with computer graphics coming in, it became quite impossible to do that. If you're on a major label you can't do this, you can't do that and say: 'That's the back cover.' The computer graphics and the art department can't handle it, because it doesn't fit on the bloody computer, does it? That was half of it; the other half was why bleeding bother anyway, because people are going to pinch ideas. I remember one guy from Liverpool, this fanzine guy, once said to me, 'There are more ideas on one of your inside covers than there are on three entire Echo & The Bunnymen albums.' I thought that was cool, you know, it made me think.

"I have always hated computers, you know. I think that has been made obvious in a lot of Fall recordings. Computers are a piece of shit, really."

The Ostrich, barely alive that night, was slowly settling to a gentle close. The landlady, unseen until this moment, confronted us politely, tapping her watch – it was 11.40 – before stating, "Congratulations . . . you are the last two left in the pub."

We realised, or rather I did, that we had also been the first two in there on that snail-paced evening, during which Mark had devoured eight cans and myself, eight glasses of wine, while hurtling through a vast array of Fall experiences. Outside the Ripper-esque, pea-souper fog still hinted at a gloomier Salfordian past, and the unlikely silence prevailed still. The conversation swayed outside the realms of this book, with Mark asking me about my many and varied experiences with ex-wives, a conversation that closed with us concluding that, between us, we had developed a very curious assembly of ex-partners.

"Do they ever come out of the blue after years of total silence?" he asked me.

"Yes Mark . . . and they now come flying at you unexpectedly on Friends Reunited."

"Friends Reunited?" he exclaimed. "What's that?"

And in the gloom, I explained the full horror of an Internet that causes your past to come hurtling back at you, picking you off when you least expect it.

"Well that won't bother me, will it?" he exclaimed, genuinely pleased. "I knew I was right all along. That is exactly why I always hated computers and I will not look at the Internet, not ever. That would be my ultimate nightmare. That's positively evil. It's bad enough when ex-girlfriends track you down with a bottle of wine, but to come at you via a computer! My mam thinks I shouldn't worry. She says it's good that girls are still interested."

The Woodthorpe, Prestwich. Summer 1981

Great and gothic. Big, dark and bold. Mark's home pub. Etched into the edge of Heaton Park, featured earlier in this book and, many, many times, flickering in many, many memories. Check it out on The Fall's loose and jittery 'Ghost In My House' video. You might catch a whiff of paranoia in those clips. The Woodthorpe always seemed, to my wandering mind at least, to have been plucked out of Scotland, which is, presumably, why Mark always found the place so strangely comforting.

Amusing landlord. Always knew Mark. Always asked if the wife was OK.

And once, sitting in the back room, Mark had turned our chairs around, lest we actually had to suffer the pained faces in the room. As such, we both stared blankly at the wall. It was a small but remarkable act of defiance. We couldn't be bothered, it seemed, with Salford's day-to-day trivialities.

The cassette recorder, a lumpen beast in the days prior to Dictaphones, let alone digital recordings, chunky, brown and ugly, procured from Stockport market for a price of around £4.99, seemed to satisfy Mark's desire for Neanderthal gadgetry. A number of times, while I was en route for bar action, he snapped it on and mumbled into the mike.

Things like this.

"Inspector Middles is on the case, dragging the waters of the canal, an old raincoat. He misses no tricks, he seeks the clues . . .

hahhhhaaaa!!!!" (In a comedic, creepy, sneery tone.)
Those were the days!

Slates (Rough Trade 10″ LP), 1981

Middle Mass/An Older Lover/Prole Art Threat/Fit And Working Again/Slates, Slags etc./Leave The Capitol

A strange little disc this one. Strangely out of time. Strangely aloof. *Slates*, a verbal broadside slapping onto the record rack, displayed a maturity that surprised even the most ardent of Fall fans. The language remained, and it must be noted that 'Prole Art Threat', arguably the archetypal early Fall song, simmered away, three songs in. However, it did sit rather uneasily among the pack. One thinks most obviously of 'An Older Lover', which saw Mark spinning around a curious thread of detached romance, cynicism spitting from his words, spilling bile into a world of cheap love in the office, of insecure and unfaithful sales reps driving up motorways, perhaps the most intriguing anti-love song ever written.

"He take an older lover, take an older lover, take an older lover . . . he'll soon get tired of heeeerrrrrr!"

And pinned all around this spiked outburst, came various glances at domestic life from a number of unexpected angles.

Mark: "I think it is right to say that I was expanding at a great pace at that point. Until then I had been self-governed to some extent. I mean, I always thought that I looked beyond . . . way beyond any of the other groups around, in terms of lyrics anyway. Most of them did tend to produce the expected. One band would go one particular way and all the others would follow. But I was starting to realise that there were no rules at all about any of this. A lot of people never really caught onto that fact about The Fall. And I realised that I could write about anything. It didn't matter. In fact, it was so easy, so obvious to do that. That always makes me smile, to be honest, just how fucking conservative all those so-called 'alternative' groups really were. And it was just the simplest thing in the world to use a bit of imagination and stand out from the crowd."

In Britain at least, if nowhere else, there was distrust in the air. The summer of 1981 saw sporadic rioting that began with small pockets of inner-city unrest, and tumbled over in domino copycat fashion out into the suburbs.

If one can see beyond The Specials' fortuitous 'Ghost Town', which at least grasped the state of calm that would precede an uprising, then the British music scene was rather too concerned with exploding from an underground base into risible Eighties glam and while the era was rather more fun and, indeed, rather more profound than clips on *Top Of The Pops 2* might suggest, there was little general concern within the music business about anything other than desperately grasping the next rung before it would be cruelly snatched away in favour of something younger, something in leg warmers, something with bigger hair.

For The Fall, the career dangers seemed obvious as Mark's peers weirdly transformed into a sellable pop state. Julian Cope, who began his musical life in a state of studied conservatism, was rapidly unfolding into a bizarre attention seeking monster, and as his head expanded, so did his trousers, so did his boots and so did his expectations. Likewise, one might note, Ian McCulloch's scouse ripostes were now hurled from beneath an increasingly precarious mop and Robert Smith, yet another sullen teen from a grey, overtly sincere band, speedily morphed into arguably the most grotesque caricature of all, grasping the Eighties for all it was worth, surging gleefully into the pop world. Not, perhaps, that anyone could seriously blame these bands. None would be happy progressing through life carrying the fading legacy of Britain's post punk underground on their backs. The time was right, it was all there for the taking and nobody looked back.

77 – *Early Years* – 79 (Step Forward SFLP6, September 1981 LP), 1977

Repetition/Bingo-Master's Break-Out!/Psycho Mafia/Various Times/It's The New Thing/Rowche Rumble/In My Area/ Dice Man/Psykick Dancehall No. 2/2nd Dark Age/Fiery Jack

Mark: "If there is one thing, though, that I can't stomach, it's all that retrospective shite. That's something that I have never been into and never will. It represents a trainspotter mentality, little men collecting things. I don't like that at all. I am proud of what we have done and I listen to old music all the time, more so now than ever before, but I don't trawl through back catalogues, not even of the people I most admire. The Fall are about the present and always will be. Some bands are about the past and some are always striving for the future, to further their careers. The Fall are here, now, in the present. That's the whole point. It's really not that difficult, is it?"

Stuck in the present, then. Stuck in a British music scene that was segueing from dark to light, into pop, into the yellow. Almost overnight the review pages of the *NME* changed. No more a barrage of self-produced singles, no longer the lowbrow aesthetic. All of a sudden, in the now, the major labels rose to gather around the lauded 'Single of the Week' spot, and formerly solemn and erstwhile pop-loathing hacks twisted into lovers of the pale and the light. Outrageously positive reviews would be poured over Dollar and Bucks Fizz. Hi-gloss would gather column inches. Where, one wondered, would that leave Mark E. Smith. When I interviewed Mark for *Sounds* in 1981, it seemed significant that on the flip side of The Fall's allotted page, was a bristling little write-up championing the emerging Martin Fry, an ex-Stockport punk riding Trevor Horn's fast track to chart success. Not without wit, not without a certain panache either, but it was curious to read a barrage of interviews that celebrated a move into the mainstream while forcibly stressing a no-sell-out strategy. Indeed.

Flip that particular piece and your eyes move from a smartly blazered and polo-neck sweatered Fry to a memorable image of Mark standing in Mark Lane, carrying a suitcase and looking like someone who had stepped out of a Burton's window just five years previously. Wide-collared jacket, crumpled collared white shirt . . . cords possibly. It was an unusual image, even for Mark, who had seemingly stepped away from that much loved sardonic leer that allowed him to shine, even while wearing that diamond pattern,

Bury market jumper. But here he looked likely to sell you a Dansette cassette player or some equal chunk of grim audio equipment. Here he looked quite the antithesis of all that was about to mushroom. Here was Mark, not a step behind at all, a step beyond perhaps . . . most definitely a step sideways.

Fear not, I am not about to reiterate much of what was, in all honesty, a poorly written piece and, given the myriad of other music press interviews which ran from the profound to the pretentious and often wavered between the two, there are a couple of moments that continue to intrigue me now, as, indeed, they did then.

What follows is proof that Mark's wisdom has crossed the decades with elegant ease, for the following quotes appeared in the pages of *Sounds* in an interview conducted by yours truly. They are now framed retrospectively, of course, but first I need to add a little rock 'n'roll background. This rather grim interview was actually preceded, seven days earlier, by an attempted *Sounds* interview, when yours truly fell from his senses, if only for a while, and thoroughly disgraced himself. It is not something that I am remotely proud of but I do remind myself of such days, whenever some balding moron in an ageing Ford belts past me, all hi-fi boom and steely leer. It began the night before, the night before I met Mark Smith, in a studio in Stockport, deep within darkened catacombs beneath a defunct mill on Underbank, latterly a network of rehearsal rooms and at least one low-tech recording studio. In this unholy shell, I talked about The Fall with The Distractions. It was one of the things you did in 1981. Either that, or the absolute reverse. The Distractions latched strongly onto The Fall and, to some extent, the respect was proven to be mutual.

On this night, as on many similar nights, the darker forces within The Distractions line-up pushed something into my hand . . . a square of blotting paper, presumably soaked in acid. I am not sure but then, if not now, such things did the rounds in Stockport and Manchester.

"For the interview . . . tomorrow," one of them smiled, before informing me casually that Charles Shaar Murray would be interviewing them in a few weeks' time. Whatever. They had become dream peddlers. The Distractions, as Murray sagely noted, were good for dreams.

Driving through Manchester at 11 am the next morning proved uneventful. Disappointingly so, as it happens, as I had dropped the acid while passing through Romiley, and had figured on – at least – a bit of street warping by the time I reached Bury New Road. However, perhaps mercifully, it was not to be; not even as I floated to Mark and Kay's door, my arms flopping like rubber, my ears plucking sounds from – seemingly – miles away . . . snippets of conversation, bits of noise. Not exactly a psychedelic dream of Timothy Leary proportions, but segueing towards the surreal anyway. Which, for a while at least, seemed remarkably apt.

Mark greeted me at the door. Smiling. Purposeful. Full of banter. Full of America, as it happened, The Fall having just returned, triumphant, from a lengthy and eventful surge through small-to-medium gig circuits, twisting through New York to the Deep South, picking up all manner of misfits and creeps along the way.

He seemed full of it that day, full of mischief, full of pride.

Upstairs Kay launched at me. Arms grasping, full of hug fun, as if wanting to touch base after a dangerous adventure, as if wanting some reassurance that something mundane, and from Stockport, could still arrive at their doorstep, still hunting an interview, still with feet planted firmly on the ground. Ironic then as, by the time I had walked into the kitchen, by the time the first cup of coffee had touched my lips, I was already seeping through the ceiling, fighting to stay on the couch, fighting to retain some kind of reality, clutching the table, clutching the coffee cup, not allowing the conversation to stray for one instant, not allowing a moment to wander, to float. Mark was talking in slow motion, Kay was ushering me into the bathroom, where two lines of speed lay temptingly on the mirror. Even in my state, I could sense that this might be unwise. Not their fault, of course, for they offered the gift kindly and hoped it might kick me into some kind of verbal animation.

In the pub – and the pubs were open all day – I was transported ever higher, while Mark continually deflected local, lowbrow sycophancy with ease and he was looking at me, slightly curiously.

"I can't interview you," I slurred. "Would be silly . . ."

"I think, Mick, that we had better do this next week," he stated. "But when's your deadline?"

One week later, a second attempt, sitting in The Foresters Arms, once again soaking in the very Fallish hues. Greens, browns . . . pub hues, packed and lively at the dead end of a working week, with wage packets torn open, football performances to dissect. Martin Fry, one strongly sensed, wouldn't be in such a place, rather more at home perhaps, in the then voguish black'n'chrome, up-bracket burger joint on Marylebone Road, most likely. We were chatting about such things when . . .

"Hey," an oil-encrusted trainee mechanic exclaimed, striding purposefully over to Kay Carroll.

"Hey . . . I was in this flat in Hulme the other night and I picked up a copy of this LP. And there was this guy on the back cover, drinking a pint and I thought . . . hey . . . that's me mate from the pub. That's Mark . . . was chatting to him the other night. That's amazing. I had no idea you did that, Mark . . . I just had no idea."

And, later, there was another one, from another one.

"Mark . . . Jim from the off-licence told me that you'd been to Las Vegas. That's fantastic. What did you think of it? Me and the wife always had an ambition to go to Las Vegas. To see those places where Elvis played. We are saving up so one day we can go. How could you afford it? Was it a holiday or was it with that band? Did you like it Mark . . . did you?"

The Fall, it transpired, had just returned from a mammoth seven-week American tour. And here they were, Mark and Kay, heads swimming with observations from across the pond, brimful of anecdotes. Still lacking the kind of money that most of the artisans in The Foresters Arms would command, but building rapidly in terms of experience. In terms of influence too, I strongly sensed. But there still seemed something rather incongruous about the very notion of The Fall in America.

"Yeah, it was very strange in the States, in 1981. We went over there not really knowing what to expect. It was a two-way thing, as well. The venue owners didn't know what to expect and were very surprised by the result. As were we, to some extent. Some of the gigs were very odd."

Myron's Ballroom, Los Angeles, California. July 7, 1981

English Scheme/Jawbone And The Air-Rifle/Prole Art Threat/
The N.W.R.A./Your Heart Out/No Xmas For John Quays/
Hip Priest/C'n'C-S Mithering/Lie Dream Of A Casino Soul/
Totally Wired/Leave The Capitol/How I Wrote 'Elastic Man'

(Supported by The Flesheaters and Blurt . . . curiously enough.)

Mark: "Like in LA it was just so fuckin' weird. For us and for the crowd in a sense, but I remember the manager of the hall walking up to us after the gig and shaking his head and saying: 'We've never had junkies in the audience before . . . we have never had whores in the crowd, man.' It wasn't that he necessarily disapproved though, I just don't think he could understand where the core of our appeal lay. And, to be honest, neither could I. Neither could I. But that was fucking great for us . . . it would be a nightmare for a record company marketing man. I do understand that and, frankly, I sense that will always be the problem with The Fall. Because we don't appeal to an identifiable group of people. Like loads of Fall fans in fucking long coats or any of that shite. Fall fans cut right across society. They can be plumbers and whores and junkies – and fucking newsagents. Quite often – and this always amazes me – the only thing they have in common is the fact that they don't look like they are a fan of anything. And that's fucking great as far as I am concerned. That's fucking great because they are really into us. They understand full well what we are about and don't rely on music press shit or peer groups or age or class or absolutely anything. But I do admit it was amazing to discover that this was the case, not only in the UK, but right across America as well. I mean the size of the crowd varied from place to place but in a way the crowds didn't. They were just a fucking really strange mix of people, which was just fucking brilliant. Wonderful to see guys in Hawaiian shirts just standing there and really listening while I would be singing about Wigan Casino or something."

Mark, in this interview and beyond – way beyond actually – showed little sympathy towards the British bands of the day and their insatiable ambition to break America. To be fair to them, it's possible that bands such as The Clash were pushed firmly towards the US stadium circuit by management and record companies alike . . . and why not? Surely a fresh British injection into a vast circuit that still seemed to be overrun by AOR couldn't be such a bad thing for both the bands and, not to put too fine a point on it, for the American rock fans as well. Rather The Clash than Foreigner, surely?

Mark: "The Clash. The fucking Clash? Ha. We played with The Clash in New York. That was a great indication of the real and the plastic. They . . . The Clash . . . they brought this whole London scene over to America. It was like all the little creeps and trendies who hang around the backstage areas in London, all those fucking wankers had been transported to New York where they were toadying around The Clash and trying to seem really important. It was hideous to witness because The Clash were just going for the big time rock'n'roll trip, precisely the kind of stuff they always professed to be so totally against. It was gruesome. I mean, The Clash treated people like cattle. The whole set-up was to treat the people who came to see them like cattle and the whole audience became cattle. There was no mutual respect at all. It was a real old-style submissive audience deal and the fact was that there were no interesting people at the show at all. They were all just heavy rock fans. Black T-shirts, jeans. I mean, that's OK . . . I am not knocking that but we are used to playing to a real mix. This lot were all just into Led Zeppelin or The Rolling Stones. Which just proved to me that it was all the same as The Clash anyway. In fact, they might as well be listening to the Stones because all The Clash have become is a bad version, a bad copy of the Stones. I really don't see the point in that . . . other than to make money, of course. The fans, as it turned out, had no idea what was going on. They thought we were The Clash at first and they were really getting into it. It was just going well, then The Clash turned the PA off because we were going down too well. And we were too because we were offering them something that was genuinely different, something totally unexpected. It was like they had been waiting for so long for something original to come along and they understood us straight away. I mean, we didn't pamper them either and, in true style, we played what we wanted to play and they completely got it. When The Clash saw that, it must have scared them a bit. It was really funny because afterwards Joe Strummer came up to me and said, 'Hi . . . you are Mark Smith, aren't you. You can't stand to talk to me, can you?' That wasn't true. He was completely wrong about that. I have nothing personal against Joe Strummer. He's a nice bloke and all that. It was just that he was so irresponsible. The Clash didn't give a toss about their audience. All they were interested in was numbers and becoming the biggest band ever. Pathetic . . . really pathetic to see an English so-called punk band behaving like that.

"Because of the English-band attitude, I went all around America putting England down. If they ask me about English music, as they did all the time, I just told them that it was a load of crap, frankly. That they might as well stick with REO fucking Speedwagon or something because the English bands are just bad versions of the same old stuff. I am not anti-English. In fact I am English and very, very proud of it and I see nothing wrong with that. But the English bands really believe they are selling something special. What they don't realise, what they can't grasp is that the Americans buy it like it was a Hawaiian trip or something. Most Americans regard England as a small European state, but the English bands go around thinking that they are from some kind of king state.

"But that is where the switch is. I put down the English band attitude but the people I want to represent are not something to be sold off lightly. England is where all the real art in the world comes from, basically. How can you not be proud of that? But all those fucking English bands going round pretending to be Cockneys is just not on. The Clash were really selling this plastic England. They looked like English minstrels. It was just so fucking embarrassing. 'Oh let's go and look at those skinny limeys dancing around like idiots.' That was the American attitude. Cute England.

"I changed my mind completely about John Lydon around this time. He's produced a crock of shit, it's just shit, basically shit. Rather cynical shit as well. I don't blame him . . . you read interviews with him, he puts his case across rather well. I think it's what he wants to do, I suppose. It's just this attitude . . . I don't know, it doesn't sound good mainly, you got to start from there. That single . . . he does well in Britain, people buy it. It's like Tom Petty, it's just like Tom Petty. He sounds real silly, because his voice doesn't fit in with the music. What I hate about it . . . my younger sister goes out with a guy 18, 19, never had a job, no hope, and I gave him all my old Sex Pistols stuff and he's mad on it . . . now screwing with the kids like that, I don't like it . . . using Ginger Baker, and all that fucking . . . I'm not against those blokes, it's just that the sound is shit. The sound to me is revolting. We've got a guy in our band, Simon, he's a brilliant musician, he went to the College of Music. It's all session men's tricks, duum, dum, duum, you know, the bass that you hear on every fucking record, you know the $300-an-hour guys . . . with his voice over it, it just sounds crazy, and his rubbish lyrics that he's used about four or five times. That's what I hated about the late Public Image. I mean there's a certain resentment there from me of course, because I used to like him, also why should that guy get away with stuff that I throw in the bin."

City Gardens, Trenton, New Jersey. June 12, 1981

Impression Of J. Temperance/Deer Park/Leave The Capitol/
Fortress/Totally Wired/Hip Priest/2nd Dark Age/Fantastic Life/
Lie Dream Of A Casino Soul/Fit And Working Again/Jawbone
And The Air-Rifle/Session Musician/Container Drivers/
Middle Mass/Prole Art Threat

Cute as England might have seemed from across the pond, the tensions of Blighty were real enough for those who lived in the firing line, for those cowering in Moss Side blocks of flats or the owners of burning cars on the streets of Toxteth. The irony wasn't lost on Mark E. Smith.

Mark: "I was just sitting in this hotel and I saw this guy wander past with a newspaper that was screaming headlines about the Manchester riots. It was all really over-the-top stuff, as usual. But I admit, I just panicked. I thought, 'Christ, the north has risen at last and here's me sitting in fucking Atlanta.' How ironic was that? I ran out to find the nearest paper stall. It was, like, six miles away. I was feverish. I just devoured all the articles and couldn't wait to get back home. It really painted this picture of a whole country burning. I know the riots were serious but the reality didn't match the headlines. We came back expecting to see the place devastated but it was like, it was like beautiful England. I wasn't really disappointed but the rioting did ease a lot of tension in Manchester. The truth is that it was genuinely horrible just before we went away. You could really feel the tension, just hanging in the air. It was obvious that something big was going to happen. You would have had to have been an idiot not to notice this. But the rioting did seem to ease a lot of tension. In Manchester at least. It all seemed a lot more loose after we returned.

"Good things come out of everything. Like the recession. The guys in my local pub are really nice and genuine because they have to be . . . without a job. If you haven't got a job and you can't genuinely get a job, then you have nothing to feel ashamed about. And the point I am making – and I know because, when I was on the dole, nobody tried harder than me to get work, which is how The Fall came about, really – but the point is that, if you are in that position, it strips you of any pretensions. And that is not always a bad thing. Because you have to be yourself. That's why I like some of those guys and I certainly have more respect for them than many of the idiots I meet in the music business. Funny thing is, if these guys did have a job and money then they would all drive Ford Capris and would pick up girls. That would become their entire life. But I get on better with them as it is, you know. These pub guys tell you a lot about the English way. It's like, 'Let's start the revolution when the pubs shut.' It's inbred. You can't change it. The English have great suss and a great sense of humour. Like in those riots, the vandals smashed the windows but it was these guys, the pub clientele . . .

these guys did the looting, just because it was there. There was no malice. That's just the English scheme."

I was constantly reminded, sitting with Mark in the Woodthorpe, the Forester's or the Ostrich, in 1977, 1981, 1995 and 2003, spinning stories about old times, that Mark doesn't really like old times. "If you want to write about Deeply fucking Vale then that's up to you but I am not going to read that bit," he says, and I believe him. It would be a shame, though, because I liked the Deeply Vale bit but it reminded me of all those stories.

Mark will never forgive me for saying this, but The Fall sometimes remind me of The Grateful Dead. What a long, strange trip it has been – The Fall, I mean, not The Dead.

Question: Is there actually any difference between 'Dead Heads' and 'Fall Heads'? (And, if you are reading this book, you are almost certainly in the latter category and, most certainly also, loath the former category.)

Mark: "Obviously . . . I have always reacted against that. That's my one worry with this book, Mick. I said this at the beginning. I don't want it to be trainspotterish, release by release crap."

Mick: "Don't worry Mark. It won't be."

Mark: "Must be alive."

Mick: "Will be."

Mark: "I don't want it to include all the albums and singles, all retro like. Just do the bits that are natural, that are of real interest to you, not the best bits, just the bits that mean something to you, and please, not all those band members."

Mick: "No. Won't do. Haven't mentioned loads of them. Big ones, too. Even Jim Watts was only mentioned on leaving! No Marcia."

Mark: "And please, not Marc Riley."

Mick: "Ah . . . now there we have a problem . . . remember that time at The Hacienda?"

It was the first time I had met Marc Riley. He viewed me with suspicion. He had known me by name and, no doubt, through chatter with Mark and Kay – Mick's comin' round tonight . . . 'spose we will be in the pub if you need us, Marc, etc. – but not, curiously, in the flesh. Oh, once or twice, when he simmered in the corner of some dressing room. Too lost, I sensed, in his own work. He always had to concentrate . . . Marc. I recalled him, and quite fondly, shortly after falling from school and into The Fall, looking gawky, geeky, shy and uncertain; casting endless nervous glances, looking towards Mark for direction. And this was during group photo shoots with Kevin Cummins or Paul Slattery circling, snapping away, trying to tempt the heart of Marc Riley forward.

"Oh Marc's not shy at all . . . he's a fuckin' nut," stated Kay. "Especially when drinking and he drinks a fucking lot. Me and Mark can't keep up with him, that's how bad it gets . . . great though . . . he added a lot of fun into the band. A real load of fun."

But I never saw it. Too distant. The Fall trundled away in their surreal world of downbeat clubs, ferociously loyal fans, trainspotter nerds, intellectual aesthetes, plumbers and waitresses, pimps and prostitutes, with Riley gaining the most intense education one could imagine, meeting life head on, be it in New Zealand or Arkansas, without the comforting barrier of money. Can't have been easy, sometimes, to live among the locals. Surely, if in a band, and a hit band at that, one would be forgiven for wanting to retreat? Mark often did. Not so much Riley, who seemed to take so much on board, despite falling out, and somewhat messily, with Mark on at least one occasion.

I knew something of this. Had even spoken to Riley . . . on the phone, while he was sweltering in the heat of, I think, the midwest. Seemed friendly enough at the time, excitedly telling me about his growing role in Fall songwriting. Perhaps at that point I should have heeded the warning. Beware bass players bearing grandiose ideas of songwriting. Not my battle. Don't really care. But Marc Riley did and, in later years, would attempt to glean payback. Maybe deserved, maybe not. Don't know. Asked Mark. His reply in a few lines.

The first time ever I saw Marc Riley he was collecting money on the door at Manchester's Cypress Tavern. On the bill that night, The Distractions. With Mike Finney preening away to great effect, and Mark and Kay bouncing among the crowd. Great night . . . a night off. One strongly sensed that Riley was relishing his new found role as small-time gig promoter . . . seemed nice enough.

The next time I met him he was sitting pintside in the aptly named Old Garrett pub. It was a post-Fall Riley and echoes of his 'disagreements' with Mark E. Smith had long since stopped bouncing around the music press gossip pages. By this time his own band, The Creepers, had become a reality and, flushed with the interest and financial shunt of his cohort, Jim Khambatta, he had instigated 'In Tape Records', a latter-day stab at punkish DIYism . . . and a mixed batch – some excellent, some downright irksome – would flow onto the label in the jangly mess of the mid-Eighties indie scene. Riley was ebullient, on that occasion and, flushed with an alarming number of midday pints, he enthused about all manner of influences, from Captain Beefheart to Johnny Cash, who he would later interview for a local radio station. But mostly, he enthused about The Creepers and their first single, 'Jumper Clown' which had fluttered briefly within The Fall's set, even opening the show on some occasions.

'Jumper Clown' was a fat, portly pop song driven by enthusiasm and appeared to point towards an intriguing future for The Creepers. The portents were good. Many people, Dave Haslem among them, still believe that the germ of artistic promise flourished to full extent during the mid-Eighties' days of Marc Riley & The Creepers. Personally, I thought Riley too talented to be shunting around with such a shambolic and directionless unit. I mentioned this, at some point, in one or two reviews within the pages of *Sounds*. I sense these reviews didn't sit too well on Marc Riley's shoulders and I can certainly understand the angst of a musician who sees his dreams dented by the artless musings of some drifting rock hack who still carried a torch for his former band. He made this point rather clear, in the summer of 1985, following the trashing of Marc Riley & The Creepers' spirited open-air set at Manchester's International Youth Year Festival where they were surrounded by the embryonic talents of Simply Red, James, Easterhouse and a huddle of mid-Eighties wannabes. In such company, I found The Creepers lacked necessary direction. Nevertheless, it wasn't actually myself who penned the review that clouded Riley's face to thunderous hatred inside The

Hacienda. Indeed, I recall him hurtling towards me, like some cartoon hoodlum, eyes blackened with fury, a man with a point to make and fair enough. The point was made. Following that, and for some years, friends of mine would warn me away from Marc Riley.

"I don't know why Mick, but he just doesn't like you."

Curiously enough, in later years, I found him effortlessly amenable, whether working for Manchester record promoter Tony Michaelides or later still in his hugely successful Lard role, blossoming in the shadow of Mark Radcliffe. I even sensed a joyous victory in this unlikely glory . . . always knew he had some kind of power within him and felt genuinely pleased. I last saw him in the studios of New Broadcasting House or maybe on some eternal Manchester to London train, sitting amid BBC gubbins, Mark and Lard melting with the ordinary folk, Lard smiling, Radcliffe grim.

Was never sure about Mark's position on this, though.

Mark E. Smith: "Doesn't bother me, one way or another now. It did at one point, though. How weird do you think it was for me when, during one of The Fall's lower spells, to be travelling along Oxford, Manchester – or perhaps London, come to that – to be confronted by a giant poster of Marc Riley. That did freak me out for a while, I can't deny. It was such a strange thing to have happened. Not, of course, that I have ever actually heard him on the radio. But I am sure he is very good. It's just a different world, really."

MIDDLE MASS

The evil is not in extremes
It's in the aftermath
The middle mass
After the fact
Vulturous in the aftermath

Summer close season
A quiet dope and cider man
But during the season
Hard drug and cider mates

The Whole World Is A John Peel Session

The boy is like a tape loop
The boy is like a uh-uh

Not much contact
Drinking, the men wait
They are set at nought
Because cripple states a holy state
Because cripple states a holy state
The Wehrmacht never got in here
The Wehrmacht never got in here
The Wehrmacht never got in here
The Wehrmacht never got in here
Thought it took us six years
The Wehrmacht never got in here
And living here you whisper, bub
And living here you whisper, bub!

This boy is like a tape loop
And he has soft mitts
But he's the last domain
Of a very black, back-room brain
He learned a word today
The word's misanthropy
And he's running to and from
The cats from tin pan alley
And he's running with and from
The cats from tin pan alley
And going down the alley
Take the cats from the alley
Up to them
The alley's full of cats from tin pan

Come into the back room Brian
And meet
The middle mass
The middle mass
Vulturous in the aftermath
Middle mass

It has been noted, though not by Mark, who flatly refuses to comment, that Middle Mass, from *Slates*, was about a 'fall out with Marc Riley'. Riley, it transpired, had spent some time living in London's famous Denmark Street or, as musicians tend to refer to it, Tin Pan Alley. Riley apparently enjoyed the Sex Pistols geographical connotations of this short, evocative street, where every British musician has wandered to admire the window displays of expensive guitars, above which shark-toothed music publishers in offices once bartered songs they hoped might reach the 'hit parade'. Riley stayed in a flat with Mike Gaines, a singer songwriter, allegedly not unfond of occasional narcotics. For a while, when Riley was in The Fall, there were murmurings of Riley and Gaines forming a band or, at least, writing material together. Smith wasn't fond of Gaines . . . whatever, it was cause for a minor band bust-up with Smith berating Riley for preferring to work with Gaines and Riley repeatedly referring to Smith as "a misanthropic old git". Smith's Middle Mass was, seemingly, the perfect aesthetic response. Soft mitts, indeed!

Perverted By Language LP. December, 1983

Eat Y'self Fitter/Neighbourhood Of Infinity/Garden/Hotel Bloedel/
Smile/I Feel Voxish/Tempo House/Hexen Definitive-Strife Knot

I recall sitting, in a post-divorce flatlet, in Heaton Moor which is as Bohemian as Stockport is ever likely to get, slumped cross-legged and peering into a cheap bottle of wine. It was as low as one could get, to be honest. Fallen nastily from a marital plain, fallen from employment too, with freelance work dripping from an emptying barrel and with State benefits barely stretching halfway into each week, no matter what they say. Unemployment never worked for me.

I recall splitting open Mark E. Smith's letter. It had arrived that morning, swiftly received after I had spilled the beans about the marriage bust-up. Had spent weeks listening alternately to Elvis Costello and The Fall and I had noticed, as a deadening Christmas approached, a certain upbeat drive seeping into the band's music and, in particular, into Mark's lyrics.

Perverted By Language was the album of the moment, and Mark's letter echoed the upbeat tone that I – and seemingly only I – had noticed.

". . . Mick . . . Brix now firmly in the band and it's the best time of my life, mate! Don't worry about your break-up. To be honest, I never thought it would last . . . nothing personal, just a hunch. I think it's for the best. Things happen for a reason. I had just about given up on women . . . completely, really. I was wrapped in the band and just didn't have anything to do with them at all. I thought I was happy like that as well. Like an island. But then things happen . . . a chance meeting and suddenly there is colour back in your world. Brix is the best thing that ever happened to me. No doubt about that. Funny thing, women are normally negative where the band is concerned, but I also think she is the best thing that has ever happened to The Fall. She is a fantastic musician and keeps the other guys on their toes. Perfect but personally she is more than that, Mick. She monitors my drinking (good naturedly). She will never win completely on that score, but she is respectful of me and me of her . . . so don't worry, Mick. Things will change. Very pleased with album but the newer stuff will be much, much better. Are you coming to The Hacienda gig? See you down there. Been a good year though . . . see bit in NME*!!!"*

The 'Bit' In The *NME* By Mark E. Smith

THIS YEAR, the group that sneers at laughing fate broke down in a quaint place three kilometres outside Dachau for five days, skint and starved, escaping only through the use of a bogus credit card to get to Yugoslavia, not worth it at all despite what these leftist musicians say. (Of course gigs are packed!) Returned home to bankrupt record co. then slipped again into a more sinister one. Went abroad and developed xenophobia. Marriage saved vocalist's neck. Attacked for tax. Spurned retrospect. Future very bright, hiding retirement. Now number 6, age average 22.5.

OTHERWISE, it's the cyclical tone of 1983 that strikes me the most. Viewed through miserable eyes, much familiarity here: Music Vaudeville still. Manned as ever by cockney musicians in disguise, supplemented by Lancashire-Scotch deserters. But there's more to it. Loads of crafted 'good pop' lyrics, Serious, Pal, in their statement of non-conviction in this living desert, etc. but subtly appealing to humanity in the same way as a hospital does. Nothing new, except this is of the groups' own accord! So, I have to proclaim 1983 – THE YEAR OF THE TOADIES. A good laugh though was seeing all the serious/literal musicians go 'Lite' (in wake of lager and cigarettes) as the scrambling for market position heated up. A musical version of the GOD-JOB Interviewer hoax practised on schools TV – i.e. declining market, etc. look at so & so, he did it – this paid off to 'those concerned.' Competition fierce, and groups as clean and accommodating as never before! Independent labels feel secure enough to pick, choose and shove around even. Early senile fantasies of groups sure to be quenched for their staff, who're comfy in the knowledge that the Y.T.S. of rock is the Soviet conscription-well of GB.

More disturbing was this panic-hitting journalist too – semi-established hacks and even their betters fighting for and adopting name scattering with redick prose, bruise purple and its insecurity. Smash Hits *realise this I think. Also funny is the proliferation of faggots in the top pop lot. I have a theory that this is due to AIDS scare, resulting in said groups having more energy derived from celibacy.*

Be seeing you.
A prompting Xmas to our friends.
MARK E. SMITH (for THE FALL)

EAT Y'SELF FITTER

I'm in the furniture trade
Got a new job today
But stick the cretin
On the number-three lathe

Went down the town
To a HM club
The sign had a cross
Through a couple well-dressed
They looked at my coat
They looked at my hair
An Easy Rider coot

The Whole World Is A John Peel Session

Grabbed the edge of my coat
Said: 'You're too smart for here'
I said: 'I'll see the manager'

He was the manager
Eat y'self fitter
Up the stairs mister
Eat y'self fitter

Analytics have got
My type worked out
Analytics on me
The poison render
I grope about
And when I go out
My mind splits
My eyes doth hurt
The musical chairs
Have been swallowed up
By a cuddly group
Who land and rub off
Hoping that
Whatever it is
Will land and drop off

I met a hero of mine
I shook his hand
Got trapped in the door
Felt a fool, I tell ya

Charmed to meet ya
Eat y'self fitter
Up the stairs mister
Eat y'self fitter

Became a recluse
And bought a computer
Set it up in the home
Elusive big one

The Fall

On the screen
Saw the Holy Ghost, I swear
On the screen

Where's the cursor?
Where's the eraser?
Where's the cursor?
Where's the eraser?
G-O-H-O-H-O-9-O
G-O-H-O-H-O-9-O
G-O-H-O-H-O-9-O
H-O-9-O-G-O-H-O

What's a computer?
Eat y'self fitter
What's a computer?
Eat y'self fitter

The Kevin Ayers scene
South of France
Plush velvet
Aback! Aback!
Aback! Aback!
Levis Fridays
Greek holidays
Barratt heritance X3

Mit-Dem! X3
Don't wanna be a mit-dem! X4

Pick the fleas mister
Eat y'self fitter
Eat y'self fitter?
Eat y'self fitter

Who tells you what
To tape on your vid. chip
How do you know the progs you miss
Are worse than those you single out?

The Whole World Is A John Peel Session

And what'll you do when the rental's up?
And your bottom rack is full of vids
Of programs you will nay look at
The way they act is, oh, sheer delight
Cardboard copyright
Make it right
Panic in Sudan
Panic in Wardour
Panic in Granadaland
Panic all over
By the wretched timesheeters
Of my delight
One starry night
The powers that be will have to meet
And have no choice but to . . .

Eat each other
Eat y'self fitter
Eat each other?
Eat y'self fitter

(Eat y'self fitter)

Portly and with good grace
The secret straight-back ogre entered
His brain aflame
With all the dreams
It had conjured X4

Mit-dem!
Don't wanna be a mit-dem! X4

The centimetre square
Eat y'self fitter
Said it purged fear
Eat y'self fitter

(Eat y'self fitter)

Hacienda, Manchester. December 17, 1983

Perverted By Language/Garden/Marquis Cha-Cha/2 x 4/Words Of Expectation/Ludd Gang/Smile/Smile Part 2/Draygo's Guilt/ Oh! Brother/Clear Off!/Eat Y'self Fitter/I Feel Voxish/ Kicker Conspiracy/Wings/Totally Wired

I finished the evening clinging to a Hacienda bollard, to be honest. Never felt wholly comfortable in there. Grabbed Fall manager Richard Thomas' arm, which wasn't the steadiest arm at the best of times, and fell down the stairs in a state of some embarrassment. Am not saying, "Hey, look at me, I was a real hip drunk cat!" because it wasn't quite like that. Never was, at Fall gigs. The band were on solid form, though. The first time I had seen Brix. Plays with female gusto, aggression, even. Scared the hell out of me. Sexual element of The Fall had been of a rather more subtle nature until this point. I could see how this new influence would be tremendously powerful. 'Smile', in particular, leaped from the pack, as it often did. Better than the curiously muted performance on *The Tube*. Better by far.

At the set's conclusion, I sat down in the Kim Philby Bar, listening to Tony Wilson ranting on and on about how The Fall should have been a Factory band. About how they actually were a Factory band in every way except that they weren't on the label. If you can work that out, you are considerably more perceptive than me. However, as the band were embroiled in the cashless act of making a half-hour video for Ikon, Factory's downbeat video wing, then one sensed that relations between Factory and The Fall were on a reasonably friendly basis. (Personally, I never really saw The Fall in the same light as any of the Factory bands . . . none of them. It was a world apart. When The Fall played with Joy Division it was always like an uneasy meeting of opposites. Fans, too, would be recognisably different. This had been particularly noticeable since 1982, when elements of Factory had attempted to embrace the new age of glam, and The Fall were seemingly devoid of any trace of fad or fashion.)

Hence . . .

Hex Enduction Hour, LP. March, 1982

The Classical/Jawbone And The Air-Rifle/Hip Priest/Fortress/ Deer Park/Mere Pseud Mag. Ed./Winter (Hostel-Maxi)/Winter 2/ Just Step S'ways/Who Makes The Nazis?/Iceland/And This Day

The world was changing fast. Rock was shading rapidly into pop. The second glam age had already begun in earnest. This lightening had already heavily flavoured the music press. On the 'Singles' pages, almost overnight, the independent labels had drained steadily away and young, po-faced, short-back-and-sided rock writers had suddenly started to grapple with a new pop sensibility, whatever that meant. Well, what it meant, in London at least, was that writers once attuned to the avant-garde, who had suddenly started to live and love the life in Maida Vale – stand up and take a bow, Paul Morley – had started to grimace at the thought of a pint of beer or a DIY post-punk single . . . now they were hanging onto the shirt-tails of the pop mavericks. Morley's initially unlikely association with Trevor Horn would, within 18 months, bear fruit with the appalling Frankie Goes To Hollywood but, for the time being, he would drift among the shadows of ABC videos . . . gushing lavish praise onto the Martyn Fry-Trevor Horn collaboration that had already produced 'Poison Arrow' and was set to blossom in 1982's giant pop romance extravaganza, *The Lexicon Of Love*. Suddenly all was big and bright and glittery and glam. The trash aesthetic had taken a stronghold and even more earnest young men, like Fall fanatic Ian Penman, would hurtle warped prose at the likes of August Darnell and hail the birth of a new exotic dance music. The world, or so it seems, was waltzing down to the Camden Palace in leg warmers.

People wore yellow without embarrassment.

Bleached hair trickled over shoulders . . . bronzed muscles bulged from singlets. Intelligent people were caught without socks. Hairdressers smiled. *The Face* fell into foul fashion. Rock hadn't died . . . but it had decided to get dressed for dinner.

The student bars of Manchester reverberated to New Order's 'Everybody's Gone Green'. Factory boss Tony Wilson talked a great deal about the new computer music his finest band were suddenly pumping out of the rehearsal rooms. Over in New York, in The Paradise Garage nightclub, a new breed of disco dancing was rampant. Out on the streets, a blacker, urban breakbeat was struggling free. It was a time of transition.

Where exactly did that leave The Fall?

Mark: "Stuff like that never really bothered me. In fact, I loved it during the spells when they wouldn't want to write about us. It used to amuse me to see people who had been writing reams of gushing journalese about The Fall be suddenly transformed and even start to aim nasty little remarks. It was just like flies but, during the late Seventies, it was so obvious that that was going to happen. All these journalists had their free holidays. Suddenly they caught a glimpse of a bit of glamour. Suddenly they thought they had actually made it. No way were they interested in music for its own artistic merit. They were absolutely no different from the musicians, some of whom joined The Fall, and then decided that they wanted the big time – and would become big rock star idiots, if only in their own heads. Same thing happened with the journalists. Their egos just carried them away. It was pathetic to see, to be honest, and you knew that it would end in some kind of disaster. That they would all come running back, tails between their legs. And so they did. But, looking back over those periods, and there have been periods where nobody wanted to know The Fall at all, I think they were where we were at our best and I was certainly happier, it was like the sycophancy had evaporated and we could get on with what we really wanted to do. It was fine by me."

Ironically, it would be during those periods when the spotlight flickered on the pop end of the spectrum that The Fall often became their most commercially inaccessible. No surprise that in November 1982, at the very peak of the pastel-coloured-trouser pop boom, The Fall would release their most stubbornly awkward record to date, *Room To Live*. Wedged in at the start of that same year was their most stark album to date, the haunting, often disturbing *Hex Enduction Hour*, which continued the drive into the eclectic that had begun with *Slates*.

The words of 'Hip Priest', arguably the most misquoted song in The Fall's massive repertoire, indicate an obvious belligerence but also, I suggest, faint signs of insecurity . . . though Mark will strongly deny this.

HIP PRIEST

He's not appreciated
He's not appreciated
He's not appreciated

Drink the long draught, Dan,
for the Hip Priest

I said drink the long draught, Dan,
for the Hip Priest!

He's not appreciated
He's not appreciated

White collar hits motorway services
It's the Hip Priest
From the eyes he can see, they know
It's the Hip Priest

He's not appreciated

It's purple psychology
Not just an old lady's

That's hip hip hip hip hit hit hit Hip Priest

That's hip hip hip hip hit hit hit Hip Priest

And he's gonna make an appearance
He's gonna make an appearance

Was shown in a freakshow early on
And drunk from small brown bottles since I was so long

Cause I'm a Hip Priest
Cause I'm a Hip Priest
People only need me when they're down and gone to seed
Cause I'm a Hip Priest
Cause I'm a Hip Priest

It's appreciation half won
And they hate their allegiance to hip preacher one
Hip Priest

I got my last clean dirty shirt outta the wardrobe
I got my last clean dirty shirt outta the wardrobe
And all the good people know

That's hip hip hip hip hit hit hit Hip Priest

All the young groups know
All the young groups know
They can't ever take advantage because I'm a Hip Priest
I was as clean as a packet of chocolate chips

That's hip hip hip hip hit hit hit Hip Priest

And if the good people knew they would say
He's not appreciated
He's not appreciated

So drink the long draught, Dan,
for the Hip Priest

DEER PARK

I took a walk down West 11
I had to wade through 500 European punks
In an off-licence I rubbed up with some oiks [1]
Who threw some change on the Asian counter
And asked polite if that covered two lagers
A hospital discharge asked me where he could crash

The Whole World Is A John Peel Session

Have you been to the English Deer Park?
It's a large type artist ranch
This is where C Wilson wrote Ritual in the Dark
Have you been to the English Deer Park?

Spare a thought for the sleeping promo dept.
They haven't had an idea in two years
Dollars and Deutschmarks keep the company on its feet
Say have you ever had a chance to meet
Fat Captain Beefheart imitators with zits?
Who is the King Shag Corpse?

Have you been to the English Deer Park?
It's a large type minstrel ranch
This is where C Wilson wrote Ritual in the Dark
Have you been to the English Deer Park?

The young blackies get screwed up the worst
They've gone over to the Hampstead house suss
In the English system they implicitly trust
See the A&R civil servants
They get a sex thrill out of a sixteenth of Moroccan
They get a sex thrill out of a sixteenth of Moroccan

Have you been to the English Deer Park?
It's a large type artist ranch
This is where C Wilson wrote Ritual in the Dark
Have you been to the English Deer Park?

Yes, dear chap, it hasn't changed that much
It's still a subculture art-dealer jerk-off
Yes, dear chap, it hasn't changed that much
It's still a subculture art-dealer jerk-off

Have you been to the English Deer Park?
It's a large type minstrel ranch
This is where C Wilson wrote Ritual in the Dark
Have you been to the English Deer Park?

Have you been to the English Deer Park?
It's a large type minstrel ranch
This is where loads of punks congregate in the dark
Have you been to the English Deer Park?

Have you been to the English Deer Park?
It's a large type minstrel ranch
This is where C Wilson wrote Ritual in the Dark
Have you been to the English Deer Park?

Hey tourist it wasn't quite like what you thought
Hey Manchester group that wasn't what you thought
Hey Scottish group that wasn't quite like what you thought
Hey Manchester group that wasn't what you thought
Hey Scottish group that wasn't quite like what you thought
Quite like what you thought

Hey Midlands, scooped yer, how d'you ever get the job?
Hey Manchester group from it wasn't quite like what you thought
Quite like what you thought
Guess what
Guess guess guess . . .
Guess what

Polytechnic, Manchester. March 27, 1982

Joker Hysterical Face/I'm Into CB/Mere Pseud Mag. Ed./Flat Of Angles/Who Makes The Nazis?/Wings/Solicitor In Studio/Fit And Working Again/The Classical/Lie Dream Of A Casino Soul/ Hexen Definitive-Strife Knot/And This Day/Look, Know/ Prole Art Threat/Deer Park

There was a fight, a schoolyard brawl. A small man, craggy and quaffed, punched beyond his weight. They moved swiftly, like a cartoon rumble, out of the bar and towards the stage, fists rained in from every which way. Almost comically, plastic pint pots were hurled into the fray and above it, leering down at the pathetic huddle, the giant eerie figure of Denis the Menace, painted flat and bright onto the backdrop, and in front of Denis, the bold gaze of Mark E. Smith. Unhappy with the distraction, he spat more venom than usual into 'Lie Dream Of Casino Soul'. The song spinning from another era, homing in on the vagaries of Wigan, where speed-filled all-nighters were also spiced by the undercurrent of potential violence and where reality faded at the crush by the door, where values were twisted and the spinning, swirling, sweating dancer was both rich man and artist, temporarily adored by the girls in the corner, forgotten the moment the sunlight returned.

Out at Blackpool Mecca, down at The Torch in Stoke-on-Trent, at Manchester's Twisted Wheel, a false currency prevailed, where records would change hands at extraordinary prices and DJs would offer a glimpse of a time when they would grasp the limelight.

"I just suppose it goes to show, the lie dream of a casino soul . . ."

Propping up the corner, seedy men with seedy record stalls, flogging wares in the heat of the hour.

Mark ('82): "It's of the 'rock' sort of thing today. I want to be didactic; I want to be opinionated, I don't think because we're having a fucking hard time everybody should stop having opinions and start getting into good time stuff. I think people in hard times need brain stimulation more than anytime. 'Having a good time till the bomb drops' or 'looking good when the bomb drops', or suchlike nonsense, is the de rigueur pose to pursue.

"Bands smaller than us have got these sort of clone people walking about. Seen that in the Bunneymen audience. I find that very, very disturbing and God help anyone who turns up dressed like me! Should that ever happen, which is pretty unlikely, but you never know these days. Everything is seen as fashion in 1982. But it's good for us.

"We've started getting people who'll stand by us. I've talked to loads of people who come to see us who just don't like any other groups, which is great. I mean, they haven't got FALL written over their chests and everything, but they say, 'Oh, I like you, and I like a bit of reggae and a bit of . . . you know.' These are people who are comfortable within their own identity. They don't need to have my stupid fucking face on their overpriced T-shirts to feel good about themselves. And they like the band for what the band is. For the music. They take that and they leave. They don't want The Fall to permeate their every waking moment. They don't want to be part of a Fall club. That would be horrible.

"There's a very large number – some people are surprised at just how large a number – of disaffected music-loving folk who just aren't bothered about 'looking good' or buying the latest clothes, no matter what the economic climate's like and what the music barons and their handmaiden press dictate, and who find little to connect with in more transparent musical/stylistic practices. For many of them, The Fall are still the only honest group around, the only ones who don't condescend, who don't try and manipulate them.

"Fuckin' crap. Bullshit. I mean, the whole scene's gone back seven years, 'cos some people are out of work. We've always been poor. It hasn't made any difference to us. Y'know, it's what really shits me up. I mean, like, Teardrop Explodes – escapist fuckin' rubbish! I'm not knockin' it, I never have. I've always loved that type of stuff. But, y'know, when you start gettin' knocked for tryin' to fuckin' say somethin'.

"We're having a bit of a difficult time 'cos people are coming along and sort of liking us, as opposed to the last two years, where it's just been getting up everybody's backs. Gotta change your tune, which we can do. I mean, we have sort of broken that myth down, we are doing it, eventually. We're getting more and more of your average rock audience – it's getting quite heavy in a way – and we've got to start on them as well or you're just preaching to the converted all the time. There's no way I'm gonna go on now and just fuckin' barrack 'em, 'cos you're getting 500 people in a hall and they've all come to see you. It's no use just saying 'fuck it' like we used to be able to.

"It's hard to define, y'know? It's probably just people with an open mind. I think we are getting a lot more voyeurs just coming to see if Mark'll start on somebody, or if we'll get hit, or something. I mean, everybody knows about the split between the North and the South in England, but 'The North Will Rise Again' wasn't a political statement, it's a story, like a science-fiction story. The way I wrote it was from a few dreams I had after playing the north a lot – it's about what would happen if there was a revolution. It's purely fantasy, science-fiction stuff.

"I felt we were in danger of turning into some sort of big band, like the sort of epic rock sound that the Bunnymen were moving towards at the time, and that's never been the idea of The Fall. That's why *Room To Live* was such a necessary album.

"We've just seen too much, right from the early days, of idiots like Stiff Little Fingers shooting way up beyond us where you could see they had no real ability, now dullards like Heaven 17 hitting the heights with the most pathetic versions of what The Fall did years ago. I do hate looking back in the sense of glorifying the past, but I do think you have to be aware of the fact that The Fall have always been ahead of their time, because it's that which gives us the impetus to move forward."

Deadening Sunday, The Peveril Of The Peak pub, Manchester. July 1985

I always think fondly of 1985 in Manchester. Nobody outside the city seemed to notice what was happening? It was a springtime, of sorts, a whole tumble of bad bands and intriguing ones, too. None-theless, an energy existed back then that seemed to hint that anything was possible – and it was, too. It was a great year to be lingering with intent!

Face cragged into a semi-squint, a wily wisdom, a wisdom beyond his years, seeps from the corner of his eyes, his faint sneer seems fondly mocking, Salfordian vowels clashing with my rounded 'Cheshtone'. As if in a film, a stylistic film, where steam rises from the steel sheen of a wet street, and relentless raindrops add to the effect, unforgiving, relentless, adding to, rather than defeating the silence.

No café bars gleam on the corners. No lofts, theme clubs or Bridgwater Halls in 1985. No Comedy Stores or Loafs, no Tampopo or Waggamama, no Printworks or Selfridges, no Trafford Centre, no Academy.

Just the empty half-can shell of G-MEX, just a Hacienda filling slowly, just a deep street leading to Colin Sinclair's Boardwalk, reclaimed by the owner and his father from the dusty grandeur of a ghostly Victorian school. And in there, down on Little Peter Street, amid the Knott Mill shadows, the rebirth of Manchester has begun in earnest, with a small huddle of rehearsal rooms, a deserted theatre and a rush of downbeat and mostly penniless activity.

More fun though, more fun than it had been since the late Seventies, with long shadows cast by The Smiths, New Order, The Fall and the emergent Simply Red. With The International Club, in Longsight, reclaimed from its dubious life as a semi-gangster-owned cabaret; latterly a venue in resurgence, pushing a new Manchester breed, not afraid to pick up guitars again, not afraid to write and listen to songs.

Manchester, mid-1985, was nicely adrift in the shadows. Despite the allure of the big three, the music press by and large ignored the city completely, relenting only occasionally by offering freelancers little chinks of patronising space. Indeed the *NME*, commenting on the lost and messy Manchester glossy rock mag of the era, *Muze* magazine – on which the author of this book admits to some involvement – noted "*Muze* was a Manchester 'zine when there was no Manchester scene." Curious, indeed, to note that, because the all-encompassing *NME* preferred to ignore Manchester at the time, it would later be able to proudly proclaim that nothing was happening at all.

Of course, for better or worse, Madchester and the latter-day Manchester resurgence was firmly rooted in 1985, in actuality the most important year in Manchester's musical history. If you were there, either involved and in deep or merely drifting along to the occasional gig, you were lucky enough to find yourself submerged in relentless, refreshing, invigorating optimism. Which is one view. In a few lines Mark, speaking from within the centre of that year, will unleash a verbal assault on the 'scene' . . . but I wasn't so sure. I enjoyed the backwater atmosphere. I enjoyed the way that, given the reactionary booking policy undertaken by Roger Eagle at The International Club, Manchester had pulled back from the funk and electro beats dominating the mush of sound that was The Hacienda and, without losing face, had started to enjoy guitar bands once more, home-made and trickling into town. In The International's relatively small space came R.E.M., Red Hot Chili Peppers, Green On Red, The Replacements. I enjoyed also the vigour and hope employed by Colin Sinclair at the Boardwalk Club, reclaimed from the crumbling wreck of a Victorian school, and fired with the prospect of a flourishing future. But The International held the key.

The International, Manchester. July 19, 1985

Copped It/Wings/Couldn't Get Ahead/Petty Thief Lout/No Bulbs/
Gut Of The Quantifier/Spoilt Victorian Child/Barmy/Elves/
Lay Of The Land

It was, for a series of reasons, a classic. Before the set, a shunt around the 500-strong crowd was enough to realise that anyone who wanted to be someone but wasn't quite at the required level was there, encircling Piccadilly Radio DJ Tony Michaelides, pushing for a mention: elements of Stone Roses, Chameleons, Happy Mondays, James, Easterhouse, all hogging to the rear, casting eyes Fall-wards without allowing themselves to be seen to be actually enjoying the proceedings, not that it mattered one way or another. It was a gig that finally proved to me that there may or may not have been a scene and then there was The Fall. Striding gleefully onto the stage, relaxed, confident, spiced by Brix's sex appeal, chomping guitars and sneering vocals. It was vintage stuff: 'Couldn't Get Ahead', all funked up and chunky, the rolling prettiness of 'No Bulbs' and the concluding parochial weirdness of 'Lay Of The Land'.

By mid-1985, The Fall had found themselves, in Manchester at least, surrounded by a new breed, in part a ragged, dysfunctional, greying breed, typified by Easterhouse & Laugh, Desert Wolves and, ironically enough, the ferociously erratic Marc Riley & The Creepers, and The Fall were there, quite literally, in the subterranean confines of The Boardwalk, where dulled music would seep from behind practice-room doors, where The Stone Roses and Happy

Mondays would be polishing their attacks, where John Robb's Membranes would be lodged quaintly in a punk dream and James would be picking a sensitive route through folksy weirdness and jazzers Kalima and The Jazz Defekters would be grasping for a certain besuited chic. And among them, in rehearsal, milling around the pool table, The Fall, distinctive and ethereal veterans by this point, with Brix loving the life, living some kind of dream.

And, on this particular day, meeting Mark seemed a noticeably surreal affair. Manchester, despite the embryonic musical resurgence – wholly unnoticed by the *NME* – seemed aloof, noticeably unhinged, yet as proudly parochial as at any time in recent history.

In stark contrast to the latter-day city, finding an open hostelry proved difficult, even though we were locked in that thin sandwich of time where, in pre-Nineties Britain, it was legally permitted to imbibe. So we smashed our way into The Peveril Of The Peak and I noted that Mark had changed . . . changed due, in one sense, to the smartening influence of his wife. His Crombie, for that's what it was, beheld a certain sheen that would have been way beyond his clothes of yesteryear. Pushing out defiantly from the bottom, however, were two studded leather boots, not at all *de rigueur* in the anti-rockist, post-New Order Mancunia but great fun nonetheless, and a strong hint that this mysterious thin, dark stranger was involved, in some bizarre way, in the music business.

Then again, maybe he wasn't. At the time, and somewhat embarrassingly, I believe I called him ". . . the most influential figure ever to grace the youth culture of our fair city . . ." I apologise. Firstly for using the term 'youth culture' and then for the absurdity of that statement (and goddamn those who seek to keep such statements alive via the evil, evil, internet).

Anyway, I digress. We decided to drive Mark home . . . or, at least, towards his Sedgeley Park abode and, naturally, into the welcoming arms of a Prestwich hostelry, where, after doubling up at the bar, he stood enigmatically in the shadows of the wooden corridor, framed by dour interiors, smiling through wave after wave of football chat. I still believed, at this point, that The Fall were without doubt the most uncompromising rock band in the world, the only band in the world and so they may well have been and, certainly, that was the position their fans believed they held, and yet, on this day, he seemed to be curiously alone. Couldn't quite put my finger on it, at least not beyond the chip he was cradling in regard to the unfolding scene of Manchester. I noted, courageously I thought, that The Fall played to smaller audiences in this new Manchester than in any other town.

Mark agreed: "Yeah, yeah . . . I know. I know that we are not popular around here and that's just great. Suits me fine, you know. I just can't believe all these new bands, all the bands in The Boardwalk there, all these bands are falling for the same old shit. I learnt a hell of a lot in the past. I would watch situations like The Distractions . . . remember?"

How could I forget?

"Yeah, er, yeah . . . The Distractions. I thought it was hilarious how that all fell through. You see it happen time and time again, people expecting to be . . . like the next big thing like, for God's sake, that band at the moment . . . Tarzanz Milkmen (long forgotten Mancunian poppy dimbos). Just cabaret. Which would be OK but they are crap cabaret. They haven't even got the guts to go out and just play cover versions. Many times, in the past, I have been offered five-year contracts and I have just thrown them back. I have never signed anything like that and never will. It cost us money, initially. It meant that we had to endure a certain hardship and there were a number of Fall band members who just could not cope with that. Well, that just showed me that they were in it for the wrong reasons."

I countered that, contract or not, a band has to create a method of survival. Surely even Mark couldn't blame any emergent band from grasping that pay cheque – only natural – and rather different for most, if not all other bands. Part of the very nature of The Fall was their rolling repertoire, their habit of performing sets that precede their releases by, at the very least, six months. The Fall can get away with that. To some degree it is expected. But not so for the rapidly emerging local band who has, quite possibly, just one short desperate stab at recognition. The Distractions were a case in point.

Mark: "We are survivalists. That's the main reason why this band has seen so many changes over the years. People like Marc Riley became content to play *Live At The Witch Trials* all the time. You know . . . just sit back and rest. That is all Marc Riley wanted to do and, in that respect, he was never in tune with what The Fall were about. We would have just become a greatest hits package. I was starting to develop characters in the lyrics, starting to try all kinds of things and all he wanted to do was to play fucking 'Music Scene'. Just look at how far we travelled, from *Live At The Witch Trials* to *The Wonderful And Frightening World Of* . . . last year. You don't do that by sitting back and being Marc Riley and pampering some audience who want to hear the fucking hits."

With Mark still languishing in the shadows of the corridor . . . and listening to him throwing gentle broadsides at The Smiths – "They are just a watered-down version of The Fall . . ." (agreed) – I mentioned to him that, since the arrival of Brix Smith, The Fall had been reborn, had started to flourish after such a spirited injection. There was a sexual thrust that had become wholly apparent at The International gig, a truly wondrous and frightening performance and an evening that seemed to prove just how much responsibility Mark had delegated to his wife, who guided the band on a more traditional, certainly more Stateside approach, as Mark seemed content to stand away from stage centre and watch a while. I had never seen him happier.

Indeed, had The Fall ever sounded so . . . vital?

Mark: "Yeah. I would agree with all that. This is a much happier band than ever before. I feel very proud with the output nowadays . . . we are even happy with our label, Beggars Banquet. That is certainly a rarity for The Fall. We have never really got on with anyone since Step Forward, I guess. But Beggars . . . well, they know what they are doing and they certainly seem to understand what it is we are doing and how much control we need and all that kind of obvious freedom stuff. They do the hard work in the background and leave us to chart our own course. We may make mistakes by doing that. I will certainly admit that, but, in making mistakes, you then start to find yourself moving in another direction. The mistake

Mark in the late 80's. "I don't socialise that much though, I spend most of my time avoiding people if I can and avoiding the music industry above all, 'cos I hate all that rubbish." (*LFI*)

The Fall as yuppie dream! (l-r) Simon Wolstencroft, MES, Hanley, Scanlon. (*Steve Double/Retna*)

Shane McGowan, MES and Nick Cave, *NME* summit, 1989. Would make for an interesting evening! (*Bleddyn Butcher/Rex Features*)

Extricate - The Fall in 1990. MES, Bramah, Scanlon, Wolstencroft, Marcia Schofield, Hanley.
(*Ebet Roberts/Redferns*)

"I Want You": Mark with Inspiral Carpets on *Top Of The Pops*, 1993. (*BBC*)

Belligerent with Bracewell. A culture clash at the ICA, 8 March 1994. (*Harry Borden/IPG*)

Three girl Fall. Brix (and pug) returns with Julia Nagle (left), Steve Hanley, MES, Karl Burns and Lucy Rimmer. A curious dynamic, to say the least. (*Hayley Madden/SIN*)

Mark posing for an *NME* feature, 'Pop Stars In Suits', 1997. (*Steve Double/Retna*)

"The Fall are always different, always the same. They are the band by which, in our house, all things are measured" - John Peel. (*LFI*)

"I have never held any truck with the notion that rock'n'roll is an easy option for people, because it isn't. Not if it is done correctly. Not if it is done for the right reasons…" (*Mick Hutson/Redferns*)

With lifelong friend, Michael Clarke. The two had worked together on the play and album, *I Am Kurious Oranj*, in 1988. "I regarded it as a very satisfactory experiment," said MES. "I was aware that we would attract criticism, and I didn't care a shit about that." (*Philip Meech/Retna*)

Accepting the *NME*'s Godlike Genius Award with sardonic grace. (*Roger Sargent/NME/IPC Syndication*)

"Once something is written I like to either change it or just move on. That is what makes me feel comfortable. That is why so many band members have left because most musicians are lazy and just want to learn something once and play it over and over again. That is never what The Fall would do. That would destroy me." (*Angela Lubrano*)

The Fall in late 2002, (l-r) Jim Watts, MES, Ben Pritchard and Dave Milner (*Red Dawn*)

Onstage in San Diego 2003, with wife Elena on keyboards. (*Cole Coonce*)

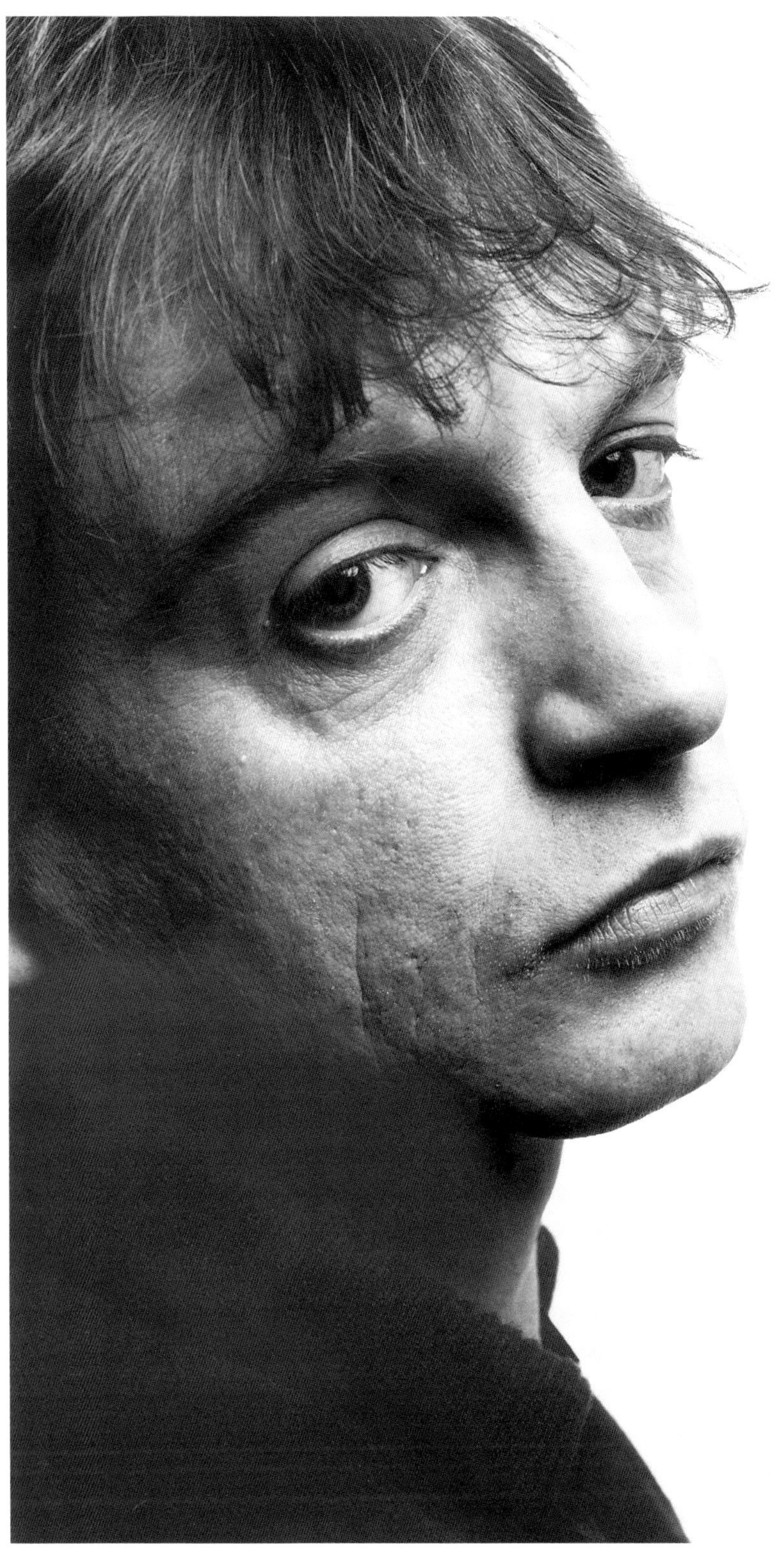

"I'm getting thin... from idiots who write rock books..." (*Harry Borden/IPG*)

becomes part of the overall process. And that's absolutely what we have always wanted to do. And Beggars allow us to do that. And if we decide to do something unusual, Beggars will act quickly and will support us. That takes a certain degree of suss . . . unlike say, well, unlike Rough Trade . . . well, Geoff Travis is just an idiot."

Rolling sweetly around the corner, avoiding those who chide too loudly, avoiding those who Mark deems it necessary to abuse as well, we arrive back at Mark's house, where Brix is tending goldfish and coming across all suburban, watching televised showjumping, her heartland Californian vowels cutting through the Salfordian air. She is hyper, enthusiastic about everything. She wallows in unlikely domesticity. The atmosphere within the house, within the battleship grey walls, is noticeably relaxed. Two cats prowl the carpets, lazily revelling in their dominance.

How did this come to be?

Brix: "You mean, how did I come to meet Mark?"

Well, if you like.

Brix: "It's a long story. I met him in a club where The Fall had been playing. I was all alone and very pissed off at the time. We fell in love immediately. But my love affair with The Fall had begun an awful lot earlier. I had played in a few bands in America and I was getting bored with the scene over there. I mean, I just was. There wasn't anything wrong with it, not locally or across the States, but you naturally get bored with the things you know. You get too comfortable. One of the things that made me start playing in bands was to stop myself getting too comfortable. That's what rock'n'roll is all about and that's why it is also a good thing, in a sense, that most bands struggle. Even bands that are regarded as hit bands often struggle. But it is fantastic because that gives you the edge . . . it gives you the edge when you realise that there are fantastic prizes to get . . . but that was what drove most people on. They want to be rich. But when I came across The Fall, I realised that there was another dimension to it all. That there was something truly valuable that lay way beyond going for the hits. A friend lent me a copy of *Slates*. I didn't know much about The Fall. Actually, that's not true. I didn't know anything about The Fall. When my friend played me *Slates*, at first I thought it was just some more hardcore, because I had been listening to that a lot . . . all the kids had these hardcore records. Which were OK . . . and , no, I hadn't heard of The Fall and then . . . then it just hit me. *Slates* just never left my record deck. I had never heard anything like it in my life. It completely changed my life and the way I felt about music. I must be like . . . well like someone in England hearing 'Anarchy In The UK' for the first time in 1976. I just couldn't understand how a record could sound so . . . so different. It was as simple as that. Because all that hardcore stuff had sounded the same. I knew instantly that I just had to meet the band. There was no two ways about it. I set my sights on The Fall straight away. And then, the moment I met Mark, I fell in love. And I think he did too. That was a bit of a surprise because, despite what a few people might say about me, I didn't approach The Fall with a view to getting in bed with one of them. That never crossed my mind. That came as much a surprise to me as to anybody else."

Kay Carroll: "No . . . I mean, Brix. C'mon, maan. It was fucking obvious what happened there. I'm not attacking her personally . . . as I don't know her. But she is one of those typical American girls who know what they want and just go and use their sexuality to the hilt to get it. I'm not even saying that is a bad thing. But I know that is what happened. She just wanted to marry a rock'n'roll star. And that's what she ended up doing. Marrying a rock'n'roll star. It was as simple as that."

Brix appeared oddly shy on this day, our first meeting. Quite the antithesis of my expectation which was some kind of blonde hair, blonde teeth, blonde life, go-getter girl, with savage blank-out lines reserved for those not famous enough to warrant her attention, for those who would waste her time. That was the image, at least, though it didn't seem to equate with the girl in front of me. Even her blonde hair had, on this day, been tucked inside an oriental black wig, and her famed precocity was also hidden behind some darkness, some domesticity. She seemed perfectly at home. Safe, perhaps, in the knowledge that her ferocious ambition had recently split into two, allowing her solo ego to be soothed by her activities in her own band, The Adult Net, a not altogether unbecoming troupe of varying musicians from the shadows of other Manchester bands.

But she seemed curiously simplistic, owning up to harbouring heroes, among them the barefooted runner Zola Budd, a curious choice I thought; surely not because she decked Decker – Mary, that is, the ultimate symbol of American blonde ambition?

And animals. Brix adores animals, takes daily horse rides across Heaton Park, yet otherwise rarely venturing out. In fact, this *intense* Brix-orientated period would see Mark venturing out less and less, not even into Salford's teaming hostelries . . . well, not so much as before, not every night anyway. Mark and Brix, perhaps understandably considering the number of seedy nightclubs their job took them to, seemed perfectly happy to exist quietly, in a curious calm, with Mark sipping whisky and scribbling lyrics, with Brix playing with the cats, with Brix asking Mark to kiss the cats goodbye before leaving to procure fresh stocks of cigarettes. Cosiness abounded . . . yes?

Mark: "Yeah, yeah . . . content . . . yeah . . . very content. I am making a living doing what I like and I work bloody hard at it. Always have done. That's the trouble with so many bands. They see rock'n'roll as an excuse to fucking laze about all day, as a soft, easy option. And it's not. Not if done properly."

Well you would expect that, that work ethic seeping through the cracks of a rock'n'roll lifestyle once more. That and the continuing mistrust of the music press. Here it comes again.

Mark: "Well, the *NME* can only put us in the same little box all the time. They need us more than we need them. I always used those right-wing comments to wind them up because I always knew how narrow-minded they were. I remember all those Dave McCullouch pieces in *Sounds*. He would come up to see us on his 200 quid a week staff job . . . he would drink my last cup of soup and would go away and tell the world that we had sold out. He just didn't know what he was talking about. I was glad, actually, when he fell to earth and went on the dole. I was glad when he tried to change everything by running a record label – by instigating Blanco Y Negro – and, you know, he just couldn't do it. It just proved everything to me. People find it so easy to knock us but they couldn't do it themselves, not in a million fucking years."

The Hacienda, Manchester. October 9, 1985

Mansion/instrumental blast/Bombast/Couldn't Get Ahead/
What You Need/The Man Whose Head Expanded/Barmy/L.A./
Dktr. Faustus/2 x 4/I Am Damo Suzuki/Gut Of The Quantifier/
Spoilt Victorian Child/Kicker Conspiracy/Lay Of The Land

Three months on and despite a seemingly invigorated set, in contrast to The International, within The Hacienda's enveloping cool, it just didn't gel. *The Wonderful And Frightening World Of The Fall* was pared down and settled into the live set, but although they appeared spirited, intense even, The Hacienda drained their energy.

Before the gig, deep within the rubber, chrome and ironic glamour of the dressing rooms – certainly more prestigious in terms of feel, style and ambience than The International's hideous backstage huddle of decayed teak tables – Brix was hamming it before the mirror, pouting and posing to fun effect. But there had been some kind of an altercation. Steven Hanley and Craig Scanlon were sulking in the corner, Mark was scowling at a journalist, one of those oikish "eerrr I might be doing this for the *NME* . . ." types, fired by enthusiasm, devoid of questions, desperately fighting to feel at home. Generally and famously, Mark treats such grasping youngsters very well indeed, even dropping a few headline grabbers for good measure, adopting the traditional wisdom handed down from clued-up rock stars through the ages (Lennon, Townshend, Bowie) that the chances of a piece being published and occupying plenty of column inches would be greatly enhanced if it were blessed with contentious quotes. It's not so inspiring, backstage at The Hac, where Mike Pickering hangs in the shadows, explaining his liking for house music, bemoaning the fact that his own musical excursions always seemed to hit the rocks of record company apathy, explaining all this to an unconcerned Fall. (Of course, Mike P's angst would be softened by the million-selling success of M People – but that was a universe away.)

This was The Fall under par. Odd, as I had visited their Boardwalk rehearsal rooms two days earlier, and found high spirits and gleeful antics . . . Brix in a wig and Mark looking on lovingly, or so it had seemed.

On stage at The Hacienda they, too, hit a few rocks. Later, downstairs in the Kim Philby bar, Mark and Brix still managed to enjoy the flush of star treatment, encircled by vulture-like fanzine editors. It was a good time, we all felt, to test the power of the club's appalling cocktail menu. And so we did. End of story.

Dancing To Distraction

U.S. 80'S–90'S

Had a run-in with Boston Immigration
And to my name had an aversion
Nervous droplets
Due to sleeping tablets

No beer
No cigarettes
Slam, spikes, gin, cigarettes
Beer in ban

The cops are tops

Welcome to the 80's–90's
Welcome to U.S. 80's–90's

I'm the big-shot original rapper
But it's time for me to get off this crapper

Welcome to the U.S. 80's–90's

No beer
No cigarettes
Spikes, gin, cigarettes
Whisky

The Fall

Like cones of silence

Welcome to the U.S. 80's–90's
Like 50s, 1890s

Kentucky dead keep pouring down
By death stadium
No more amused dressing room
My ambition, but one chance in three million Jack
Like cones of silence

Cast aside over-inflation theory of the panic insists
Welcome to the U.S. 80's–90's
Look at page 19, small column, lower right-hand side
Welcome to the 1980s

I think I was snottily perusing the pages of *The Face* magazine when I first encountered the name Michael Clarke. We were not in a good humour by this time – mid-Eighties – we had long since tired of the fact that *The Face*, initially an excellent and innovative rock magazine fuelled by the enthusiasm of editor Nick Logan, had succumbed to the vagaries of the fashion world and, within the cleanliness of designer Neville Brody, had twisted into a Covent Garden hi–fash rag, where music fell swiftly from grace. No chance then of encountering the likes of The Fall within these pages. For my part, having written a few dodgy articles for the early editions, I sighed meekly and looked for other places to write about . . . or read about . . . The Fall.

But, obviously, I still sneaked a peak at *The Face*. There he was, prancing around with a plastic penis. I probably sneered. Typical *Face* crap. Give me Bury. Give me a badly dressed indie outfit.

Michael Clarke, who was 22 at the time, spent his formative years in Aberdeen, hence the Highland Fling, it seems. At 13, his talent was shimmering enough to catch the attention of The Royal Ballet, who offered him a place at their coveted White Lodge, an establishment dedicated to transforming ugly ducklings into, and sometimes literally, dancing swans. Four years later, Clarke opted to join the rather more *moderne* Ballet Rambert, who seemed more solicitous of his growing avant-garde muse. By the time he had touched his twenties, his talent had taken him to New York and Paris under the tutorage of Karole Armitage, who created the backdrop for Clarke's punkish notions of modern dance. Some called it postmodernism. Personally, I never understood what on earth that meant, let alone cared. But Clarke's reputation grew and, within him, a desire to take dance to the more remote outposts of modern music. Hence, his seeking out one of his ultimate modern musical heroes, Mark E. Smith.

Clarke, and the dance company that had formed around his talent, began to experiment and soon included one or two dances to Fall songs within their touring repertoire. It seemed an odd combination, to say the least: the delicacy of ballet, albeit of the 'postmodernist' ilk, and the raw edges of The Fall. Nevertheless, it seemed to work well and they soon started filtering songs from *The Wonderful And Frightening World Of . . .* into their programme.

Mark. "I really liked Michael's work from the start. I got asked a lot of questions about it. About how Michael came from a completely different world than us. How can someone from London's dance scene be into The Fall in the first place. You would have to ask him that. I never thought of it as camp, to be honest. Michael was doing something that was very theatrical and that appealed to me because I had been thinking about the theatrical side of things a bit more. And we went to see Michael dancing to Fall songs, and it all seemed perfectly natural to me."

Clarke was attracting mountains of venomous press by this time, but perusing dance notices in *The Guardian* wasn't a favourite pastime with the black bedenimmed Mancunian rock audience of the mid-Eighties. Had we done so, and had we read the words of Dick Witts, by now fleetingly writing for Manchester's *City Life* magazine, we would have realised that Clarke had split the dance fraternity, whoever they may have been, into two jagged chunks, old and new wave. In rock speak he was Pistols to Zeppelin, brilliant, iconoclastic and, apparently, well worth talking about, if not actually seeing in the flesh. And many did see him, in London, in Edinburgh and, soon enough, in Manchester. Audiences were flocking to see Michael

Clarke, all camped up with curiosity provided by writers such as *The Guardian*'s Mary Clarke, who opined: "Michael Clarke, idol of the media (Royal ballet rebel) is packing them in at London's Riverside Studios, as he does everywhere else, but why all the fuss? He is a wonderful dancer. Highland as well as ballet, but what he dances is shocking only in that it is such a sinful waste of a good dancer."

And, rather sweetly I think, in the *Financial Times*: "Mr Clarke makes a form of punk dance responding to the ear-splitting din provided by a group called The Fall (who still have a long way to plummet) with costuming for Mr Clarke and his partner by Leigh Bowery, which contrives to be crassly transvestite without the wit or street chic of punks' infantile regalia."

Wonderful. Love the phrase 'infantile regalia'.

Michael Clarke and Company would twice bring their artistry to Manchester's Royal Northern College of Music, where they would dance beautifully to the music of The Fall and, on their second visit, to Ljubljana punk heroes Laibach. It was fascinating, too, to gaze across and watch an audience every bit as bizarre as the music . . . and the dancing . . . and the reaction between one and the other.

Hey! Luciani

Down by The Thames, with a backdrop of Hammersmith Bridge, is a building where things happen, a building crammed with the screaming ghosts of a thousand television egos, and where canteen staff – should they not recognise you as some bit-part actor from the shadows of *Minder* – several episodes were filmed in and around this location – will eternally pour scorn on ragged northern nobodies. This is Riverside Studios where, 20 years earlier, The Sex Pistols, with equipment nicked from nearby Hammersmith Odeon, would steal rehearsal space and, much later, Chris Evans' tyrannical control over Ginger Productions would transform the concept of televised sycophancy and post-pub lunacy.

It was therefore quite the most bizarre setting, one might reasonably presume, for Mark Smith and The Fall to present *Hey! Luciani*, the alternative play that expanded from the confines of the song,

'Hey! Luciani', a typical Mark-ish plot, where reality leaked into the absurd, and streaks of dark surrealism are allowed to further fog the entire affair. The initial plot involves the poisoning of Pope John Paul I after he had tried to revolutionise the papacy and stamp out the Vatican's unholy involvement in protection rackets, drug trafficking, gun running and general organised crime. This whole tumble of 'facts' – and they were facts too – were culled from Mark's fascination with David Yelland's book, *In God's Name*, detailing this particular Papal scandal.

And what better arena than a theatrical community where basic affectation had twisted into the realms of the perverse, where all notions of reality had flown out the window, and the luvviness that pervaded the stages of London, from The Barbican to Hammersmith, had lodged firmly in the minds of every bearded, corduroy-clad *Guardian* reading thinker in theatreville? What better arena for a Mark E. Smith play? Scoff all you like, but at least he would get a fair reception from this lot, who are at the very least well accustomed to being confronted by the avant-garde (unlike, it should be noted, the rock audiences of Britain who, contrary to common belief, tend to be quite astoundingly conservative – be they Mancunian or Glaswegian, they just want to rock). But transpose The Fall into the theatre and curious things would happen in December 1986, at Hammersmith's Riverside Studios where *Hey! Luciani*, Mark's first play, would settle into the arena of theatrical notices, for better or worse.

Rather poetically, as the audience were chewing their sushi in some chromed Hammersmith eaterie, Mark would be encamped in The Blue Anchor, a noteworthy Thameside establishment in the shadow of Hammersmith Bridge that supplies a wide variety of real ale to muscular oarsmen, more often than not served up by tanned, blonde, beautiful Australians, a state of affairs that instilled within Mark E. Smith, the germ of another idea, another song.

'Hey! Luciani', as I stated, is a song, but Fall songs have a tendency to stretch beyond their format and ask questions, stir the imagination. Sometimes, as would soon be the case with Mark's second on-stage theatrical event, *I Am Kurious Oranj*, the song in question would dip deeply into Mark's fascination with history. History is important to

Mark E. Smith. It fuels his muse. It stirs his imagination. It's there, always, embedded into his every thought. Some might say, and they often do, that history pulls and tugs at everybody . . . alas, if only it did. One of the great tragedies of Britain at this point in time is the generation who have evolved without, it so often seems, any grasp of historical value whatsoever; lost, shallow, drifting – a whole generation watching pop video porn, over and over again, with no notion or remote interest in how they came into being. Mark E. Smith, by sheer weight of his writing, has always railed against this. Historical figures have always made shadowy entrances into his songs. At times, it might be noted, they can be rather superfluous but, more often than not, they will add fire, depth and intrigue. (Too much grasp of historical fact, with no sense of objectivity can, of course, be even more dangerous . . . see 'Powder Keg'.)

So 'Hey! Luciani' was a song expanded, pushed out to the limits with some comedic props: a toytown papal balcony, a deathbed, an igloo, and indeed, and famously, Michael Clarke dancing the devil. On the most immediate level, the spectacular was impossible to ignore, if impossible to decipher. Weird stuff happened. Glam commandoes fronted by a gun-toting, body-stocking clad Brix – certainly a twist on the standard image of The Fall – with a prance of Leigh Bowery and Mark unleashing torrents of extraordinary word-play. "Caterpillars, full and wriggling, with translucent suckers and tail hairs about my size . . ."

A dummy of Martin Bormann slid into place. An overhead screen displayed images of . . . well of vomit, hands in chains, mutilation, fire, maggots feasting on eyes . . . and why do maggots always seem to feast on eyes?

HEY! LUCIANI

Arboretum.
I said Luciani
The future's here today
I said Hey! Luciani
Pope of three three days

The Whole World Is A John Peel Session

They made out you were an ultra nut
And had no time for your Christianity
You paid with your life for their treachery
The future's here today
The future's here to stay
Luciani

Hey! Luciani
Jesus has gone away
I said Hey! Luciani
Meet the Church, Bank, S.A.

They said you were of peasant stock
And one day the curia murdered you
Your hermeneutics are through
And on that fruited plain
The corporate bishops' graze
Exit church of poverty and pain
The future's here today
The future's here to stay

Hey! Luciani
A pop star in your cell
I said Hey! Luciani
A Polish son of Hell

You were the first John Paul I
How is it your 'Christian' is gone?
Can you see it from your grave?
The TV snowstorm on top,
The brass Holy Grail
Imitation for sale
The future's here today
Luciani

And all the cowls are black
On an inquisition rack
The future's here today
The future's here to stay
Luciani

The *NME* – represented by the Peak District resident and television head Len Brown – refused to be sucked into the vortex, and offered a heavy slice of considered critique by dismissing it as a "heap of shite" which would be an admirable viewpoint if delivered by a brickie from Dagenham but rather odd from someone immersed in the lunatic vagaries of Granada Television.

Nevertheless, in writing and presenting *Hey! Luciani*, there is no doubt that Mark opened himself up to understandable criticism. Where his writing works to eerie perfection within the realms of a song, it should be noted that a play demands too much from the audience and it's difficult to deliver lines like "the Earth is made up of Terylene patches" (think about that for a second) without laying yourself wide open to condemnation. Then again, you could always relax and simply watch the spectacle, watch Leigh Bowery and Brix Smith and Michael Clarke and Mark E. Smith and simply accept the entire thing for the unfathomable spectacle it was. *Hey! Luciani*, I propose, was actually a triumph, although I can fully understand those who refused to travel across the divide from song to play.*

I Am Kurious Oranj, London, Sadler's Wells

Then there was the second in the double bill where The Fall, sensing the extraordinary in the realms of theatrical absurdity, simply 'went for it'. All was colour and bombast, a virtual onstage whirling kaleidoscope, where the historical notion of a play about Dutch King William of Orange's 300th anniversary of his ascendancy to the English throne – well, that exact notion – did tend to drift a little amongst the colour and splendour. Or maybe that was the point, after all.

Michael Clarke, Leigh Bowery, The Fall. One of these three entered garbed as a tin of Heinz Baked Beans. Brix was pouting and

* Actually, there are plenty of Fall songs that might be similarly expanded. Indeed, tell me there isn't a play within 'Spectre Vs. Rector', 'Dead Beat Descendant' or 'I Am Damo Suzuki'. Just a thought.

preening while exemplifying the American dream, dressed in a swimming costume and sitting astride a giant Big Mac. It was spectacle, whether one could make sense of it, or not. But as the night wore on, and as the basic, raw music of The Fall seeped into the Sadler's Wells' rafters, it became clear that it was less of a spectacle, less of a theatrical event in any kind of traditional way, and more an experiment, once again, in stretching the songs until they became inhabited by figure and colour and lovely madness. Although many remained bewildered, it had become clear that this was The Fall in a new context. True to their innovatory heart, they had charged the boundaries. If nothing else and, if taken in the correct spirit, it was iconoclastic.

Whatever it was, it was clear that any charges of a new polished Fall, a sell-out, a softening . . . any of these recurring charges would be banished from the confused and confusing array of notices that would follow in broadsheets and music press alike in its wake. Cool, though, how the whole thing was based around the still sheer primitive edges of the music. Dance may have been the medium but if you closed your eyes and dreamt that you were back in some darkened cellar club, drinking stomach-churning beer, if you did that, it was sheer, hard ass rock'n'roll. And there is a great moment, from the *I Am Kurious Oranj* video, where the viewer is urged to do just that, and allow the simple backbeat of 'Wrong Place, Right Time' to simply take control.

And it was primitive, too. At times, the music surged back to the beautiful primal thrust of the Velvets – which didn't quite transfer, sadly, onto the accompanying album – and it was captivating to see how, in particular, Michael Clarke and his troupe coped with it all.

Mark: "I don't really like speaking about the plays. It was a perfectly natural expansion for me, and they worked on a level that satisfied me totally. It was great to see The Fall surrounded and helped by such a lot of really talented people. Some people got it, some people didn't. It was always going to be that way. I never saw them as any kind of new direction though. In everything we do, we use imagination so, in a way, it wasn't anything different for us. But I was conscious that it could have got out of hand if we continued down that line. I was quite determined to get back to basics. But it was a fantastic time, for us."

***I Am Kurious Oranj* (Beggars Banquet LP). October 1988**

New Big Prinz/Overture From 'I Am Curious Orange'/Dog Is Life/Jerusalem/Kurious Oranj/Wrong Place, Right Time/C.D. Win Fall 2088 AD/Yes, O Yes/Van Plague?/Bad News Girl/Cab It Up!

It passed almost without notice but *I Am Kurious Oranj* came during The Fall's tenth anniversary as a recording unit, and it remains intriguing to see the length of that journey, from Una Baines' out of tune twiddling on 'Bingo Master's Breakout' to the full-blown production of *Oranj* at Sadler's Wells. Who would have thought? Who would have seen the route from punk to Shakespearean grandeur . . . yes, I tease a little, but Sadler's Wells proved an intriguing breakthrough into a broadsheet land, where some people in the audience would stroke their chins and, no doubt, chat about the performance over a full-bodied claret during the following weekend's dinner parties. Had The Fall finally gained respectability, albeit in the Bohemian edge of Hampstead? Personally, I prefer to just put it all down to a little playful experimentation on Mark's part. Not too many Salfordian plumbers down the Sadler's Wells.

Mark: "I regarded it as a very satisfactory experiment. I was aware that we would attract criticism, and I didn't care a shit about that. I knew, also, that we would be watched by a whole lot of people who perhaps had never heard a Fall song before, and what, exactly, is wrong with that? Again, I say that when you make music that is not in tune with commerciality, and ours never has been, you have to work really hard. I wanted to see how we could expand things; I wanted to know what would happen. It wasn't, in effect, a deliberate ploy to get into a new area. It was just fascinating to see how very clever people, like Michael and Leigh, could interpret it, and they did it . . . brilliantly, actually."

I Am Kurious Oranj, for the record, is based loosely around a commemoration of the bloodless coup by the top protestant in Europe against the controlling Catholic hierarchy. A historical statement, maybe and, although Mark has always enjoyed tinkering with the dark fringe of religion, it would be foolish to read too much into that side of things. More mischievously, the whole thing harked back to a time when people didn't mess about.

Mark: "That's right. They had the right idea. If a king was crap, they got rid of him. We could use some of that spirit today."

The first and last thing one notices about the *Kurious Oranj* album was its unlikely accessibility. If anything, the overriding theatrical context actually serves to muddy the waters a little. This was a warm-hearted rock record and the paradox at the album's heart remains hugely entertaining. If the production of *I Am Kurious Oranj* showed The Fall extending to vast artistic proportions – a dangerous game, should the notion of a concept hover too near – conversely, the album held a 'back to basics' air. Was that irony deliberate?

Mark: "We like to tease."

It might be noted that once past the title track and the garish orange sleeve – not so dramatic on the CD – the actual concept of *I Am Kurious Oranj* does tend to fade completely. Indeed, had there never been a Sadler's Wells extravaganza, had Mark not dragged poor old William of Orange kicking and screaming into the music press and broadsheets, then this would just have been regarded as another Fall album blessed with a curious title track. Hints might leak through here and there, but one hardly feels as though one is sitting through a history lecture. Some extraordinary lyricism triggers the nerves a mite. Of particular note was Mark's megaphone bark on 'Dog Is Life' (he always did enjoy the notion of a megaphone), which saw him dipping sweetly into "Pet dog, bullshit dog, shit and baby but ass lick dog . . ."*

* Mark E. Smith has a deep aversion to anything remotely canine. Always a 'cat' man, he once lingered for 20 minutes on the stairs of my house, playing cheerily with my two bemused black'n'white cats. "Mick, your cats are boooootifoool." Once, sitting in The Foresters Arms in Prestwich, a local toady Fall fan approached him with the words, "It's great that dog, isn't it Mark?" to be swiftly rebuffed by Mark's, "No it fucking isn't . . . it's the worst thing about this pub, that fucking filthy dog . . . wish they would get rid of it and get a cat!"

"Check the record, check the record, check the guy's track record," goes the chant that precedes the opening track, 'New Big Prinz', and while nobody really knows if it refers to William of Orange or Mark himself – arguably both – it would echo down the years and surface like an old friend during a hundred Fall gigs, occasionally performed by passers-by such as Ed Blaney or no small number of Fall fans attempting to catch the vibe of Jon The Postman and what's more, the album's finest track 'Cab It Up!' appeared to be about congestion and idiocy of London life and, indeed, the arrogance of Londoners who cast a cynical smirk at any kind of northern edge. No bile, really, just a simple, simple pisstake!

NEW BIG PRINZ

Rockin' records
Rockin' records
Rock the record
Rockin' records
The guy's rock records

Big priest

Rockin' records
Rock the records
Rock rock records

Drink the long
Drink the long draught
Drink the long draught for big priest

Drink the long draught down
Drink the long
Drink the long draught
Big priest

He is not (appreciated)

The Whole World Is A John Peel Session

Drink the long
Drink the long draught
Drink the long draught for big priest

Rock the records
Check the record
Check the guy's track record
Check the record
Check the guy's track record

DOG IS LIFE/JERUSALEM

You don't see rabbits being walked down the street
And you don't see many cats on leads
Dogs pet dogs dogs rapacious wet dogs
Owner of dogs slow-witted dog owner
Owner of rabid dog saving fare for tunnel
Euro-dream of civil, civil liberation for dogs
Society secret society inevitable nightmare
Of drift dog pet dogs street bullshit
Dog shit baby bit ass-lick dog mirror
Dead tiger shot and checked out by dog
Big tea-chest-fucker dog
Black collar sends East German refugee back switch and crap pathetic
Of earth-like lousy dog role model for infidel doghouse continent
Most citadel dog-eye mirror hypnotic school slaver and learn
Rot from dog on grass and over nervous delicate dog
Detracts light from indiscrepant non-dog-lover
Dog pet dog come home to ya
Come home we'll talk shit to ya
Dog the pet-owner-owner blistered hanging there death dog
Plato of the human example and copier dogmaster pet mourner
Dog is life

And did those feet in ancient times,
Walk upon mountains green?
And was the holy Lamb of God,
On England's pleasant pastures seen?

The Fall

And did the Countenance Divine,
Shine forth on clouded hills?
And was Jerusalem
In the dark Satanic Mills? [1]

JERUSALEM

It was the fault of the government
I was walking down the street
When I tripped up on a discarded banana skin
And on my way down I caught the side of my head
On a protruding brick chip
It was the government's fault
It was the fault of the government
I was very let down
From the budget I was expecting a one million quid handout
I was very disappointed
It was the government's fault
It was the fault of the government

I became semi-automatic type person
And I didn't have a pen
And I didn't have a condom
It was the fault of the government
I think I'll emigrate to Sweden or Poland
And get looked after properly by government

Jerusalem

Bring Bow of burning gold:
Bring Arrows of desire:
Bring me Spear: O clouds unfold!

And though I rest from Mental Fight,
And though sword sleeps in hand
I will not rest til Jerusalem is built

In Englands green and pleasant Land.

WRONG PLACE, RIGHT TIME

Wrong place right time
I used to think I could do what I wanted to
Right time for me alone
Walk the streets of complete full homes

Wrong place, but I'm bound
To stick with what I intend to see through
See you, in wrong place
Right time but there's miles in between

I keep on knocking but there's no bugger in
I have to sing gothic, boo hoo

See me, a new reign
A new reign not to be forgotten
Right place, right time
Right time and Britain is mine
That day, on way
And all peasants will know Oranj

Peasants smile: big shine
Very happy under rule of Oranj
You can whine under rule of Oranj

Mike Clarke: sez I bastard
He is deranged, I am William of Oranj
Go insane in Holland!
I can't wait to taste anthrax turf again
Big Wren: homage Oranj
I am Oranj I have paid dues to the one
Who's #1 in heaven
As in Heaven so in Britain
(By Oranj I am Oranj I am one)

Can't dance can't sing
Cursed forever is William of Oranj
Can't dance can't sing

Cursed forever is William of Oranj
Can't dance can't sing
Cursed forever is William of Oranj
Can't dance can't sing
Cursed forever is William of Oranj
Cursed forever is William of Oranj
Cursed forever is William of Oranj
Cursed forever is William of Oranj
Cursed forever is William of Oranj

Notes from the Theatrical Programme from the Kings Theatre, Edinburgh:

Mark E. Smith is the leader and main songwriter of The Fall group, and under his steerage they have released 14 LPs, including bootlegs. He was born in Salford in 1958 and left his job on the docks there to form The Fall at the age of 18. An eternal thorn in the side of rock music and its press, it is claimed he has single-handedly changed the course of underground music with his pen and sheer bloody-mindedness. The Fall to him is life and passion through which he can filter his original words, music and ideas. There are no rules and boundaries in his group. He has had a lyric book published in Germany and in 1986 he wrote and directed the play "Hey! Luciani" (The Times, Life and Codex of Albino Luciani), a music comedy which centres around the mysterious death of Pope John Paul I, a brave work relentlessly plagiarised since by scores of 'new' US novelists and moribund UK pop acts. "Rock music is too easy for people," he states, "yet the possibilities are infinite." A history buff and admirer of Michael Clarke, "I Am Curious, Orange" spawned the idea of a thematic delving into the foibles and little-known psyche of William of Orange.

The Fall released their first album in 1979. Renowned for their innovatory qualities, they still remain unique and apart, begrudgingly admired by a rapidly decomposing 'rock' world for their omnipresent influence on music plus musicians of all ranges and ages. Led since the beginning by Mark E. Smith, lyricist/vocalist and feared commentator, The Fall surprisingly notched up three top 40 singles in 1987/88. Their latest line-up consists of six people, all of whom are creative composers, average age 24 years old.

Personnel: Mark E. Smith (lead vocal/Type FX), Stephen Hanley (bass guitar), Brix Smith (lead guitar/vocals), Craig Scanlon (rhythm/acoustic guitar), Marcia Schofield (keyboards/FX) and Simon Wolstencroft (drums). Described as the definitive British group and the only English group worth listening to, The Fall nevertheless contain two US citizens, Brix and Marcia, who in the past two years have added a unique creative angle that is fringed with a spot of glamour. Their latest release is "The Frenz Experiment" LP (February 1988). Brix also touts her own group, the Adult Net. "I Am Curious, Orange" is the first live collaboration entered into with Michael Clarke and Company, and heralds yet another dynamic period in Fall history.

JOE TOTALE XV, Vancouver. May 1988

Sandwiched rather strangely between the twin capers of *Hey! Luciani* and *I Am Kurious Oranj* came two years of typically intense Fall activity, spiced by unlikely action in both the singles and album charts. The biggest foray into chart territory undoubtedly arrived with The Fall's celebrated and much loathed cover of R. Dean Taylor's 'There's A Ghost In My House', a suitably perverse choice, perhaps, and enough to establish a faint and unlikely link between The Fall and Tamla Motown, to whom they came within a whisker of signing a couple of years later.*

It nudged its way to number 30 and provided a sudden burst of television exposure – the video even utilised the gothic towers of Mark's favoured watering hole, The Woodthorpe, near Heaton Park. Although Fall purists hated the disc, it built significantly on the earlier success of the 'Hey! Luciani' single (which had reached 59) and certainly paved the way for an excellent run of Fall singles.

* I don't wish to be pedantic, especially if it spoils a good story, but the 'Fall sign to Motown' story has been rather overblown. The label was, in truth, Motown UK, little more than a holding company for its American owner and The Fall interest lay rather more in the fact that it was manned by drifters from the British A&R brat pack – all of whom were big Fall fans – rather than some heartfelt desire on the part of Motown boss Berry Gordy to sign the band.

There was a point here when, after an uneasy gap, I reacquainted myself with Mark and, indeed, Brix. It was a slow process, stemming from a pub in the centre of Manchester, through two Bury New Road establishments, tumbling through three separate interviews along the way and, at one point, threatening to drift too deeply into the afternoon to actually make it intact to the house, to Brix.

"The hit record did make things easier for us," he states philosophically. "Since then it's been better for us when we play. It is weird round here. The people are dead proud of The Fall. They are genuinely pleased for us, which surprised me because, just prior to 'Ghost', I was dreading it. We do get kids standing outside the house, which I've always had to some extent but now it's nine- or ten-year-olds which I don't really like."

There were other breakthroughs this year. I, for one, never thought I'd see The Fall play Reading or, even worse, supporting U2. They only did it to make enough money not to have to work for a while and in the midst of this gig-free period – their first for nine years – The Fall released a single called, rather aptly, 'Hit The North', which saw the band in a fiery hip-hop mood. With a nod towards the scene that had replaced the northern soul phenomenon, 'Hit The North' aimed to take Smith's subversive genius back onto the northern dance floors. It was a noticeably attractive record; is it, I wondered, a play for a second hit? Smith shrugged before admitting: "Yeah, maybe. I don't see why not, there's nothing better up there."

Which is hardly the point, but never mind. There was another project at hand, a new record label which would see Smith delving into his extensive back catalogue.

"The label will be called Cog Sinister Records Limited. The first release, on November 28, will be a compilation of Fall stuff from the Rough Trade period. I don't wish to exploit this, it's simply a way of letting people get hold of old Fall stuff. I have all the old Fall tapes stored upstairs and all the publishing rights. This stems back to the days when I used to rip contracts up. I just didn't believe in them which, I'm telling you, was insanity at the time. But now it's proved worth it. It was worth starving the band for."

Believe me, The Fall have endured their fair share of lean periods. Happily, although hardly encumbered by wealth, Mark and Brix are languishing in hard-earned mild comforts. Brix slides home from an Adult Net practice session in her BMW as, get this, two leather filofaxes sit conspicuously on the table.

Brix exudes ambition. A single-minded, competitive and highly talented lady, she literally shakes with frustration at a minor setback. Apparently the present members of her spin-off band, The Adult Net (amazingly, Mike Joyce, Andy Rourke and Craig Gannon), have displayed a reluctance to go on tour with the unit. The conversation begins to drift towards the sordid demise of Joyce and Rourke's former house of employment, The Smiths. Not wishing to hear the gruesome details I drag Mark E. Smith out and away in the general direction of the local off-licence. Outside in the street a gang of repulsive 13-year-olds search for ways of causing pointless trouble. Mark E. Smith looks on with an uncharacteristically wistful air.

"I used to be just like them, causing trouble in the streets. I used to think it was really good."

He is openly proud of these kids and their unpretentious local suss. Unlike certain other Mancunian stars, Smith has not evolved into a paranoiac tragedy. He has more sense than that. He is, quite uniquely, unchanged.

Extricate. February 1990

Sing! Harpy/I'm Frank/Bill Is Dead/Black Monk Theme Part I/ Popcorn Double Feature/Telephone Thing/Hilary/Chicago, Now!/ The Littlest Rebel/And Therein . . .

Slap bang in the centre of Madchester. Crazed bums in the alleys, beer-gutted dancers in The Hacienda, Japanese 'Smiths' fans wandering around Stretford, every gawky student in town perfecting a manic dance to 'She Bangs The Drum', wild green eyes in every corner, fluorescent T-shirts in Afflecks Palace clothing emporium. It's respectability for Manchester fashion, there's sombre musos in rehearsal rooms and unholy worship of the DJ. Mark wanted and needed none of it. It was an unwelcome intrusion; a lie, too, and all in the daft pretence of fun.

There had been problems. The vacuum left by Brix, both personal and musical, still weighed rather heavily, even if Mark had moved swiftly on in terms of both love and musicianship. I saw Mark around Manchester a great deal in 1990. He would be haunting the corridors on Princess Street, where his recordings would be tended by record promoter Tony Michaelides, pushing Fall singles on to multitudinous local radio playlists. 'Telephone Thing' hovered over the airwaves in Leeds and Humberside.

Bob Dickinson, local writer, sullen artist, poet, ranter, a cappella singer, radio and television producer, man of the underground and – a rarity in such areas – all-round decent man of intelligence. Dickinson wanted to get The Fall on television, somehow, somewhere and in some crazy format. Bob had spent years attempting to push his curiously reluctant bosses at Granada Television into producing worthy music shows and had almost always come up against doors slammed shut in the wake of Tony Wilson's courageous endeavours. Manchester, such as it was, provided some kind of fresh impetus, although it was too little, too late and too cheap. Madchester had slipped through Granada Television's fingers and, although many who worked there were music orientated, had completely ignored the burgeoning Manchester scene that began in earnest in the mid-Eighties and, left to its own devices, pushed towards some kind of explosion, however irritating.

The Fall, of course, were there all along, boasting 13 years of prominence on the Manchester scene and the world stage, yet they remained largely unsupported by the television giant on the doorstep. OK, there were a few clips, here and there: a televised Fall session for Wilson's *What's On* in the early days; and a short interview, again with Wilson, during the *Frenz Experiment* days. "It was a very worthwhile experiment," said Mark. Nothing to speak of, nothing much to write about.

Then, in 1990, and for reasons that still escape me, Mark decided that if Granada were going to make a film about The Fall, it would have to involve this writer as some kind of wandering quizmaster, hurtling bizarre questions into the mix, with Mark providing off-the-cuff, unscripted answers. We met Bob Dickinson to discuss it down in the Granada canteen and an outline, of sorts, was duly presented and apparently accepted. It was loose, loose as hell actually, but no looser than the actual filming which turned out to be a fiasco. Nevertheless it brought Mark E. Smith into the profoundly undecorated shell of my then house in Romiley, Stockport, where, grabbing cans of Boddingtons and puffing profusely, he slumped over my overworked Amstrad and, with occasional interjections from yours truly, bashed out an extraordinary script, so unworkable that, had Granada accepted it, would probably have succeeded in creating television of a genuinely intriguing nature. Alas, the powers that be, no doubt with good sense, slammed the idea and turned their attention to, oh I don't know, probably Happy Mondays. It didn't matter in the least.

Extricate was the album of the moment.

HILARY

Hilary
Where's the sixty quid you borrowed off me for the gas?
I won't give you a kiss
Hilary
Hey Hilary
New Faces on Saturday at six
brought you back to me
Hilary
I'm sure it was you in the new Audi
Outside Simsbury's
Hilary
Remember when you needed three caps of speed
to get out of bed
and now you're on ecstasy
Hilary
With your daft African pop
and that wine you call bull's blood

Hilary
I thank the lord that you still don't live next to me
Hilary

CHICAGO, NOW!

Do you work hard?
Do you work hard?
You don't!
You don't!
You don't! Chicago, now!
Do you work hard?
Do you try hard?
You don't. Chicago, now!
All is commission time
Commission C.T. time
Set down, setting down
C.T. time
Chicago, now!
Work hard.
Do you try hard?
Dear crew
Try hard.
Chicago, now!
That's it: you don't.
That's it: you don't.
Chicago, now!
Chicago, now!
Step down
Setting down, just setting down
see their butt all over the street
you just go up and meet
Just setting down.
Chicago, now!
Hi-de-hi-de-hi-de-ho.

One of my favourite chunks of Mark E. Smith prose is included here at Mark's request. It's a travelogue and proof, if proof were needed, that a book-length study such as this would be a fine thing indeed. It was from the 'just married to Brix' era and published in the sadly defunct *Melody Maker.*

MUNICH

I asked this bloke why there were no historical things in Munich and he kindly showed me around. I asked him where the 1923 Putsch *was and he pointed it out and then he took me for a drink in the place where the Red Rose was, that was the student underground against the Nazis – the same street where the Nazi party was formed strangely enough.*

He then took us to the Spear Disco at the old Nazi Party headquarters, it was really hard to get in but we were with him so we were OK. It was fine until they knew we were British.

It was very sub-Gothic inside and all made up in the style of 45 years ago. No flags, but pretty much what The Hacienda wants to look like really. The people who run the disco are very protective, they don't let British rock groups in. I don't blame them either.

Bavarian hotel staff are the rudest in the world. They make London hotel staff look almost human. Almost good mannered.

AUSTRIA

In Austria we came across the 1938/88 sculpture which is very smart. When you first see it, it looks like a workman on a ladder fixing the date, then you realise it's just a statue and the first half of the eight is permanently slipped to make it read 1938. Otherwise Austria is very weird. Nobody goes there any more, a lot of people boycott it after that Terence Trent D'Arby thing.

AMERICA

Like Russia, the USA regards any genuine artistic creativity as serious mental illness. Both countries' bands sport clownish uniforms. Both countries contain vast multitudes of bourgeois-like, bored white-collar types balanced off with equal numbers of uneducated meat animals.

The slimy peasant reptile Gorbachov is on everybody's lips. As Brix's

Russian grandparents once pointed out, it's the Russian peasant mentality that . . . like in a Yorkshire town, the guy that's most admired is the guy that's toughest, best at sport, or most handsome; well in Russia it's the guy who can get away with the biggest lies. It's true, anyone will tell you, it's the man who can get away with the biggest bullshit. I'm not saying it's an evil thing, just that it's the way they are.

As in Britain, in America the only stimulation to be had is dwelling over hideous and cowardly crimes and inventing new ones like two and a half million dollar fines for possession of a roach. Culturally moribund Homestead records. Big Black are crap, dude!

CLEVELAND

Met the in-laws, drove all night. Walked all night. Walked right into the black part of Cleveland with Brix's parents and all the bars are full, loads of Jesse Jackson posters. And the in-laws were saying, 'We shouldn't really walk down here,' and this big six foot six guy jumps out of an alley with a leather jacket on, and I'd been going, 'It's alright the English can walk anywhere,' and then this guy jumps out and it looks like he's ready to mug us and I go, 'Uuuuurgh!' And he goes, 'Mark E. Smith, my maan, 'Repetition'.' He'd just seen me through the bar window and turns out he'd been a fan for years. He was quoting from Zig Zag *in '78 and asking me about members of the band who I couldn't even remember.*

As is rapidly becoming the case in the United Kingdom, the US is composed of fine unique people with infinite talents ruled and bullied by indecisive publicity seeking political incompetents who are allied with the hopeless and un-intelligent media, bullshit academics, and a Martian-like led civil service.

There's a senile generation existing and a Pete Townshend one entrenched and still coming in. Inadequate, irreligious groping about in Eastern liquefied thought, 'health' adoration, bastardised conservatism, filtered through Catholic/German religious hang-ups. Devoted to only one cause: the equalisation and standardisation of the human into some form of meat animal. This is only how I see it sometimes!!!!

Back 10 hours in England. Off to the shops I pass the butcher and painter and decorator fixing a car. "How are you?"

"Not bad, I'm knackered, I've just been on tour for ages."

"You liar," they said. "We know you're really off to the pub."

I am seriously moved. It's nice to have someone be seriously nice to you, because in the States you have to pay them to be nice to you. I don't mean that, because I like Americans, but you get this 'soul' thing.

We tour with Luxuria who are a fine bunch of men if too obviously Brits in America. I avoid conversation with them as they talk about Oscar Wilde, Kerouac and Julian Cope in loud voices. They're forming some sort of beatnik alliance with Phil and Marcia from our party. In trying to re-educate these victims of hippie lecturers I leave Lenny Bruce scripts, and Franco and Gogol biographies around but to no avail.

There is continual media moaning and harping on about 13-year-old crack dealers. The media doesn't seem to realise that we are in a scoff-law situation here, and if they relaxed their drinking laws people would errm . . . well I don't know what people would do. In bars, as is the usual, all the band were asked for ID. I saw bald people being asked for their ID. No ID, no drink. Explaining that you are one of HM's free subjects usually ends in threats to call the police – the Fascist/Irish Gestapo that passes for a police force in Boston, that miserable city.

I hear the drinking age has been hitched up by another two years in most states, some as high as 23. But again a lot of Yanks don't leave school until they're 32 (i.e. Big Black, Sonic Youth). Brix is classed as a dropout because she left college at 21!

Due to the usual hygiene frenzy accelerated by AIDS the US now finds that voyeurism and masturbation is in. And in otherwise excellent magazines like Forced Exposure *pacifism is touted as some kind of alternative. The views and opinions in this article are not necessarily concurrent with those of other FALL members.*

VANCOUVER

Nice Commonwealth-type people, good to eat real food, but also here as in Britain, there's an exploitation of crime and danger. However, one of the most interesting things about America is the danger, death, excitement and improvisation of the place.

After seven days in the US, THE FALL is sober from rank beer, joke-less and palate-dead. I like the USA, I like the old USA, Buggs Bunny, etc.

TRIP FROM VANCOUVER TO SAN FRANCISCO

Me and Simon in quite a weird state chanting, 'Squid Lord, Squid Lord' beating fly swatters and demanding the sacrifice of Ed, the monitor slag, for working with Marc Almond and Morrissey in the past. And daring to wake up and interrupt our continual playing of the Hairspray *soundtrack. We stop after a 16-hour drive on a sun-drenched beach. Euphoria. The coach driver is nuts as he left England in 1962, and he still has that attitude. Really ancient British attitudes. Really weird how people change. Like another race. Talking about 'Bloody Huns' and 'bloody' this and 'bloody' that, steak 'n' kidney pies.*

It's a shame for the Americans because it's like being on one long ferry crossing for the rest of your life. I've got some great mates there, but you don't feel enriched in any way for going there.

HOLLAND

On arrival write vicious anti-dog rant, although I haven't seen one in ages. What actually sparks it off was hearing English cricket commentary on hotel's TV. This was depressing after the bliss of six weeks of TV in foreign languages, where you can make it up yourself. Was convinced in Austria that the US and Iran were at full-scale war. From past experience do not ask questions about politics in Holland, all you get is deep-world psychiatry of the situation, and its relevance to Holland's world role.

SLOPPY GUIDE TO FOREIGN WRITERS AND MEDIA

The KRAUTS, like me, also make it all up – World War III and penguin's eating habits are of equal importance. All their press men have a healthy nose for pretension. With ruthless mockery their mags take any opportunity to reprint the dafter excesses of UK rock mags, i.e. "The NMEMMSOUNDS says 'This group will resound for years to come' – the man is a mental hermit!" or my personal favourite: "Typically, Smith's play was greeted with incomprehension by the obsolete British bourgeois-liberal art critic establishment!" Yeah! And I don't even know him!

AMERICANS, quite rightly, avoid or can't grasp any form of news except for their superb sports coverage and mind-bending ideas of the finance scribe, who is fused on the astral plane with false real values. Liquid hollow-room projections and indivisible well devouring and/or disobedient real estate. US rock interviewers are on the whole stimulating, but also tiring, being too nosy by half.

GREEK news and its reportage is always perceptive. Their hacks spend most of the time being intellectual superbrains that often leave me gasping in awe. Somehow the typical British Record Mirror, etc. pop lad is in need of basic speech and thought therapy, who thinks that all words are the same thing anyway and join together easily with HA HA HO HE and strings of dots is not in the same Spartan class.

CANADIANS write about interesting detail and seriously worry about British rock and pop morality.

The AUSTRALIAN mainstream writer thinks you've got a cheek messing about putting words on vinyl, etc. 'What's all that about?' they ask when they could be out pulling some pools racket or in NEW ZEALAND's case re-reading Jane Eyre for the 50th time.

Honestly, all FRENCH hacks start by repeatedly saying how unknown, unsuccessful, irrelevant and doomed your career is, in world-leading, modern, Universe-creating frogswamp, and ask you to explain the lack of beatnik imbecility in your Reaganite-Stalanistic, English-thick 'lyric statements'. Walking out or punching out does not work, as they do the same or phone the police. Best action is to ask them what's the bees-knees and then suppress tears of laughter as they gush for hours on the Cure/Bolshoi/Damned's deep, root-tapping of something that is deep inside them, as literal, artistic scarf-wearing frog-spawn – something beyond all words, my pupil Anglais.

The ITALIANS, with true style, only have soccer-news. Their journalists are so cool they have not heard of any group ever, yet know everything about mad obscure artists like their own lot and Lewis, Celine, etc. Quite right.

HOLLAND *continued*

On tour, if alone at night, I knock out lists of things to do – these quickly become hysterical enraged notes packed with vicious unkeepable equipment and spiritual demands of my compatriots. These make hilarious reading in the sober morning, i.e.:

6) EMPHASIS NARRATIVE
NO SPACEY HI-FI CRAP
UNFORMULATED AS ON US TOUR
Or the unbelievable
7) BAND excellent – 100 per cent improvement in sound, group and crew imperative.
10) WHY no change-over? PUNISH
Or: Trevor (Long, tour manager) pop-in and keep EVERYBODY else out. We do not work for them.

On a night off have a convoluted discussion with an acid-house type bloke about merits of Dutch 'freedom' and British 'oppression'. I even broke my 'no talking to men in cycle shorts' rule for this. I've had to hint strongly to our party that 'pot banned on Dutch tour-dates' rule still in force. (Due to worst, and first, Fall show ever in Eindhoven circa 1980.) Send potential rule-breakers on useless errands and tasks. Mainly for our up-and-coming ballet here. Am deliberately being vague about visual theme, mainly because I've no idea, and with clothes, my concentration evaporates after 15 seconds. So, categorically and firmly state: black, white, brown, Amish.

Force Andrew (Berry) into this rule – he is perfect, disappearing 10 hours at a time returning with square metres of useless, cheap material. He is this week's honorary Fall Stylist – hiding any spare clothes out of sight and mischief.

We catch a 6 am ferry with a group who are fronted by a superstar from a famous group (Queen). They shout, and like all Covent Garden rockers, try and be rebellious in public. My Armani pullover is some kind of fashion faux pas to these Canterbury Revenge middle-class hard rockers.

Hilariously and without any prompting they launch into rabid defence about playing with this star, saying how talented they are in their own right, etc. how great he is – he even comes on their bus sometimes. We ask if they have an oxygen tent for these occasions and say he sounds like a fine leader of men.

They are insolent in the main, though, and me and the lads are ashamed to be in the same business, but we're tired as we actually did some work in Europe, and have slight revenge as the young Customs lads appear to be Fall fans and examine us quickly, while HMC detain this mentally retarded other group and search their ridiculous rock steel suitcases and cassette holders. We leave Dover 30 minutes before the justifiably angry seamen of Britain descend and paralyse the port.

"Just look at them, wearing fucking shorts," exclaimed Mark, voicing his disapproval at the *NME* affectation of the day.

We were sitting amid the chrome and wood 'splendour' of Manchester's Factory owned Dry Bar, at some point in the early Nineties, on an occasion – I think – when A Certain Ratio were having some kind of new release bash. All the old wags of rock Mancunia were duly milling and drinking the wine and smiling the smile. Madchester was now just about to fade. "Thank God," we all said, and a trickle of *NME* scribes surrounded a central table. James Brown, flicking hair from his face, resplendent in suitable smugness and, no doubt, enjoying the hedonism that would soon earn him a fortune, and Roger Morton chatting and bobbing with Clint Boon and Gretton and Pickering and Erasmus and Bob Dickinson, CP Lee and Bruce Mitchell. Rather too easily, Mark and I were swallowed into their midst but something rather odd was transpiring here. Tony Wilson, more often than not a gentle soul despite his lovable tendency to shout off at the merest click of a Dictaphone, stormed up to Mark and screamed torrid abuse before storming away, seemingly satisfied. Mark just looked at me and smiled. "I have no idea what that was about . . . hah haaah!"

It was, I suspected, something to do with an earlier sharing of opinions that had occurred while Mark's vision was somewhat clouded by alcohol though Mark genuinely did have 'no idea' what caused the Wilson storm. And it was soon to subside, with the *NME* contingent unaware of it anyway.

"Just look at them, wearing fucking shorts."

Shirts, black shorts, sullen faces!

"They look so self-important, don't they?" humphed Craig Cash, then a young unheard of DJ on Stockport's KFM Radio who hovered near with his close companion, Terry Christian of Stretford, oikish rogue blessed with a sly smile, like Cash, like Vic Reeves and, while we are on the subject, Jeremy Vine.

Ho hum.

But the shorts were an issue. They seemingly rankled.

Mark: "He had shorts . . . that Dele Fedele . . . from the *NME*. Pestering me at Reading. . . ."

At Reading?

Mark: "Reading was . . . well, I wouldn't like to be in that scene. It was really depressing to see 20,000 Quo fans all aged about 35 and all pissed out of their heads. There were about 3,000 people at the front to see us and 20,000 behind them throwing stuff. As far as U2 is concerned, I didn't want to play it. We actually played to do them a favour as the previous band dropped out, but the press attacked us for playing for the money. To feel the hatred from the U2 fans was great. I know U2 are all religious and we must have seemed like a bunch of Satanists to that crowd. They bombarded us but we didn't care, we could handle it. Incidentally, the Mission flopped after us, as they did at Reading . . . ha! Well, the idea was to play those big gigs and then stop playing until January."

It started with a cassette tape, arriving in the post from New Jersey, I think. Or Boston. Must have been 1986/7. I hadn't heard from Kay Carroll for six years or so and neither had Mark. I loved Kay so, despite the fallout it was nice to get the tape. There was a rather lovely letter attached, telling how her family had sent over copies of the *Manchester Evening News*, and she had noticed my name from some story or other and had forged contact via the paper, and she wanted me to listen to the tape.

And so I did.

She was sitting in her living room. Chatting to her lover. And then, into the tape, she told me how she had always felt bad about leaving The Fall in that predicament but . . . well, she had to go. Get out quick, she said . . . and I could hear a waver in her voice, a wobble in her vowels but Kay, bless her, fell into a torrent of Kay-style words that reminded me, so much, of the time she fell into an argument in The Foresters Arms, defending British Royalty and quoting Thomas Hardy to three electricians and a plasterer . . . and I knew that Mark had fallen out with her and, to this day, remains unhappy about what happened but that was beyond my knowledge at the time. It was so lovely to hear her voice – it was a brotherly love, in case you are wondering – and suddenly, she broke away. The television blasted from the corner of the room – Iggy Pop, "It's Iggy. Oh Mick, it's Iggeeeeee!!!! OOOOhhh how weird!!!" she screamed, and the tape clicked to a halt!

Three months later I opened the door of my Romiley flat and there stood Kay, unannounced, complete with beaming smile and boyfriend. Kay and a whole bundle of memories.

It was weird too because I had seen Mark the day before, and we had spoken about Kay. Someone had told him that she was back in Prestwich, seeking people out, but I hadn't expected her in Romiley, Stockport, with boyfriend.

At the pub we melted into wearying nostalgia. Mark wouldn't have liked it.

So I didn't tell him (like the way I wouldn't tell him about my Grateful Dead albums). She was ebullient, though annoyed that, in 1983, we had missed each other in New York. And then I never saw her again.

I mentioned this impromptu visit to Marc Riley during his spell as a record plugger. "She came to see me too," he said. "I think she did the rounds."

But she never went to see Mark.

7

The Avenues Of Influence

There is a Marks & Spencer in Prestwich now, a posh one, too. I suppose it's quite fitting when you think about it. How come it took them so long? The problem is, year by year, day by day, it gets more and more difficult to see the old Prestwich should you wish to, not that I ever have. But even Fall album covers, even Fall songs, seem to scream from a bygone age. It's a concept that would, no doubt, offend Mr Smith. Or maybe not.

Mark: "We've had a lot of Prestwich buildings on our covers over the years. Especially in the early days. They were put there for a reason, an obvious reason, really. It was because I really liked them. They were beautiful buildings and now old Fall album covers are a bit like an archive of old Prestwich because every building I ever have from Prestwich on the back of my covers gets fucking pulled down. The church on *Grotesque* is probably one of the few photographs left of the thing. Like the building on *Elastic Man* was pulled down, the building on . . . which one was it . . . *Hex Enduction Hour*? Was it *Hex*? Yes, that was pulled down; the building on *Dragnet* was pulled down. Hah! I started to get a bit paranoid about it at one stage. I thought we might be the kiss of death. All those buildings that I cherished were just pulled down . . . just like that. We'd come back off tour and another one would be bloody gone."

History, heart, soul . . . all crumbling away in the name of regeneration.

An extraordinary legacy of buildings has enriched the area where an extraordinary array of inter-denominational churches has added a certain poignancy to the area where, to Mark's disgust, one senses, Prestwich was officially classed a 'rural' area until 1901, when Heaton Park and surrounding grounds were sold to Manchester Corporation. It wasn't until after World War One, when the progressive Lloyd George government instigated a 'Homes for Heroes' policy, that the greenbelt land was swiftly transformed into a contemporary estate, the 1920 equivalent of a 'new town' development. The standard architectural features of that era would echo down the ages, adding a distinctive 'feel' to the area; a string 'feel' that has only started to weaken in recent years as the Manchester and Salford regeneration extends along Bury New Road. Nevertheless, that 'feel' remains, and has its affect as soon as you pull off the M62 and drive past the Tesco and Marks & Spencer, deep into the area. The same feel is immortalised on the album sleeves and in the music of The Fall.

It is difficult, perhaps even impossible, to think of a single living artist, in the rock spectrum at least, where a locality is so deeply embedded within their work; within the lyrics, naturally, but, on a more general level, within the flickering thought patterns that inform the work from day one of the band and, in the case of Mark, from before the band. When I was talking to Irene Smith, she told me that Mark had a curious quality, where he would drift off alone, be it when he was reading a book or playing football out on the street; to drift off unconcerned with tending the goal made from two humps of coats in the road, and into an aloof, dreamlike state. He was oikish, grubby and scuff-kneed in the Salfordian tradition, but he was soaking something in, nonetheless.

At the start of this book, and in almost matter-of-fact fashion, I mentioned that while Mark was wandering between Rydal Water and Ambleside, wandering through the black of night, he saw two Druid-like figures deep in the woods that seemed to follow him awhile before drifting back to whatever strange task they had at hand. It was easy to dismiss this for a number of reasons. Partly, one must confess, because the encounter arrived at the end of an evening fuelled by lager and Lagavulin and, as Mark later admitted, fired further by the tight neurosis that arrives when sleep patterns break down. Even Mark acknowledged that it might have been either a student prank – The Lake District is eternally bubbling with such pranks – or little more than the result of his feverish imagination, forced into overtime by lack of sleep. Even if that is the case, then it says an awful lot about an imagination that has spilled over, so entertainingly, so inspiringly into the continuing music of The Fall. If that is all . . . then that is a great deal.

But I sensed then, as I have always sensed around Mark, that there is something more.

Mark doesn't like talking about his psychic edge but spend any reasonable period of time in his company and you will sense that there is something else. I have no idea what it might be. I have not read widely in terms of psychic phenomena and, apart from a few intriguing instances, have no reason to believe that I, too, have any psychic gift whatsoever.

This is frustrating because I can't tune into people. However, there are times when people have tuned into me, and there are times when a message, of sorts, has been received.

There was a curious instance in 1995 in Essex, a county which, for much of the Nineties, featured strongly in my personal life. The pubs that pepper the countryside around Chelmsford saw a great deal of myself during a pre-Britpop lull in my personal musicality, when I was approaching middle-aged tedium with a weakening air of defiance and a growing sense that rock'n'roll was not quite as all encompassing as I had previously believed. (I have since revised that opinion, incidentally. Hence this book. Hence my deep love of rock'n'roll, be it Gene Vincent, The White Stripes, Lucinda Williams or, indeed, The Fall.)

But, for a while, I was lost. Lost in Essex. Which is a terrible place to lose oneself, given the unusually large proportion of males wearing flecked gym trousers and singlets. If the importance of this information is lost on you, may I return to the notion that long-term Fall fans, that strange breed apparently loathed by Mark – though I don't always buy his ageist insistence that one has to be a young blood to be true to the cause – do tend to drift away, sometimes for years, sometimes for over a decade before returning to the flock, no doubt comforted by the knowledge that there really isn't anything better out there; and, no doubt, regretting those drunken nights spent trying to recapture a youthful spirit with a Kula Shaker album and a chunk of bad dope sold to you by a 13-year-old; no doubt wondering what it was that once seemed so exciting and, with The Fall, so illuminating.

And there I was in Essex, driving aimlessly up the A12, from Chelmsford, vaguely in the direction of Colchester to visit a distant relative. I have no idea why I turned left away from the town centre in the direction of the University of Essex. Why would I? It was a traffic light. It may have been nothing more than a sudden dip in concentration, some kind of internal freak-out. I just don't know. But somehow I was pulling to a halt within the university campus. Why should I drive there?

Why did I not curse under my breath, berate myself for making a wrong turn and do a U to get back to where I was going? But I didn't. I parked the car and – I swear – walked across to the student compound where, to my utter astonishment, a poster informed me that The Fall would be performing that very evening. It was too much of a coincidence to ignore. How could I? My distant relative would understand, probably . . . possibly.

This had happened once, just once before, although back then it hadn't involved The Fall. It was back in the punk swirl of 1977, in Manchester. On a Sunday night at The Electric Circus, we had interviewed new-wave pretenders, The Vibrators, in the steamy post-gig dressing room. Four days later, returning from London, shunting up the M6, we decided to pull off the motorway and settle on the nearest pub. And in that pub, somewhere around Stafford, we walked straight into The Vibrators, who invited us to the gig they were playing, that night, at the Top Rank Suite. Weird and weirder still, there never seemed to be any reason behind the coincidence.

And neither was there any particular reason behind the similar affair, in Colchester.

Essex University. March 24, 1990

Error Orrori/And Therein/Jerusalem/Sing! Harpy/I'm Frank/ Telephone Thing/Hilary/Hit The North/Bill Is Dead/Black Monk Theme/Popcorn Double Feature/Dead Beat Descendant/ British People In Hot Weather/Bremen Nacht/Tuff Life Boogie/ Mr Pharmacist

For two hours I mingled meekly in the blackened cube at Essex University. Attempts to gain privileges backstage proved fruitless. With no 'guest list' advantage, I was lost amid a large and swelling crowd, all students, of course, all out for a congenial Saturday night binge, regardless of the band who would grace the stage that night. Could have been Felt, could have been anyone . . . but wasn't. When the time came it was thrilling to see a Fall of Mark E., Craig Scanlan, Steve Hanley and Simon Wolstencroft. I don't recall seeing Martin Bramah, who had returned to fill the post-Brix void but I do recall, most clearly, a thrilling 'Popcorn Double Feature', which instigated a huge stageward sway of sweaty studenthood and an equally thrilling finale courtesy of the eminently danceable, 'Mr Pharmacist', which saw me casting middle-aged reserve to the wind and spinning gleefully into the crowd.

Curiously, when I nudged into this particular post-gig dressing room, Mark greeted me with an astounding degree of nonchalance. "Hey Mark. How yer doin . . . great gig . . . etc." And, no doubt, a string of empty post-gig compliments.

I was greeted with a rather staid, "Oh hi Mick . . . yeah glad you enjoyed it, cocker."

No, "What are you doing in Essex?" No, "Where have you been for three years?" Just nothing beyond a relaxed acceptance, which seemed rather eerie to me. When I mentioned this story to Mark, months later, while sitting – as per – in a downbeat Manchester drinking-den, he merely smiled and added a curious, "Oh yeah. I remember that night. That kind of thing happens quite a lot, to be honest Mick. I never like to make much of it, because I just don't think that people ever believe me, but it's not an unusual situation.

You were in the area and picked up some kind of signal. It's not a big deal. Do you believe in stuff like that?"

Well, I believed it after that. However, I did wonder why Mark's admirable method of selling Fall tickets by psychic messaging didn't work that time The Fall played in Los Angeles on an evening where I had been sitting in an Indian restaurant in Santa Monica, less than five miles away, totally unaware. Perhaps it doesn't always work. Perhaps it doesn't work in America!

Since 'Psykick Dancehall', psychic experience has remained a constant presence in the lyrics of Mark E. Smith. Literally, in places, but adding an extra poignancy, I sense, to practically everything Mark E. Smith has ever written, in particular during spells when his sixth sense has guided him through areas of a historical nature. History sits strongly with Mark E. Smith. It is part of his make-up. It is thoroughly contemporary to him and, as in all areas of art, science and literature, the relevance of history is a vital aspect of anyone wishing to push into new areas. As crass as it may sound, you have to look to the past to be able to glimpse the future. And an awareness of the past remains vital. Good to see that Mark carries that awareness so splendidly, his knowledge more solidly reassured than many history graduates who, more often than not, have a knowledge that has been sectioned due to curriculum necessity. Mark, who has always taken a great delight in discovering facts for their own sake, and not merely to further a career by pushing blindly through examinations, retains a rare and healthy fascination with history . . . and with lots of other things. On numerous occasions I have caught him with unlikely books, from biographies of Napoleon, Roman Polanski, William Blake and Alistair Crowley to the wilder areas of obscure sci-fi.

Can you think of another band with such diverse influences and such powerful imagery? I recall Mark sending me an acetate of 'Jerusalem' with "A present from Blake . . . via Mark E. Smith" scrawled on the outside.

Blake seemed a fitting connection, somehow, a fitting influence. Blake, it should be noted, alongside his predecessor, John Milton, is the greatest religious poet in the English language. What is particularly interesting here is that Blake deliberately side-stepped the aesthetic trappings of any distinctive organised faith, be it Catholic or Anglican, and pursued a religious awakening all of his own. His famous words, "I must create a system or be enslaved by another man's" certainly resonate through the centuries.

As Mark told *Melody Maker*: "He [Blake] was a real workhorse for his time. I thought he was great, especially what he did and how he managed to do it for that period of history. He wrote 'Jerusalem' and all his other stuff about himself but the thing is, he used to paint stuff behind the writing and then print it out on copper, totally the reverse of what he was meant to be doing. He'd do paintings with, like, a verse over it and then print it up himself. Amazing, really, when you think about it. I suppose my favourite work by him is 'Ghost Of A Flea'. Ha ha ha ha! What a title! What I like about it is that it's just like a really, really grotesque painting. I like something grotesque in an artist."

Blake is an unusual avenue of influence for a rock band, to say the least, particularly one named after a Camus novel. But the Camus connection is no mere affectation either, although it might be admitted that old Albert's name has tripped off rather too many rock star tongues during the past 30 years or so. The lounge at the Kingswood Road flat would be brimming with feverishly devoured Camus titles and it was Kay Carroll who tuned this writer in to his lesser work, *A Happy Death*, because, she said, ". . . it is one step beyond the more obvious Camus titles," meaning, one senses, *The Outsider, The Fall, The Plague* and the scrappily confused though eternally hip *The Rebel.*

Camus held an appeal that lay beyond simple lines of text. Although I would prefer to put aside the hugely overstated, overused, overvalued word 'existentialism' (lest I be accused of fanzine-like juvenile enthusiasm, and I have been accused of worse) his eternal link with rock music was forged by his tendency to comment on and celebrate the utter pointlessness of life. On book jackets, the face of Albert Camus is eternally seen with a Gitane dangling from the corner of his mouth. He was, unquestionably, the ultimate hip smoker and café philosopher and nobody looked so cool, surrounded by swirls of smoke and, no doubt, immersed in the sweet smell of

Cognac. In *The Outsider* (*L'Étranger*) Camus succinctly presented generation after generation of hip young studenthood with the eternally appealing concept of alienation and crossed it with a sense of the absurd. This could be the basis for simplistic, sexually driven rock'n'roll and it is certainly the mix that is shot through the work of Mark E. Smith, even if Smith's own reading matter is 25 years further down the line. One should always read Camus and, I guess, Kerouac, Burroughs and Sartre, while still in the flush of youth and rather less prone to cynicism. And if you are going to choose just one Camus book in which to dip your toes, *The Fall* is the choppy, accessible tale of one man's fall from a lofty society position, though, for what it's worth, the finest Camus novel is *The Plague* (*La Peste*) with its comforting notions that life is a plague and people are merely victims, condemned to a continuous downward spiral of futile revolt. Try sound tracking it with The Fall's *Bend Sinister*.

If images of Prestwich will forever be synonymous with the earlier Fall albums, then the extraordinary work of Pascal Legras has undoubtedly established an instantly recognisable visual link with later recordings. Always dipped in the absurd, always striking and, for my money, always worth staring at for a considerable length of time, they tend to change in terms of shape and visual attack. The more you look, the bigger the paintings become. Rather like a Fall album, in fact.

Mark: "Pascal is amazing, just fantastic. It's incredible that he came to us. I love his work and it seems to enhance The Fall beautifully. I had never heard of him myself at first and he does all our covers for free, man. He started just after 'White Lightning' with *Shift-Work*. He's just like a sublime genius; all his work looks well ahead of its time. I don't have that much contact with him though, because he's from Normandy and he lives in Paris and I can hardly understand a word he's saying to be honest but he's great. There have been times when I have wondered why he made the connection in the first place. He never moans about me when I mess about with his stuff, because I do. Can you imagine any other serious artists agreeing to that? Of course I mess about with things, change the angle and things like that. But I'm just like his editor or something like that. The ideas come from him or, before that, maybe they come from The Fall, too. It goes round in a cycle. I started using him after he called me up out of the blue – don't know how he got my number – and said, 'Can I do some Fall covers?' So I gave him the usual stuff about sending some paintings in. I get that 10 times a week, to be honest. I really do and mostly it's just completely unsuitable. Well, most of it is complete crap, but I don't mind. I like the fact that people paint to The Fall. I like the fact that people write books to The Fall. Whether they are any good or not is another matter, but it's great that we have that effect on people. But Pascal is a proper artist, you know, his work's in the Louvre in Paris and that. It's amazing, really. It's incredible."

Can you imagine anybody painting to Oasis? Can you imagine writing a novel to the sound of Paul Weller? I had a friend, once, who wrote a vegetarian cookbook to the sound of Joni Mitchell (who is another intriguing connection because her albums, in particular the jazzed post *Hissing Of Summer Lawns* albums, also strongly featured on Mark and Kay's record player). And, possibly because Joni Mitchell herself is an artist of considerable quality, there is a strong, visual element to her work . . . and one can certainly imagine visual creativity taking place to the sound of, say, Mingus. Joni's talent for twisting a song around the words, rather than vice versa, also echoes in a number of Fall recordings, though the influence is certainly mild.

Mark once intriguingly supplied *Melody Maker* with this information when asked to list his base influences:

MIKE 'THE HAIRCUT' HILL AND JR

"These are my North Manchester friends and they're quite important to me because they're always there for me when I'm depressed or under the weather or pissed off. They come round and cheer me up, not always the easiest of tasks. Heh heh heh! I haven't got many friends but these are good lads. They're only in their mid-20s and they're not really into The Fall that much. They like grunge and speed metal and all that, but they look out for me, y'know. They always pop around and check I'm alright. I don't socialise

that much though, I spend most of my time avoiding people if I can and avoiding the music industry above all, 'cos I hate all that rubbish, the bit. I think I met these lads when the wife bought a car off one of them."

It might also be noted that beyond the Mark E. Smith of The Fall lies life on another level. His non-music friends who, one strongly senses, would be the exact same people who would have been his friends had he followed his father into the plumbing business. They have also filtered, albeit heavily disguised, into his lyricism, though whether they know it or not is a matter of considerable doubt.

When, in the spring of 2002, Mark encountered me in a rather morose, lovelorn state, following a particularly gruelling emotional rejection, his advice to me was, "You want to come with me and my mates, though you mustn't write about them. We have some amazing nights, incredible nights. They are wonderful, really. Really strong and funny characters and they never talk about The Fall. I don't think they are interested at all, which is perfect for me. I relax in situations like that. It's just refreshing to get away from the music business, you know. Sometimes I just wish it wasn't there because it just clouds the real issues. So it's great to have friends who are just friends. I value that really highly even if, in recent times, I have been living more of a hermetic life . . . although, obviously I'm not alone now that Elena is with me."

And sometimes . . . just sometimes one does tend to wonder why Mark chose the rock life in the first place. As a plumber or shipping clerk or docker's mate, he could have stayed indoors at night, could have written books, could have written amazing books.

Mark: "I don't know. Do you think so? As I have said, I have edged near to that and I am a bit odd about the publishing industry. I don't want to write books. Music has always been the best medium for me. Writing lyrics is what I got into rock music for. To me, a song's never finished and it's never good enough, that's why I don't write lyrics down. Once they're down on paper, you can't change 'em, and I like to change 'em, even just before I'm going on stage. I am changing lyrics all the time. They are completely fluid. I can change and scribble and then change my mind, try it out at some gig in fucking Doncaster and, if I don't like it, change it. Lyrics change shape and meaning all the time. That's the beauty of the music being so simple and tight. I love writing. It's my only pleasure. I'm compulsive. My problem's knowing when to shut up on a song. I can't put that bleeding pen down, so I hone it, try to get it as simple as possible. That is something I have learned over the years. I know how to edit. Anyway, it's crap that you don't get literature in the format of rock music. You do. You can get intelligent lyrics in rock music and you always have done. Ray Davies did it. Lou Reed is absolute classic, most of the time. Better than any American novelist. Hank Williams is excellent, a moral parable in 90 seconds. Perfect. That's the beauty of the rock lyric. It is very powerful. You don't have to be pretentious or rant on and on like Dylan. He can't write for toffee. I have always said that. A lot of writing is psychic, really. As I have said, I used to be a bit of a psychic when I was a teenager, but since then I've taken that . . . I won't call it a gift . . . but I have tried to divert it into my work, so I'll often write a song and I don't know what it means till six months later. That is the basic reason for what I do, you know. Once something is written I like to either change it or just move on. That is what makes me feel comfortable. That is why so many band members have left because most musicians are lazy and just want to learn something once and play it over and over again. That is never what The Fall would do. That would destroy me.

"I do craft my songs, but not in terms of worrying about details like that. It stops you writing if you get into that. The funny thing is I think in rhyme all the time and a lot of the time when I'm cutting and honing lyrics what I have to do is unrhyme them. Dostoevsky's a brilliant writer, Gogol, and none of their stuff rhymes but it's pure poetry to me. It's sweet, hard, it buzzes with words. That is something I have done . . . but just naturally. I was doing it before I realised it."

Perfectly naturally . . . walking around Prestwich, words buzzing in the head . . . words clashing . . . falling into rhythm . . . falling out of rhythm . . . Fall songs form this way . . . any poetry . . .

Hard not to think of days in 1979, driving some downbeat banger around London, tape clapped into the buzz of the car stereo, blasting out The Fall's extraordinary *Live At Acklam Hall* recording, raw and yet crackling with clarity, and within the intimacy of the car, evoking the sounds and smells of a dark, damp venue, simmering in beer culture . . . and in that car, soaking in some of the most extraordinary rock lyrics ever presented onstage, soaking in 'Spectre Vs. Rector' while driving through St John's Wood.

SPECTRE VS. RECTOR

MR James be born be born
Yog Sothoth rape me lord
Sludge hai choi [blah blah]
MR James be born be born
Yog Sothoth rape me lord
Van Greenway [blah blah]
Sludge hai choi [blah blah]
Part one: spectre versus rector
The rector lived in Hampshire
The spectre was from Chorazina
In evil dust in the air
The rector locked his doors
Part two: detective drives through Hampshire
Stops because of the fog there
And thinks a visit to the rector
And meanwhile and meanwhile
Spectre possesses rector
Rector becomes spectre
Sludge hai choi [blah blah]
Sludge hai choi [blah blah]
Enter inspector
Even as he spoke a dust devil suddenly arose and struck him
Part four: detective versus rector
Detective versus rector possessed by spectre
Spectre blows him against the wall
Says "Die latin this is your fall
I've waited since Caesar for this"
Damn Latin my hate is crisp
I'll rip your fat body to pieces

MR James be born be born
Yog Sothoth rape me lord
Van Greenway [blah blah]
Scene five, scene five
Comes a hero
Soul possessed a thousand times
Only he could rescue rector
Only he could save inspector
And this hero was a strange man
"Those flowers, take them away" he said
"They're only funeral decorations
And oh this is a drudge nation
A nation of no imagination
A stupid man is their ideal
They shun me and think me unclean,
unclean"
I have saved a thousand souls
They cannot even save their own
I'm soaked in blood but always good
It's like I drunk myself sober
I get better as I get older
MR James be born be born
Yog Sothoth rape me lord
Van Greenway [blah blah]
Sludge hai choi [blah blah]
Sludge hai choi [blah blah]
Part six:
That was his kick from life
That's how he pads out his life
Selling his soul to the devil
And the spectre enters hero
But the possession is ineffectual
But the possession is ineffectual
And the possession is ineffectual
And MR James be born be born
Yog Sothoth rape me lord
Van Greenway [blah blah]
Sludge hai choi [blah blah]
Sludge hai choi [blah blah]

I said Sludge hai choi [blah blah]
Last scene:
Hero and inspector walk from the scene
Is the spectre banished forever?
The inspector is half insane
The hero runs back into the mountains
The hero goes back into the mountains
He was an exorcist but he was exhausted
An exorcist but he was exhausted
He racked on his bed all night long
MR James be born be born
Yog Sothoth rape me lord
Van Greenway [blah blah]
Sludge hai choi [blah blah]
Sludge hai choi [blah blah]

[M.R. James was a nineteenth century ghost story writer. Yog Sogoth is a character in H.P. Lovecraft's horror stories. Demon possession is a common theme in Fall songs – see 'Lay Of The Land', 'Impression Of J. Temperance', 'Jawbone And The Air-Rifle', 'Elves', 'Bug Day'.]

I spent a long time. Wasted a lot of days allowing the line "The possession was ineffectual" to bounce around my head. Couldn't imagine a Spandau Ballet song containing such a statement. I could, though, imagine Dylan in similar mode, which is where myself and Mark disagree. 'Lily, Rosemary & The Jack Of Hearts' from *Blood On The Tracks* had a great deal in common with The Fall, complete, as it is, with black surreal word play and gloriously warped characters.

But to admire Spectre Vs. Rector, to really admire it, you had to be there, kind of. It only worked to fulsome effect if you could see the grimace on the soundman's face. If you could sense the unease of the audience, especially those who had chanced upon the band after scanning *NME* or *Sounds* . . . that was always necessary to gain fuller effect. Catch them when they were expecting something that might sound appropriate from a band supporting Siouxsie & The Banshees

. . . and that happened a great deal and the truth of it was that The Fall had little in common with any of the artists with whom they shared their audience. Most spectacularly, one thinks of John Lydon, now horribly relegated into a sad pantomime but, in 1979, carrying the avant-garde baton with the grotesquely overrated PIL who fell swiftly from promise . . . and as they drained away, one could sense Mark's respect also draining.

It is true to note that Mark's vocal attack – its initial hard phrasing anyway – owed much to Rotten (as opposed to Lydon) and he made no bones about that, often citing The Sex Pistols as the only punk band worthy of more than a couple of minutes of his time. He adored 'Holidays In The Sun', arguably the Pistols' finest moment, and would sit in his armchair listening to Sex Pistols live bootlegs, Kim Fowley's *Sunset Boulevard* and Patti Smith's *Easter* while dreaming of ways to expand his lyricism without losing the attack of rock 'n'roll phrasing. It was curious to see Smith parting from Lydon, in this respect, with the latter unable to discover a depth beyond laying down the odd clashing, striking phrase . . . and that would soon come to be the most glaring difference. The reason you are reading this book right now, and the reason The Fall's latest album, *Country On The Click* – as I write, teetering on the brink of release, albeit a frustratingly delayed release – still retains a vitality, unprecedented in an artist pushing into his 26th working year . . . the reason is very, very simple.

And, then again, almost as if to prove the point, the release date of *Country On The Click* is pushed deeper and deeper into the year, Mark still unhappy with the mix and, no doubt, the fact that the initial recordings were temporarily lost and, so typical of The Fall, where once Action Records were going to release it and were so vigorous in the build-up to the album, now don't seem to be the ones who are going to release it at all. But by the time you read this, surely . . . surely, *Country On The Click*, complete with the thumping, baseball cap wearing 'Theme From Sparta FC' will have seeped into your living room walls on numerous occasions but, as I write and as the band are locked in rehearsals prior to an impending US tour, it all seems so uncertain yet again.

Maybe that is just how it should be. Maybe it really is the best place to leave it . . . right there in a ball of uncertainty.

As for Mark!

He remains curious.

He remains interested.

He remains beyond curriculum.

He scribbles notes.

And throws them away.

He refuses to bow to sweeping technology.

And in that he may be alone . . .

Alone in the field of rock'n'roll, at least.

Or nearly.

And increasingly distanced.

And he still lives it . . .

Lives like Mark E. Smith

Because it is

That simple.

And tonight I can go to the pub with Mark

And enjoy the force of his character . . .

As ever.

And . . . no doubt . . . we will encounter broadsides

From characters of Salford . . . reverential or aggressive

And Mark will watch them . . . very closely

Whatever.

Mark: "A lot of Fall songs are very much of the day. Very spur of the moment, off the cuff! They come from and aim at a short concentration span. Which connects with sex. The thing is, Mick, when you wrote to me and told me that you had become a bit of a recluse. That came at a strange time because I was the same at that point and many of my friends were, too. It took me fucking ages to write and I was really upset because the band would write great tunes and I just couldn't get the lyrics. It came bit by bit through the two months we were in the studio. I go in to record with a big box of lyrics and the band have their tunes ready, but we'd be in there forever if we stuck to trying to fit one to the other. So in the end I lock the box and start writing on spec. Don't force it, that's the secret. That's what has always worked best for me. I'm better just going in the studio with nothing . . . though it's good to have a few scraps of ideas just to kick things off. I can't labour over songs. Doesn't work like that . . . drains the life from them. It's more fun like that but that doesn't mean the lyrics aren't saying anything. They're saying more than I could possibly articulate otherwise. It is weird. I have said this before, I know, but I think about it a lot myself. When I started buying records, the ones I liked were the ones I could only half-understand. What I don't like about a lot of records today is that they're too clear. There's really no fascination or mystery left."

Eloquent people talk about The Fall. Clever writers spin The Fall into extended essays.

People study The Fall . . . they do . . . at college!

Mark: "That's fucking disgusting. They should be shot."

People scrutinise Fall lyrics and spin deeper and deeper into literary theory.

Which is to miss the point.

Hugely.

Better really . . . better to listen . . . then go and have a drink.

Watch people.

Read a book.

Or write things.

Better just to accept The Fall for what they are.

And enjoy.

Mark: "Although I have done a lot of interviews . . . and I have had to do them to survive . . . and some of them have been fun . . . and I have no complaints, really. The irony is that to just talk about The Fall and myself, I can't do it, you know what I mean? Like you say, what is there to The Fall? That's what this book has been asking. But I just see it as a vacuum, you know, which isn't true. It's one of those cases where you wished you had said this; you know what I mean, just like the brain isn't connected to the mouth at all. I know what The Fall is and I don't think there is much you can do to explain it, which is why a lot that is written about us is just crap. Because there's nothing you can actually say about it really, without it being there, which is why I still have this belief . . . and I have said this over and over. I still think we're valuable. If I didn't, I wouldn't be doing this. I wouldn't be releasing records or playing gigs. It just goes on and on."

He would have made an extraordinary plumber.

Band-O-Graphy

A list of musicians who have been a part of The Fall, however briefly:

1977

March

Mark E. Smith (vocals)
Martin Bramah (guitar)
Tony Friel (bass)
Una Baines (electric piano)
Dave (drums)

May

Karl Burns (drums) joins
Dave (drums) leaves

December

Tony Friel leaves

1978

January

Jonnie Brown (bass) joins

March

Jonnie Brown leaves
Una Baines leaves
Eric Random (keyboards) joins

June

Eric Random leaves
Yvonne Pawlett (keyboards) joins
Marc Riley (bass) joins

1979

January

Karl Burns leaves
Mike Leigh (drums) joins

April

Martin Bramah leaves
Craig Scanlon (guitar) joins
Steven Hanley (bass) joins

August

Yvonne Pawlett leaves

1980

April

Mike Leigh leaves
Paul Hanley (drums) joins

October

Karl Burns (drums) joins
Kay Carroll (already manager, joins band on backing vocals)

1982

October

Marc Riley leaves
Kay Carroll leaves

1983

September

Brix E. Smith (guitar/vocals) joins
Gavin Friday (vocals) joins for one month

1984

October

Simon Rogers (bass/keyboards) joins
Paul Hanley leaves
Steven Hanley takes extended holiday

1985

June
Steven Hanley returns

1986

June
Karl Burns leaves
Simon Wolstencroft joins

1987

January
Simon Rogers leaves
Marcia Schofield (keyboards) joins

1989

June
Brix E. Smith leaves
Martin Bramah (guitar) returns

1990

July
Marcia Schofield leaves
Martin Bramah leaves
Kenny Brady (violin) joins

1991

May
Kenny Brady leaves

June
Dave Bush (keyboards) joins

1993

January
Karl Burns (drums) joins

1995

January
Brix E. Smith (guitar) joins

December
Craig Scanlon leaves
Dave Bush leaves

1996

January
Julia Nagle (keyboards) joins after trial period
Lucy Rimmer (vocals) joins
Mike Bennett (vocals) joins

October
Brix E. Smith leaves

December
Karl Burns leaves

1997

May
Karl Burns (drums) joins
Tommy Crooks joins

August
Simon Wolstencroft leaves

1998

April
Karl Burns leaves
Steven Hanley leaves
Tommy Crooks leaves
Katie Methan joins for three gigs

August
Neville Wilding (guitar) joins
Tom Head (drums) joins
Karen Leatham (bass) joins

December
Karen Leatham leaves
Adam Helal (bass) joins

2000

November
Tom Head leaves
Spencer Birtwistle (drums) joins

2001

February
Neville Wilding leaves
Adam Helal leaves
Ben Pritchard (guitar) joins
Jim Watts (bass) joins

August
Julia Nagle leaves
Brian Fanning (keyboards) joins

October
Brian Fanning leaves

November
Spencer Birtwistle leaves
Dave Milner (drums) joins

2002

September
Elena Smith (keyboards) joins

2003

March
Jim Watts leaves
Steve Evets (bass) joins

Discography

SINGLES

Bingo-Master's Break-Out!/Psycho Mafia/Repetition
Step Forward SF7, August 1978 (7")

It's The New Thing/Various Times
Step Forward SF9, November 1978 (7")

Rowche Rumble/In My Area
Step Forward SF11, July 1979 (7")

Fiery Jack/2nd Dark Age/Psykick Dancehall 2
Step Forward SF13, January 1980 (7")

How I Wrote 'Elastic Man'/City Hobgoblins
Rough Trade RT048, July 1980 (7")

Totally Wired/Putta Block
Rough Trade RT056, September 1980 (7")

Lie Dream Of A Casino Soul/Fantastic Life
Kamera ERA001, November 1981 (7")

Look, Know/I'm Into CB
Kamera ERA004, April 1982 (7")

Marquis Cha-Cha/Room To Live
Kamera ERA014, October 1982 (7")
(a few initial copies were labelled Papal Visit *on B-side)*

The Man Whose Head Expanded/Ludd Gang
Rough Trade RT133, June 1983 (7")

Kicker Conspiracy/Wings
Container Drivers/New Puritan
Rough Trade RT143, October 1983 (double 7")

Oh! Brother/God-Box
Beggars Banquet Beg110, 8 June 1984 (7")

Oh! Brother/Oh! Brother/God-Box
Beggars Banquet Beg110T, 8 June 1984 (12")

c.r.e.e.p/Pat-Trip Dispenser
Beggars Banquet Beg116, 24 August 1984 (7")

C.R.E.E.P/Pat-Trip Dispenser/c.r.e.e.p.
Beggars Banquet Beg116T, 24 August 1984 (12")

Call For Escape Route
Draygo's Guilt/Clear Off!/No Bulbs
Beggars Banquet BEG120E, 12 October 1984 (12")

No Bulbs 3/Slang King 2
Beggars Banquet BEG 120 (Bonus 7")

Couldn't Get Ahead/Rollin' Dany
Beggars Banquet BEG134, June 1985 (Double A-side 7")

Couldn't Get Ahead/Rollin' Dany/Petty (Thief) Lout
Beggars Banquet BEG134T, 21 June 1985 (12")

Cruiser's Creek/L.A.
Beggars Banquet BEG150, October 1985 (33 rpm 7")

Cruiser's Creek/L.A./Vixen
Beggars Banquet BEG150T, 11 October 1985 (12")

Living Too Late/Hot Aftershave Bop/Living Too Long
Beggars Banquet BEG165T, 7 July 1986 (12")

Living Too Late/Hot Aftershave Bop
Beggars Banquet BEG165, July 1986 (Promotional 7")

Mr Pharmacist/Lucifer Over Lancashire
Beggars Banquet BEG168, 1 September 1986 (7")

Mr Pharmacist/Lucifer Over Lancashire/Auto Tech Pilot
Beggars Banquet BEG168T, 1 September 1986 (12")

Hey! Luciani/Shoulder Pads #1B
Beggars Banquet BEG176, 8 December 1986 (7")

Hey! Luciani/Entitled/Shoulder Pads #1B
Beggars Banquet BEG176T, 8 December 1986 (12")

There's A Ghost In My House/Haf Found Bormann
Beggars Banquet BEG187, 27 April 1987 (7")

There's A Ghost In My House/Haf Found Bormann
Beggars Banquet BEG187H, April 1987 (7" With hologram sleeve)

There's A Ghost In My House/Haf Found Bormann/Sleep Debt Snatches/Mark'll Sink Us
Beggars Banquet BEG187T, 27 April 1987 (12")

There's A Ghost In My House/Hey! Luciani/Mark'll Sink Us/ Sleep Debt Snatches
Beggars Banquet BEG187C, May 1987 (MC)

Peel Sessions EP
Put Away/Mess Of My/No Xmas For John Quays/Like To Blow
Strange Fruit SFPS0, 28 June 1987 (12")
(Session recorded 27 November 1978, transmitted 6 December 1978; original limited edition came in metalicised sleeve)
Castle SFPS028 1989 (CD)
Reissue with same track listing

Hit The North Part 1/Hit The North Part 2
Beggars Banquet BEG200, 19 October 1987 (7")

Hit The North Part 1/Hit The North Part 3/Australians In Europe/ Northerns In Europe
Beggars Banquet BEG200T, 26 October 1987 (12")

Hit The North Part 1/Hit The North Part 2
Beggars Banquet BEG200P, October 1987 (7" picture disc)

Hit The North Part 4/Hit The North Part 5/Hit The North Part 1
Beggars Banquet BEG200TR, October 1987 (12")

Hit The North (Zeus B. Held Remix)/Hit The North (Extended Version)/Hit The North (Dub Version)
Beggars Banquet SOVX2410 1987 (12")

Hit The North Double Six Mix
Hit The North Part 1/Hit The North (Double Six Mix)/
Hit The North Part 4/Australians In Europe
Beggars Banquet BEG200C, October 1987 (MC)

Victoria/Tuff Life Boogie
Beggars Banquet BEG206, 18 January 1988 (7")

Victoria/Tuff Life Boogie
Beggars Banquet BEG206B, January 1988 (Boxed numbered 7" + badge + 2 lyric sheets)

Victoria/Tuff Life Boogie/Guest Informant/Twister
Beggars Banquet (12") BEG206T, 18 January 1988 (12")

Victoria/Tuff Life Boogie/Guest Informant/Twister
Beggars Banquet BEG206C, 18 January 1988 (MC)

Bremen Nacht Run Out/Mark'll Sink Us
Beggars Banquet FALL1, 29 February 1988 (7" free with The Frenz Experiment*)*

Jerusalem/Acid Priest 2088
Beggars Banquet FALL2 (7")
Big New Prinz/Wrong Place, Right Time No. 2
Beggars Banquet FALL3 (7")
(Two discs and a postcard in a box limited to 15,000, numbered and issued as FALL2B November 1988)

Jerusalem/Acid Priest 2088
Beggars Banquet FALL2 (CD)
Big New Prinz/Wrong Place, Right Time No. 2
Beggars Banquet FALL3 (CD)
(Two discs in a wallet limited to 5,000, numbered November 1988)

Big New Prinz/Wrong Place, Right Time
Beggars Banquet FALL4, 1988 (Promotional 7")

Big New Prinz/Wrong Place, Right Time
Beggars Banquet FALL4T, 1988 (Promotional 12")

Cab It Up!/Dead Beat Descendant
Beggars Banquet BEG226, June 1989 (7")

Cab It Up!/Dead Beat Descendant/Kurious Oranj (live)/
Hit The North (live)
Beggars Banquet BEG226T, 12 June 1989 (12")

Telephone Thing/British People In Hot Weather
Cog Sinister SIN4, January 1990 (7")

Telephone Thing (extended)/British People In Hot Weather/
Telephone Dub
Cog Sinister SINDJ412, January 1990 (Promotional 12")

Telephone Thing (extended)/British People In Hot Weather/
Telephone Dub
Cog Sinister SIN412, January 1990 (12")

Telephone Thing (extended)/British People In Hot Weather/
Telephone Dub
Cog Sinister SINCD4, January 1990 (CD)

Telephone Thing/British People In Hot Weather
Cog Sinister, January 1990 (Promotional MC)

Popcorn Double Feature/Butterflies 4 Brains
Cog Sinister SIN5, March 1990 (7")

Popcorn Double Feature/Arms Control Poseur/Butterflies 4 Brains
Cog Sinister SIN512, March 1990 (12")

Popcorn Double Feature/Zandra
Cog Sinister SINR5, March 1990 (7" limited to 3,000 copies)

Popcorn Double Feature/Zandra/Black Monk Theme Part II
Cog Sinister SINR512, March 1990 (12" limited to 3,000 copies)

White Lightning/Blood Outta Stone
Cog Sinister/Fontana SIN6 (Promotional single c/w small bottle of 'White Lightnin' Tequila)

White Lightning/Blood Outta Stone
Cog Sinister SIN6, 13 August 1990 (7")

White Lightning/Zagreb (Movement II)/Blood Outta Stone/
The Funeral Mix
Cog Sinister SINX612, August 1990 (12")

The Dredger EP
White Lightning/Blood Outta Stone/Zagreb (Movements I + II + III)/Life Just Bounces
Cog Sinister SIN612, August 1990 (12" limited to 5,000 copies)

White Lightning/Blood Outta Stone/Zagreb (Movements I + II + III)/Life Just Bounces
Cog Sinister SINCD6, August 1990 (CD)

High Tension Line/Xmas With Simon
Cog Sinister SIN7, December 1990 (7")

High Tension Line/Xmas With Simon/Don't Take The Pizza
Cog Sinister SIN712, December 1990 (12")

High Tension Line/Xmas With Simon/Don't Take The Pizza
Cog Sinister SIN7(12), December 1990 (Promotional MC)

So What About It?
Cog Sinister NICE1 1991 (Promotional 12" containing four remixes of the song)

Free Range/Everything Hurtz
Cog Sinister SINS8, 2 March 1992 (7")

Free Range/Everything Hurtz
Cog Sinister SIN8, 2 March 1992 (7" Limited edition 'hand-painted' sleeve)

Free Range/Return/Dangerous/Everything Hurtz
Cog Sinister SIN812, 2 March 1992 (Numbered limited edition 12")

Free Range/Return/Dangerous/Everything Hurtz
Cog Sinister SINCD8, 2 March 1992 (CD)

Ed's Babe/Pumpkin Head Xscapes/The Knight, The Devil And Death/Free Ranger
Fontana/Cog Sinister SINCD912, 22 June 1992 (12")

Ed's Babe/Pumpkin Head Xscapes/The Knight, The Devil And Death/Free Ranger
Fontana/Cog Sinister SINCD9, 22 June 1992 (CD)

The Re-Mixer/Lost In Music/A Past Gone Mad/The League Of Bald-Headed Men
Permanent/Cog Sinister, 15 February 1993 (Promotional 12")

Kimble/C'n'C-Hassle Schmuk
Strange Fruit SFPS787, 8 March 1993 (7")

Kimble/C'n'C-Hassle Schmuk/Spoilt Victorian Child/Words Of Expectation
Strange Fruit SFPS087, 8 March 1993 (12")

Kimble/Gut Of The Quantifier/Spoilt Victorian Child/Words Of Expectation
Strange Fruit SFPCD087, 8 March 1993 (CD)

Why Are People Grudgeful?/Glam Racket
Permanent/Cog Sinister 7SPERM9, 5 April 1993 (7")

Why Are People Grudgeful?/Glam Racket/The Re-Mixer/Lost In Music
Permanent/Cog Sinister 12SPERM9, 5 April 1993 (12")

Why Are People Grudgeful?/Glam Racket/The Re-Mixer/Lost In Music
Permanent/Cog Sinister CDSPERM9, 5 April 1993 (CD)

Behind The Counter/War/Cab Driver
Permanent/Cog Sinister 12SPERMD13, 13 December 1993 (12")

Behind The Counter/War/Cab Driver
Permanent/Cog Sinister CDSPERMD13, 13 December 1993 (CD)

M5/Happy Holiday/Behind The Counter (Remix)
Permanent/Cog Sinister 12SPERM13, 20 December 1993 (12")

M5/Happy Holiday/Behind The Counter (Remix)
Permanent/Cog Sinister CDSPERM13, 20 December 1993 (CD)

15 Ways/Hey! Student/The $500 Bottle Of Wine
Permanent/Cog Sinister CDSPERM14, 18 April 1994 (CD)

15 Ways/Hey! Student/The $500 Bottle Of Wine
Permanent/Cog Sinister10SPERM14, 18 April 1994 (Clear vinyl 10")

15 Ways/Hey! Student/The $500 Bottle Of Wine
Permanent/Cog Sinister 12SPERM14, 18 April 1994 (12")

The Chiselers/Chilinist
Jet JET 500, 12 February 1996 (7")

The Chiselers/Chilinist/Interlude/Chilinism
Jet JETCD 500, 12 February 1996 (CD)

The Chiselers/Chilinist/Interlude/Chilinism
Jet JETMC 500, 12 February 1996 (MC)

Masquerade – Mr Natural Mix/Masquerade – PWL Mix/
Masquerade – Album Mix
Artful 10ARTFUL1, 9 February 1998 (10")

Masquerade – Single Mix/Ivanhoes Two Pence/Spencer Must Die
Live/Ten Houses Of Eve Remix
Artful CDARTFUL1, 9 February 1998 (CD1)

Masquerade – Single Mix/Calendar/Scareball/Ol' Gang Live
Artful CXARTFUL1, 9 February 1998 (CD2)

Touch Sensitive Dance Mix/Touch Sensitive /Antidote
Artful 12ARTFUL2, 23 February 1999 (12")

Touch Sensitive/Antidote/Touch Sensitive Dance Mix
Artful CDARTFUL2, 23 February 1999 (CD)

F-'Oldin' Money/Perfect Day (new version)/Birthday Song (new mix)
Artful CDARTFUL3, 16 August 1999 (CD)

F-'Oldin' Money/The REAL Life Of The Crying Marshal (new
version)/Tom Raggazzi (new mix)
Artful CDXARTFUL3, 16 August 1999 (CD)

Rude (All The Time)/Wake Up In The City
Flitwick Records MK45 1FG 2001(7")

My Ex Class Mates Kids/New Formation Sermon/Distilled Mug Art
Voiceprint COGVP128CD

Susan Vs Youthclub/Janet vs Johnny
Action Records TAKE20, 2 December 2002 (7")

Susan Vs Youthclub/Janet Vs Johnny/Susan Vs Youthclub (remix)
Action Records TAKE20CD, 2 December 2002 (CD)

The 7″ was intended to be blue vinyl but due to a production error it was pressed in standard black. The remix on the CD was done by Vertical Smile. A one-track promo CD of Susan Vs Youthclub was issued on a blank CDR with a small white sticker on the disc giving the song title and Action's email address only.

ALBUMS

Live At The Witch Trials

Step Forward SFLP1, January 1979 (LP)

Frightened, Crap Rap 2/Like To Blow/Rebellious Jukebox/No Xmas For John Quays/Mother – Sister!/Industrial Estate/Underground Medecin/Two Steps Back/Live At The Witch Trials/Futures And Pasts/Music Scene

CD (SFLPCD1), LP (SFLP1) and MC (SFLPC1) with same track listing released 1989 on IRS records. Second re-release 1997 poor quality, mastered from vinyl.

Dragnet

Step Forward SFLP4, October 1979 (LP)

Psykick Dancehall/A Figure Walks/Printhead/Dice Man/Before The Moon Falls/Your Heart Out/Muzorewi's Daughter/Flat Of Angles/ Choc-Stock/Spectre Vs. Rector/Put Away

CD (SFLPCD4) with same track listing released 1990 on IRS records. Released again on CD by Cog Sinister (COG113) March 1999.

Totale's Turns (It's Now Or Never)

Rough Trade ROUGH10, May 1980 (live LP)

Intro – Fiery Jack/Rowche Rumble/Muzorewi's Daughter/In My Area/Choc-Stock/Spectre Vs. Rector 2/Cary Grant's Wedding/ That Man/New Puritan/No Xmas For John Quays

Reissued on CD (DOJO CD 83) with same track listing released 21 November 1992 on DOJO records. Reissued again by Castle 1998 on their Essential label with slightly different cover.

Grotesque (After The Gramme)

Rough Trade ROUGH18, November 1980 (LP)

Pay Your Rates/English Scheme/New Face In Hell/C'n'C-S Mithering/The Container Drivers/Impression Of J. Temperance/ In The Park/W.M.C.-Blob 59/Gramme Friday/The N.W.R.A.

CD CLACD 391 mastered from vinyl with same track listing released 8 November 1993 by Castle Communications. Re-released again by Cog Sinister on 29 June 1998, this time specially mastered for CD and with new art work and the following additional tracks: How I Wrote 'Elastic Man', City Hobgoblin, Totally Wired, Putta Block, Grotesque.

Slates

Rough Trade RT071, April 1981 (10" LP)

Middle Mass/An Older Lover/Prole Art Threat/Fit And Working Again/Slates, Slags etc./Leave The Capitol

Later reissued with a slightly different sleeve; Reissued by DOJO records on CD only c/w A Part Of America *in December 1992, titled:* Slates/A Part Of America Therein, 1981 (LOMA CD 10).

77 – Early Years – 79

Step Forward SFLP6, September 1981 (LP)

Repetition/Bingo-Master's Break-Out!/Psycho Mafia/Various Times/ It's The New Thing/Rowche Rumble/In My Area/Dice Man/ Psykick Dancehall No. 2/2nd Dark Age/Fiery Jack

Reissued 27 March 2000 on Cog Sinister COGVP123CD with two additional tracks from the Live At The Electric Circus *compilation:* Stepping Out *and* Last Orders.

Hex Enduction Hour

Kamera KAM005, March 1982 (LP)

The Classical/Jawbone And The Air-Rifle/Hip Priest/Fortress/ Deer Park/Mere Pseud Mag. Ed./Winter (Hostel-Maxi)/Winter 2/ Just Step S'ways/Who Makes The Nazis?/Iceland/And This Day

Reissued on LINE Records (FRG) on white vinyl and CD LICD 9.00126. Reissued 1999 on Cog Sinister COGVP119CD, with same tracklisting.

Room To Live (Undiluteable Slang Truth)

Kamera KAM011, October 1982 (LP)

Joker Hysterical Face/Marquis Cha-Cha/Hard Life In Country/ Room To Live/Detective Instinct/Solicitor In Studio/Papal Visit

Reissued on LINE Records (FRG) on black or white vinyl. This reissue also contains Lie Dream Of A Casino Soul *and* Fantastic Life.

Reissued again by Cog Sinister (COGVP105CD) March 1998 (CD) with original track listing including four-track bonus live disc Special Limited Edition EP Pt 1 *(COGVP105CD2), culled from the Derby Hall, Bury on 27 April 1982 (not Manchester Band On The Wall 1982 gig as the packaging indicates). Limited run of 1,000 (2,000?) mastered from vinyl. Tracks on live CD:* Drago's Guilt/Joker Hysterical Face/Lie Dream Of Casino Soul/Hexen Definitive-Strife Knot

A Part Of America Therein, 1981

Cottage (US) LP1, May 1982 (LP)

The N.W.R.A./Hip Priest/Totally Wired/Lie Dream Of A Casino Soul/Cash'n'Carry/An Older Lover/Deer Park/Winter

Reissued by DOJO records on CD only c/w Slates, *December 1992, titled:* Slates/A Part Of America Therein, 1981 *(LOMA CD 10)*

Perverted By Language

Rough Trade ROUGH62, December 1983 (LP)

Eat Y'self Fitter/Neighbourhood Of Infinity/Garden/Hotel Bloedel/ Smile/I Feel Voxish/Tempo House/Hexen Definitive-Strife Knot

Reissued with same track listing by LINE Records (FRG) on white vinyl and CD (LICD 9.00006); Castle Communications on CD (CLACD 392) 8 November 1993;
Cog Sinister on CD (COGVP104CD) 9 February 1998; Released again by Castle Communications ESMCD 639, 29 June 1998 with the following additional tracks:
The Man Whose Head Expanded/Ludd Gang/Kicker Conspiracy/ Wings/Pilsner Trail

In A Hole

Flying Nun (NZ) MARK1/2, 1983 (Live LP + 12")

Impression of J. Temperance/The Man Whose Head Expanded/ Room To Live/Hip Priest/Lie Dream Of A Casino Soul/Prole Art Threat/Hard Life In Country/The Classical/Mere Pseud Mag. Ed./ Marquis Cha-Cha/Backdrop/Fantastic Life/English Scheme/Joker Hysterical Face/No Xmas For John Quays/Solicitor In Studio

Reissued on Cog Sinister Records (COGVP102CD) May 1997.

The Wonderful And Frightening World Of . . .

Beggars Banquet BEGA58, October 1984 (LP)

Lay Of The Land/2 x 4/Copped It/Elves/Slang King/Bug Day/ Stephen Song/Craigness/Disney's Dream Debased

Plus on the CD version (BEGA 58 CD/BBL 58 CD) and the cassette **Escape Route From The Wonderful And Frightening World Of The Fall** *(BEG C 58):* No Bulbs/Oh! Brother/Draygo's Guilt/ God-Box/Clear Off!/C.R.E.E.P./Pat-Trip Dispenser

Hip Priest And Kamerads

Situation Two SITU/SITL13, March 1985 (LP)

Lie Dream Of A Casino Soul/The Classical/Fortress/Look, Know/ Hip Priest/Room To Live/Mere Pseud Mag. Ed./Hard Life In Country/I'm Into CB/Fantastic Life

Cassette version (SITL13) and CD version (SITL13CD) feature live versions of: Who Makes The Nazis?/Just Step S'ways/Jawbone And The Air-Rifle/And This Day

This Nation's Saving Grace

Beggars Banquet BEGA67, September 1985 (LP)

Mansion/Bombast/Barmy/What You Need/Spoilt Victorian Child/ L.A./Gut Of The Quantifier/My New House/Paint Work/I Am Damo Suzuki/To Nkroachment: Yarbles

Cassette BEGC67 also includes: Vixen/Couldn't Get Ahead/ Petty (Thief) Lout

Additional to these, the CD version BEG67CD/BBL67CD features: Rollin' Dany/Cruisers Creek

Nord-West Gas

Funf Und Vierzig (FRG) LP08, 1986 (LP)

My New House/Bombast/Disney's Dream Debased/Couldn't Get Ahead/No Bulbs/Paintwork/C.R.E.E.P./I Am Damo Suzuki/ Rollin' Dany/L.A./Barmy/Lay Of The Land

Bend Sinister

Beggars Banquet BEGA75, October 1986 (LP)

R.O.D./Dktr. Faustus/Shoulder Pads 1#/Mr Pharmacist/ Gross Chapel – British Grenadiers/U.S. 80's–90's/Terry Waite Sez/ Bournemouth Runner/Riddler!/Shoulder Pads #2

CD version BEGA75CD also contains: Living too Late/Auto-Tech Pilot

Additional to these, the cassette version BEGC75 features Town and Country Hobgoblins

Palace Of Swords Reversed

Cog Sinister COG1, December 1987 (LP)

Prole Art Threat/How I Wrote 'Elastic Man'/Totally Wired/Pay Your Rates/Putta Block/An Older Lover/Fit And Working Again/ Marquis Cha-Cha/The Man Whose Head Expanded/Neighbourhood Of Infinity (live)/Kicker Conspiracy/Wings

Plus on CD (CDCOG1) and cassette (COGC1): City Hobgoblins/Leave The Capitol

Reissued by Cog Sinister (COGVP107CD) 20 February 1998 (CD) with original CD track listing including four-track bonus live disc Special Limited Edition EP Pt 2, *with live tracks culled from the Derby Hall, Bury (April 27, 1982) (Manchester Band On The Wall gig in 1982 as the packaging indicates). Limited run of 1,000 (2,000?).*

Tracks on live CD: Look, Know/Tempo House/I'm Into CB/ Mere Pseud Mag. Ed.

The Frenz Experiment

Beggars Banquet BEGA91, 29 February 1988 (LP)

Frenz/Carry Bag Man/Get A Hotel/Victoria/Athlete Cured/In These Times/The Steak Place/Bremen Nacht/Guest Informant (excerpt)/ Oswald Defence Lawyer

Cassette BEGAC91 (which has Bremen Nacht Run Out *instead of* Bremen Nacht) *and CD BEGA91CD (which has* Bremen Nacht Alternative *instead of* Bremen Nacht) *also contains:* Guest Informant/ Tuff Life Booogie/Twister

CD also has There's A Ghost In My House/Hit The North Part 1

I Am Kurious, Oranj

Beggars Banquet BEGA96, October 1988 (LP)

New Big Prinz/Overture From 'I Am Curious Orange'/Dog Is Life/ Jerusalem/Kurious Oranj/Wrong Place, Right Time/C.D. Win Fall 2088 AD/Yes, O Yes/Van Plague?/Bad News Girl/Cab It Up!

Plus on CD (BEGA96CD) and cassette (BEGA96C): Guide Me Soft/ Last Nacht/Big New Priest

Seminal Live

Beggars Banquet BBL102, 1989 (LP)

Dead Beat Descendant/Pinball Machine/H.O.W./Squid Law/ Mollusc In Tyrol/2 x 4/Elf Prefix/L.A./Victoria/Pay Your Rates/ Introduction/Cruisers Creek

Plus on CD (BBL 102 CD): Kurious Oranj/Frenz/Hit The North/ In These Times

(All but the first five listed tracks are live recordings)

Extricate

Cog Sinister 842.204-1, 19 February 1990 (LP)

Sing! Harpy/I'm Frank/Bill Is Dead/Black Monk Theme Part I/ Popcorn Double Feature/Telephone Thing/Hilary/Chicago, Now!/ The Littlest Rebel/And Therein . . .

Plus on CD (842 204-2) and cassette (842 204-4): Arms Control Poseur/ Black Monk Theme Part II/British People In Hot Weather/Extricate

Extricate (Album Sampler) (FALL 1) contains the tracks: I'm Frank/ Telephone Thing/Bill Is Dead/Sing! Harpy

Re-released on Cog Sinister COGVP122CD, 30 April 1999 with same track listing.

458489 A Sides

Beggars Banquet BEGA111, 1990 (LP)

Oh! Brother/C.R.E.E.P./No Bulbs 3/Rollin' Dany/Couldn't Get Ahead/Cruisers Creek/L.A./Living Too Late/Hit The North Part 1/ Mr Pharmacist/Hey! Luciani/There's A Ghost In My House/Victoria/ Big New Prinz/Wrong Place, Right Time No. 2/Jerusalem/ Dead Beat Descendant

Also on cassette (BEGC111) and CD (BEGA111CD)

458489 B Sides

Beggars Banquet BEGA116, 31 December 1990 (Double LP)

God-Box/Pat-Trip Dispenser/Slang King 2/Draygo's Guilt/Clear Off!/No Bulbs/Petty Thief Lout/Vixen/Hot Aftershave Bop/Living Too Long/Lucifer Over Lancashire/Auto Tech Pilot/Entitled/ Shoulder Pads #1B/Sleep Debt Snatches/Mark'll Sink Us/Haf Found Bormann/Northerners In Europe/Hit The North Part 2/Guest Informant/Tuff Life Boogie/Twister/Acid Priest 2088/Cab It Up!

Cassette (BEGC116) also contains: Australians In Europe

Also on double CD (BEGA116CD): Oh! Brother (12")/C.R.E.E.P. (12") *[actually c.r.e.e.p.]*/Bremen Nacht Run Out/Mark'll Sink Us *[alternative version]*/Kurious Oranj (live)/Hit The North (live)

Shift-Work

Cog Sinister/Fontana 848 594-1, April 1991 (LP)

So What About It?/Idiot Joy Showland/Edinburgh Man/ Pittsville Direkt/The Book Of Lies/The War Against Intelligence/ Shift-Work/You Haven't Found It Yet/The Mixer/A Lot Of Wind/ Rose/Sinister Waltz

Cassette (848 594-4) and CD (848 594-2) also contains: High Tension Line/White Lightning

Code: Selfish

Cog Sinister/Fontana 512 162-1, March 1992 (LP)

The Birmingham School Of Business School/Free Range/Return/ Time Enough At Last/Everything Hurtz/Immortality/Two-Face!/ Just Waiting/So-Called Dangerous/Gentlemen's Agreement/ Married, 2 Kids/Crew Filth

Also available with same track listing on CD (512 162-2) and cassette (512 162-4)

The Collection

Castle CCSCD365, March 1993 (CD)

Intro/Fiery Jack/Muzorewi's Daughter/Choc-Stock/Cary Grant's Wedding/Middle Mass/Slates, Slags etc./Leave The Capitol/ Container Drivers/Impression Of J. Temperance/W.M.C.-Blob 59/ City Hobgoblins/Totally Wired/How I Wrote 'Elastic Man'/ Hip Priest/The N.W.R.A./Smile/Medical Acceptance Gate/A Day In The Life

Also available on cassette (CCSMC365)

The Infotainment Scan

Permanent/Cog Sinister PERMLP12, 26 April 1993 (LP)

Ladybird (Green Grass)/Lost In Music/Glam-Racket/I'm Going To Spain/It's A Curse/Paranoia Man In Cheap Sh*t Room/Service/The League Of Bald-Headed Men/A Past Gone Mad/Light/Fireworks

Also available with same track listing on cassette (PERMMC12), and on CD (PERMCD12) with the following additional tracks: Why Are People Grudgeful?/League Moon Monkey Mix

BBC Radio 1 'Live In Concert'

Windsong International WINCD038, 2 August 1993 (Live CD)

Australians In Europe/Shoulder Pads/Ghost In My House/ Hey! Luciani/Terry Waite Sez/Fiery Jack/Lucifer Over Lancashire

Recorded 25 May 1987 at The Rock City, Nottingham

Middle Class Revolt

Cog Sinister/Permanent PERMLP16, 3 May 1994 (LP)

15 Ways/The Reckoning/Behind The Counter/M5#1/Surmount All Obstacles/Middle Class Revolt!/War/You're Not Up To Much/ Symbol Of Mordgan/Hey! Student/Junk Man/The $500 Bottle Of Wine/City Dweller/Shut Up!

Also available with same track listing on cassette (PERMMC16) and (CD PERMCD16)

Cerebral Caustic

Cog Sinister/Permanent PERMLP30, 27 February 1995 (LP)

The Joke/Don't Call Me Darling/Rainmaster/Feeling Numb/ Pearl City/Life Just Bounces/I'm Not Satisfied/The Aphid/Bonkers In Phoenix/One Day/North West Fashion Show/Pine Leaves

Also available with same track listing on cassette (PERMMC30) and CD (PERMCD30)

The Twenty Seven Points

Cog Sinister/Permanent PERMLP36, 7 August 1995 (Live double LP)

Mollusc In Tyrol/Return/Ladybird (Green Grass)/Idiot – Walk Out/ Ten Points/Idiot Joy Showland/Big New Prinz/Intro – Roadhouse/ The Joke/M.H.'s Jokes/British People In Hot Weather/Free Range/ Hi-Tension Line/The League Of Bald-Headed Men/95: Glam Racket/Star/Lost In Music/Prague '91/Mr Pharmacist/Cloud Of Black/Paranoid Man In Cheap Sh*t Room/Bounces – Leeds/Outro/ Passable/Glasgow Advice/Middle Class Revolt – Simon, Dave & John/Bill Is Dead/Strychnine War!/Noel's Chemical Effluence/ Three Points/You're Not Up Too Much

Also available with same track listing on double (CD PERMCD36)

The Legendary Chaos Tape

Scout Releases/Rough Trade SAR1005, 1996 (CD)

Middle Mass/Crap Rap/English Scheme/New Face In Hell/That Man/ An Older Lover/Male Slags/Prole Art Threat/Container Drivers/ Jawbone And The Air-Rifle/In The Park/Leave The Capitol/Spectre Versus Rector/Pay Your Rates/Impression Of J. Temperance

Recorded at the Acklam Hall (now Subterranea), London, 11 December 1980. Initially released in 1980 as a bootleg tape Live in London, 1980 *by Chaos Tapes (LIVE006) with same tracks but differing titles.*

Sinister Waltz

Receiver Records RRCD 209, 22 January 1996 (CD)

A Lot Of Wind/Couldn't Get Ahead/Blood Outta Stone/Arid Al's Dream/The Knight, The Devil And Death/Chicago, Now!/Birthday/ Pumpkin Head Escapes/Wings/Dktr. Faustus/Telephone Thing/

Black Monk Theme (alternative mix)/Gut Of The Quantifier/
Edinburgh Man

First in a series of three CDs featuring alternative previously unreleased versions.

Fiend With A Violin

Receiver Records RRCD 211, 19 February 1996 (CD)

I Feel Voxish/The Man Whose Head Expanded/What You Need/
L.A./Petty Thief Lout/Fiend With A Violin/Spoilt Victorian Child/
Bombast/Married, 2 Kids/Haven't Found It Yet/
Gentleman's Agreement/Fiend With A Violin (Vox)

Second in a series of three CDs featuring alternative previously unreleased/live versions. 'Fiend With A Violin' is actually '2 x 4'.

Oswald Defence Lawyer

Receiver Records RRCD 213, 15 April 1996 (CD)

Just Waiting/Oswald Defence Lawyer/Victoria/Frenz/2 x 4/
Bad News Girl/Get A Hotel/Guest Informant/Big New Prinz/
Bremen Nacht/Carry Bag Man/Bombast

Third in a series of three CDs featuring alternative previously unreleased/live version.

The Other Side Of The Fall

Receiver Records 1997 (Triple CD)

Boxed set comprising the three albums:
Sinister Waltz *Receiver Records RRCD 209*
Fiend With A Violin *Receiver Records RRCD 211*
Oswald Defence Lawyer *Receiver Records RRCD 213*

The Light User Syndrome

Jet Records JETCD 1012, 10 June 1996 (CD)

D.I.Y. Meat/Das Vulture Ans Ein Nutter-Wain/He Pep!/Hostile/
Stay Away (Old White Train)/Spinetrak/Interlude/Chilinism/
Powder Keg/Oleano/Cheetham Hill/The Coliseum/Last Chance To
Turn Around/The Ballad Of J. Drummer/Oxymoron/Secession Man

Also available with same track listing on vinyl JETLP1012 and cassette

JETMC1012. Re-released on Receiver Records RRCD264Z early 1999 with additional tracks from the single: Chiselers/Chilinist

The Fall In The City. . . .

Artful Records ARTFULCD3, 27 January 1997 (live CD)

The Joke/Aphid/Deadbeat/Feeling Numb/War/Glam Racket/ Pearl City/L.A./Don't Call Me Darling/Bill Is Dead/Behind The Counter/Edinburgh Man/Middle Class Revolt/Gut Of The Quantifier/Life Just Bounces

Recorded live at the Roadhouse, Manchester 1995

Archive Series – The Fall

Rialto Records RMCD214, May 1997 (CD)

I Feel Voxish/Guest Informant/Arid Al's Dream/Bad News Girl/ Fiend With A Violin (vox)/Edinburgh Man/Get A Hotel/ Blood Outta Stone/Carry Bag Man/Gut Of The Quantifier/ The Man Whose Head Expanded/Pumpkin Head Escapes/ Oswald Defence Lawyer/Dktr. Faustus/Just Waiting

CD features a selection from the albums Sinister Waltz, Fiend With A Violin, Oswald Defence Lawyer

The More You Seek The Less You Find

Receiver Records, 1997 (Double CD)

CD1: Edinburgh Man/Couldn't Get Ahead/Blood Outta Stone/ The Knight, The Devil And Death/Arid Al's Dream/Birthday/ Telephone Thing/Black Monk Theme/Gut Of The Quantifier/ Wings/I Feel Voxish/The Man Whose Head Expanded/ What You Need/Bombast (live version)/Married, 2 Kids/Hostile

CD2: L.A./Petty Thicf Lout/Oswald Defence Lawyer/You Haven't Found It Yet/Gentleman's Agreement/A Lot Of Wind/Just Waiting/ Victoria/2 x 4/Bad News Girl/Get A Hotel/Guest Informant/Big New Prinz/Carry Bag Man/Bombast (alternative version)/Oxymoron

CD features a further selection from the albums Sinister Waltz, Fiend With a Violin, Oswald Defence Lawyer *and a few additional tracks. Note the release is titled* The Less You Seek The More You Find *elsewhere on the cover.*

15 Ways To Leave Your Man

Receiver RRCD239, 11 August 1997 (live CD)

Chilinist/Don't Call Me Darling/15 Ways (To Leave Your Man)/ D.I.Y. Meat/Pearl City/Feeling Numb/L.A./Big New Prinz/ Mr Pharmacist/Everything Hurtz/The Mixer/Das Vulture Ans Ein Nutter-Wain/M5 6-7PM/Return/The Reckoning/Hey! Student

Recorded live in London 1996

Levitate

Artful CDX9, 29 September 1997 (LP/CD 1997)

Ten Houses Of Eve/Masquerade/Hurricane Edward/I'm A Mummy/ The Quartet Of Doc Shanley/Jap Kid/4½ Inch/Spencer Must Die/ Jungle Rock/Ol' Gang/Tragic Days/I Come And Stand At Your Door/Levitate/Everybody But Myself

Limited edition with additional CD containing: Powderkex/Christmastide/ Recipe For Fascism/Pilsner Trail/Everybody But Myself (live)

Oxymoron

Receiver RRCD246, November 1997 (CD)

Oxymoron/Powder Keg/White Lines/Pearl City/The Birmingham School Of Business School/Hostile/Glam Racket/Italiano/He Pep!/ Rainmaster/Behind The Counter/Bill Is Dead/E.S.P. Disco/ Interlude/Chilinism/Life Just Bounces

Cheetham Hill

Receiver RRCD247, November 1997

Time Enough At Last/Cheetham Hill/Free Range/The Chiselers/ U.S. 80's–90's/Spine Track/Idiot Joy Showland/Oleano/The Joke/ Ed's Babe/Hit The North/White Lightning/Secession Man/Last Exit To Brooklyn (Last Chance To Turn Around)/The Coliseum/ Eat Yourself Fitter

Yet another non-essential Receiver compilation

Smile . . . It's The Best Of

Castle CCSCD823, March 1998 (CD)

Smile/An Older Lover Etc./Rowche Rumble/D.I.Y. Meat/

Totally Wired/New Face In Hell/Prole Art Threat/New Puritan/ Tempo House/Pay Your Rates/He Pep!/Spectre Vs. Rector/ Oxymoron/Lie Dream Of A Casino Soul/Impression of J. Temperance/ No Xmas For John Quays/That Man

(Another non-essential compilation cobbled together from Grotesque, Slates, A Part Of America Therein, Totale's Turns, Perverted By Language *and* Light User Syndrome*)*

Live To Air In Melbourne '82

Cog Sinister COGVP108CD, 4 May 1998 (CD)

I Feel Voxish/Tempo House/Hard Life In Country/I'm Into C.B./ Lie Dream Of A Casino Soul/Solicitor In Studio/Marquis Cha-Cha

Recorded at Prince of Wales Hotel, Melbourne on 2 August 1982. Only the first 1,000 copies were supposed to include a second CD with the final three tracks (the encore), but the gig is split evenly over both CDs (despite what's written on the packaging). All released copies seem to have both CDs. Second CD tracks: Room To Live/Hexen Definitive/Deer Park/ Totally Wired/Joker Hysterical Face/Hip Priest

Northern Attitude

Music Club MCCD350, June 1998 (CD)

Telephone Thing/Das Vulture Ans Ein Nutter-Wain/Oxymoron/ M5 6-7PM/Powder Keg/Victoria/Edinburgh Man/Oswald Defence Lawyer/I Feel Voxish/L.A./Guest Informant/E.S.P. Disco/ Mr Pharmacist/Italiano/Fiend With A Violin/Bremen Nacht/The Man Whose Head Expanded/Bombast

Another non-essential selection of 18 tracks licensed from Trojan records, featuring tracks from Fiend With A Violin, E.S.P. Disco*, etc.*

The Post Nearly Man

Artful CD14, 6 September 1998 (CD)

The Horror In Clay/Shad Segment/The Caterer/I'm Bobby Pt 1/ The CD In Your Hand/Enigrammatic Dream/Visit Of An American Poet v 1/Segment/Visitation Of An American Poet/Visit Of An American Poet v 2/I'm Bobby Pt 2/Typewriter/Dissolute Singer/ A Lot In A Name

Album credited to "Mark E. Smith" rather than The Fall. Spoken word CD features Mark E. Smith's self-penned short stories, lyrics, poetry, keyboard and sound effects.

Live Various Years

Cog Sinister COGVP111CD, 22 September 1998 (live double CD)

Dead Beat Descendant/Big New Prinz/Why Are People Grudgeful?/ Free Range/Shift-Work/Strychnine/Das Vulture/Spine Track/Behind The Counter/Interferance/Hip Priest/Interferance (reprise)

Tracks 1,2 NYC 93; 3-6 Munich 93; 7-12 Bristol 97. Also comes with bonus live CD titled **16.04.88** (no location given but probably from the Fritz Club, Vienna, April 15, 1988): Carry A Bag Man/ Yes Oh Yes/U.S. 80's–90's

Nottingham '92

Cog Sinister COGVP110CD, 1998 (live CD)

Time Enough At Last/Blood Outta Stone/Idiot Joy Showland/ Free Range/Immortality/High Tension Line/Married, 2 Kids/ New Big Prinz/Pittsville Direkt/Return/Everything Hurtz/ The Birmingham School Of Business School/Edinburgh Man/ And Therein . . ./The War Against Intelligence

Recorded live at Trent Polytechnic, Nottingham, March 15, 1992.

The Peel Sessions

Strange Fruit SFRSCD048, 25 January 1998 (CD)

Rebellious Jukebox/Mess Of My/New Face In Hell/Winter/Smile/ Middlemass/2 x 4/Cruisers Creek/What You Need/Athlete Cured/ Dead Beat Descendant/Black Monk Theme/Idiot Joy Showland/ Free Range/Strychnine/A Past Gone Mad/M5

The Marshall Suite

Artful ARTFULCD17, 19 April 1999 (CD)

Touch Sensitive/F-'Oldin' Money/Shake-off/Bound/ This Perfect Day/(Jung Nev's) Antidotes/Inevitable/Anecdotes + Antidotes In B#/Early Life Of Crying Marshal/The Crying Marshal/ Birthday Song/Mad.Men-Eng.Dog/On My Own

Also available on MC (ARTFULMC17) with same track list, and limited edition vinyl double album (ARTFULLP17) which features an extra track: Finale: Tom Raggazzi

A Past Gone Mad

Artful ARTFULCD30, 28 February 2000 (CD)

The CD In Your Hand/Touch Sensitive/High Tension Line/Rose/ The Birmingham School Of Business/Free Range/Lost In Music/ I'm Going To Spain/It's A Curse/A Past Gone Mad/Behind The Counter/Hey! Student/Ten Houses Of Eve/F-'Oldin' Money/ Shake Off/Jung Ney's Antidotes/Bonkers In Pheonix/Bill Is Dead

Non-essential compilation of album tracks

Live 1977

Cog Sinister COGVP114CD, 27 March 2000 (CD)

Psycho Mafia/Last Orders/Repetition/Dresden Dolls/Hey Fascist/ Frightened/Industrial Estate/Stepping Out/Bingo-Master's Break-Out!/Oh! Brother/Cop It/Futures And Pasts/Louie Louie

I Am As Pure As Oranj

NMC PILOT61, 7 August 2000 (CD)

Dog Is Life/Jerusalem/Kurious Oranj/Yes Oh Yes/Hip Priest/ Wrong Place, Right Time/Acid Priest/Frenz/Bad News Girl/ Dead Beat Descendant/The Plague/Cab It Up!/Bremen Nacht

Recorded at the Edinburgh Festival, Kings Theatre, 17 August 1988

Psykick Dancehall

Eagle Records EEECD010, 7 August 2000 (3CD)

CD1: Stepping Out/Last Orders/Bingo-Master's Break-Out!/ Psycho Mafia/Repetition/It's The New Thing!/Various Times/ Frightened (from the poor quality LP-derived CD)/No Xmas For John Quays (as above)/Industrial Estate (as above)/Music Scene (as above)/ Rowche Rumble/In My Area /Psykick Dancehall/Printhead/ Dice Man/Muzorewi's Daughter/Flat Of Angles/Put Away
CD2: Fiery Jack/2nd Dark Age/How I Wrote 'Elastic Man'/Middle Mass/Crap Rap (from *Live At The Acklam Hall*)/That Man (as above)/

Male Slags (as above)/Spectre Vs. Rector (as above)/Totally Wired/ Pay Your Rates/English Scheme (from *Live At The Acklam Hall*)/New Face In Hell (as above)/Container Drivers (as above)/Prole Art Threat/ Fit And Working Again/Leave The Capitol (from *Live at the Acklam Hall*)/Lie Dream Of A Casino Soul/Fantastic Life
CD3: The Classical/Jawbone And the Air-Rifle/Hip Priest/Fortress/ Deer Park/Winter 1 (Hostel Maxi)/Just Step S'ways/And This Day/ Look, Know (cut version from the Band On Wall)/Bury Derby Hall (bonus CD)/I Feel Voxish (cut version from *Melbourne 82*)/ Marquis Cha-Cha/Hard Life In Country/The Man Whose Head Expanded/Kicker Conspiracy/

Classic archive recordings from The Fall 1977–1982. Contains nothing unavailable elsewhere. Album versions unless otherwise stated.

Live In Cambridge 1988

Voiceprint/Cog Sinister COGVP115CD, October 2000 (CD)

Shoulder Pads/2 x 4/Get A Hotel/Cab It Up!/Hit The North/ Bremen Nacht/Frenz/Pay Your Rates/Hey! Luciani/Oswald Defence Lawyer/L.A./Carry Bag Man/Victoria/Mr Pharmacist/ U.S. 80's–90's/Lucifer Over Lancashire

Live in Reykjavik 1983

Voiceprint/Cog Sinister COGVP125CD, October 2000 (CD)

Tempo House/The Classical/Eat Y'self Fitter/Hexen Definitive/ I Feel Voxish/The Man Whose Head Expanded/Garden/ Kicker Conspiracy/Look, Know/Backdrop

Backdrop

Voiceprint/Cog Sinister COGVP127CD, October 2000 (CD)

Marquis Cha-Cha/Bremen Nacht Run Out/Mark'll Sink Us (live)/ Lucifer Over Lancashire/Hey! Luciani/Wings/L.A./U.S. 80's–90's/ Guest Informant/The Man Whose Head Expanded/Backdrop/ Dresden Dolls/Strychnine/Race With The Devil/Plaster On The Hands/Uncredited Piece of MES talking about the release of How I Wrote 'Elastic Man'/City Hobgoblins

Official release of the earlier Pseudo Indie bootleg (q.v. for track details).

The Unutterable

Eagle Records EAGCD164, 6 November 2000 (CD)

Cyber Insekt/Two Librans/W.B./Sons Of Temperance/Dr. Buck's Letter/Hot Runes/Way Round/Octo Realm / Ketamine Sun/Serum/ Unutterable/Pumpkin Soup And Mashed Potatoes/Hands Up Billy/ Midwatch 1953/Devolute/Das Katerer

A World Bewitched – Best Of 1990–2000

Artful CD35, 6 February 2001 (2 CD)

CD1: Sing! Harpy (*Extricate*)/I'm A Mummy (*Levitate*)/Idiot Joy Showland (*Shift-Work*)/Powder Keg (*The Light User Syndrome*)/ M5*1 (*Middle Class Revolt*)/Inevitable (*The Marshall Suite*)/ Immortality (*Code: Selfish*)/Arid Al's Dream (*Sinister Waltz*)/ The Mixer (*Shift-Work*)/4½ Inch (*Levitate*)/The Caterer (*The Post-Nearly Man*)/One Day (*Cerebral Caustic*)/Middle Class Revolt (*Middle Class Revolt*)/Glam Racket (*The Infotainment Scan*)/Black Monk Theme (*Extricate*)/Strychnine (*Live Various Years*)/Noel's Chemical Effluence (*The Twenty Seven Points*)/Light/Fireworks (*The Infotainment Scan*)
CD2: Theme From ERROR-ORROR!/Blood Outta Stone/ Why Are People Grudgeful?/Ed's Babe/The REAL Life Of The Crying Marshall/Kimble/The Legend Of Xanadu/Seventies Night (*Edwyn Collins feat. Mark E. Smith*)/Calendar (*The Fall feat. Damon Gough, AKA Badly Drawn Boy*)/I Wanna Be Your Dog (*The Clint Boon Experience*)/I Want You (*The Inspiral Carpets feat. Mark E. Smith*)/ Repetition (*Tackhead feat. Mark E. Smith*)/The Heads Of Dead Surfers (*Long Fin Killie feat. Mark E. Smith*)/Plug Myself In (*D.O.S.E feat. Mark E. Smith*)/KB (*Elastica feat. Mark E. Smith*)/Happy Holiday/ Fistful Of Credit (*w. Mild Man Jan*)/Life Just Bounces

Compilation of album tracks and rarities

Are You Are Missing Winner

Cog Sinister, November 2001 COGVP131 (CD)

Jim's "The Fall"/Bourgeois Town/Crop-Dust/My Ex-Classmates' Kids/Kick The Can/Gotta See Jane/Ibis-Afro Man/The Acute/ Hollow Mind/Reprise: Jane – Prof Mick – Ey Bastardo

The Rough Trade Singles Box

Castle CMGBX526 SET, 15 July 2002 (5 CD)

Boxed set comprising the 4 singles released on Rough Trade:
How I Wrote 'Elastic Man'/City Hobgoblins
Totally Wired/Putta Block
The Man Whose Head Expanded/Ludd Gang
CD1: Kicker Conspiracy/Wings
CD2: Container Drivers/New Puritan

The versions of Container Drivers & New Puritan are album versions from Grotesque *and* Totale's Turns, *not the Peel Session versions that originally appeared on the single.*

2G+2

Action Records TAKE18CD, 10 June 2002 (CD)

The Joke/New Formation Sermon (studio)/My Ex-Classmates' Kids/Enigrammatic Dream/I Wake Up In The City (studio)/Kick The Can/F-'Oldin' Money/Bourgeois Town/Distilled Mug Art (studio)/Ibis Afro-Man/Mr Pharmacist/I Am Damo Suzuki

All tracks recorded live at the US November 2001 gigs, except for New Formation Sermon, Distilled Mug Art (these two were on the withdrawn The Present *EP), and I Wake Up In The City (from the limited edition Flitwick 7").*

Totally Wired – The Rough Trade Anthology

Castle CMDDD461, 15 July 2002 (double CD)

CD1: Totally Wired/New Face In Hell/Fit And Working Again/That Man/Container Drivers/Rowche Rumble/How I Wrote 'Elastic Man'/An Older Lover/Cary Grant's Wedding/Pay Your Rates/City Hobgoblins/Middle Mass/Gramme Friday/Leave The Capitol/English Scheme/New Puritan/Prole Art Threat
CD2: The N.W.R.A./The Man Whose Head Expanded/Lie Dream Of A Casino Soul/I Feel Voxish/Hip Priest/Hotel Bloedel/Winter One/Ludd Gang/Smile/Tempo House/Hexen Definitive-Strife Knot/Wings/Eat Y'self Fitter/Kicker Conspiracy

Pander! Panda! Panzer!

Action Records TAKE19CD, 23 September 2002 (CD)

Includes: Mount Street Sermon/PPP-The End/Enigrammatic Dream/Life Just Bounces/Copenhagen "Set-Up"/Dissolute Singer/Lucifer

Over Lancashire/Lakeland Opus 1/Sport Duet/Idiot Joy Showland/ "5 Previously Unreleased Sentences"

Mark E. Smith spoken word album. The CD is mastered as one continuous track.

High Tension Line

Recall/Snapper SMDCD443, 23 September 2002 (double CD)

CD1: Life Just Bounces/Idiot Joy Showland/Behind The Counter/ Hey! Student/Bonkers In Phoenix/The League Of Bald-Headed Men/ A Past Gone Mad/I Come And Stand At Your Door/Middle Class Revolt/Paranoia Man In Cheap Sh*t Room/Hurricane Edward/ The Mixer
CD2: War/Free Range/Glam Racket/Immortality/Spencer Must Die/The Birmingham School Of Business School/High Tension Line/ Don't Call Me Darling/Levitate/Cloud Of Black/Noel's Chemical Effluence/Why Are People Grudgeful?

Compilation of tracks sub-licensed from Artful.

Listening In

Cog Sinister/Voiceprint COGVP132CD, 11 November 2002 (CD)

Telephone Thing (Extended)/Butterflies 4 Brains/Zandra/Blood Outta Stone/Zagreb (Movements I + II + III)/Life Just Bounces/ The Funeral Mix/So What About It? (Remix 1)/Xmas With Simon/ Don't Take The Pizza/So What About It? (Remix 2)/Ed's Babe/ Pumpkin Head Xscapes/The Knight, The Devil And Death/ Free Ranger/So What About It? (Remix 3)/Telephone Dub

Subtitled "Lost Singles Tracks 1990–92". A compilation of B-sides and other singles tracks originally released on Phonogram.

Early Singles

Cog Sinister/Voiceprint COGVP136CD, 2 December 2002 (CD)

Bingo-Master's Break-Out!/Psycho Mafia/Repetition/It's The New Thing/Various Times/Rowche Rumble/In My Area/Fiery Jack/ 2nd Dark Age/Psykick Dancehall No. 2/Lie Dream Of A Casino Soul/ Fantastic Life/Look, Know/I'm Into C.B./Marquis Cha-Cha/ Room To Live

Compilation of A & B-sides from all the singles released on Step Forward and Kamera 1978–1982. Newly 24-bit mastered from the 7" vinyl.

MISCELLANEOUS

Short Circuit – Live At The Electric Circus

Virgin VCL5003, June 1978 (10" live LP on blue, orange or black vinyl)

Features Stepping Out/Last Orders

(Reissued in 1988, CD only (CDVCL5003))

Live in London 1980

Chaos Tapes LIVE006 (Live MC 4,000 copies only)

Middle Mass/English Scheme/New Face In Hell/That Man/
Older Lover/Slates/Gramme Friday/Container Drivers/Jawbone And The Air-Rifle/In The Park/Leave The Capitol/Spectre Vs. Rector/ Pay Your Rates/Impression Of J. Temperance

Recorded at the Acklam Hall (now Subterranea), London on 11 August 1980. Reissued in early 1996, CD only.

Dresden Dolls/Psycho Mafia/Industrial Estate

Total Eclipse DRD1 (bootleg 7")

(First 50 came with black on red insert)

Indie City

NME NMEPRO8 (promotional LP limited to 500)

Features Rowche Rumble

Speed Trials

Homestead (US) HMS011, 1984 (LP)

Features live versions of Smile/Tempo House

One Pound Ninety-Nine – A Music Sampler Of The State Of Things

Beggars Banquet/Situation Two BBB1, 1985 (LP)

Features Spoilt Victorian Child

Fruitcakes And Furry Collars

LP, mail order only from Record Mirror, *1986*

Features L.A. (live at Albany Empire, Deptford)

NME's POGO A GOGO

NME NME021, 1986 (MC)

Features Bingo-Master's Break-Out!

Vinyl Conflict 2

Melody Maker, *September 1986 (7" EP given away free with* Melody Maker*)*

Features Lucifer Over Lancashire (alternative)

Mixed Peel – The John Peel Sessions

Strange Fruit NME033, 1987 (MC given away free with NME*)*

Features Put Away

Sounds Showcase 1

Sounds SHOW 1, 28 February 1987 (7" EP given away free with Sounds*)*

Features Hey! Luciani (original)

Bugs On The Wire

Leghorn SAW399, 1987 (LP)

Features Wings (live)

Head Over Ears – A Debris Compilation

Play Hard DEC7, December 1987 (includes a copy of DEBRIS *magazine)*

Features U.S. 80's–90's (live)

Sgt. Pepper Knew My Father

Youth NMEDEPLP100, 1988 (LP)

Features A Day In The Life

Coldcut What's That Noise

Ahead Of Our Time CCUT LP, 1 April 1989 (LP)

Contains track featuring Mark E. Smith on vocals: (I'm) In Deep

Sniffin' Rock *No. 9 magazine, June 1989 has a free EP (SR006A7)*
Guest Informant (*live in Vienna*)

The Adult Net 'White Night' Beggars Banquet (BEG 164), July 1986 (7" single).
Also on 12" single (BEG 164T).
Features MES vocals on B-side Naughty But Nice

Home
Sheer Joy SHEER001, 1990 (LP)
Features a track by Mark E. Smith, M. Beddington, S. Hanley, S. Wolstencroft: Theme from ERROR-ORROR!

Winters Of Discontent – The Peel Sessions
Strange Fruit, 1991 (CD)
Features Mess Of My

The Indie Scene 1978
IBM IBMCD78, 1992 (CD)
Features Bingo-Master's Break-Out!

The Indie Scene 1979
IBM IBMCD79, 1992 (CD)
Features Rowche Rumble

The Indie Scene 1980
IBM IBMCD80, 1992 (CD)
Features Totally Wired

The Indie Scene 1983
IBM IBMCD83, 1992 (CD)
Features Kicker Conspiracy

The Indie Scene 1985
IBM IBMCD85, 1992 (CD)
Features Cruisers Creek

Manchester So Much To Answer For

(CD)

Features Eat Y'self Fitter

Radio Daze – The John Peel Sessions

Vox/Strange Fruit GIVIT3, April 1992 (MC given away free with Vox *magazine)*

Features Return

Volume Four

World's End V4CD, 1992 (CD)

Features Arid Al's Dream

Volume Eight

World's End V8CD, 1993 (CD)

Various artists CD features War

Ruby Trax

Forty NME40CD, 1992 (Triple CD)

Features Legend Of Xanadu

Young At Heart – A Kick Up The 80s, Vol. 7

Old Gold OG3626, 1992 (LP)

Features There's A Ghost In My House

Angels With Dirty Faces – The History Of Punk, Vol. 3

Old Gold OG3306, 1992 (CD)

Features Totally Wired

NME Singles Of The Week 1992

RCA/BMG NMERCACD1, 1993 (CD)

Features Free Range

RCD Classic Rock Collection, Vol. 10

(CD accompanying Rock CD *magazine Vol. 1, No. 10, June 1993)*

Features A Past Gone Mad

RCD Classic Rock Collection, Vol. 15

(CD accompanying Rock CD *magazine Vol. 1, No. 15, September 1993)*

Features There's A Ghost In My House

In Session Tonight

Strange Fruit BOOKCD 1, 1993 (CD accompanying BBC Radio 1 sessionography book)

Features Kimble

Independent Top 20

Beechwood Music TT017CD, 1993

Features Why Are People Grudgeful?

Inspiral Carpets I Want You

Mute DUNG 24 CD (CD) / DUNG 24 CDR (CD) also on 7" and MC, 21 February 1994

Features Mark E. Smith on vocals

The Nineties Collection Chapter II – The Rebirth

Fontana 515 905-2, 1993

Compilation double CD includes Telephone Thing/White Lightning

Bend It! '94

Exotica Records PELE8CD, 1994 (CD)

Features MES dialogue from his Goal TV appearance

C.R.E.E.P. SHOW

Schlick Yarbles Revisited F101, 1984 (Bootleg LP)

Lay Of The Land/Ludd Gang/Kicker Conspiracy/Smile/2 x 4/ C.R.E.E.P/Neighbourhood Of Infinity/Copped It/Garden

(Recorded live in Munich, 4 April 1986. Limited to 200 copies.)

Backdrop

Pseudo Indie Label PIL05CD, 1994 (Bootleg CD)

Marquis Cha-Cha (*Kamera 7" version*)/Bremen Nacht Run Out (*Free*

7″ with Frenz Experiment)/Mark'll Sink Us (live) (*Free 7″ with Frenz Experiment*)/Lucifer Over Lancashire (*Melody Maker free Vinyl Conflict EP version, 1986*)/Hey! Luciani (*Sounds Showcase 1 EP, 1987*)/ Wings (*live in NYC '85, from Bugs On The Wire LP, 1987*)/L.A. (*live at Albany Empire, Deptford. From Fruitcakes And Furry Collars LP, mail order only from Record Mirror, 1986*)/U.S. 80's–90's (*live in Bremen, Germany from Head Over Ears LP, 1987*)/Guest Informant (*live in Vienna, from 7″ EP with issue 9 of* Sniffin' Rock, *1989*)/The Man Whose Head Expanded (*live, from Bang Zoom tapezine No. 7, 1986*)/Backdrop (*from Fall In A Hole*)/Dresden Dolls (*unreleased rehearsal, '77* (*Total Eclipse DRD1*)/Strychnine (*from BBC Radio 1 Peel Session*)/Race With The Devil (*Gene Vincent song played as a request for John Peel at his 50th birthday party, Subterranea, London, August 29, 1989*)/Plaster On The Hands (*live at the Venue, London on 21 March 1983*)/*uncredited piece of MES talking about the release of 'How I Wrote 'Elastic Man''*/City Hobgoblins

Sharks Patrol These Waters – The Best Of Vol. Two

BOVCD2, 1995 (CD)

Various artists CD features Arid Al's Dream

D.O.S.E Featuring Mark E. Smith Plug Myself In

Coliseum Records/PWL TOGA001CD1 (CD)/TOGA001CD2 (CD) 1996

CD 1: THE SPOONFUL OF SUGAR MIXES/7″ Nero Mix/ 12″ Caligula Mix/12″ Pointblanc Intensive Care Mix/Missing Link Symphonic Instrumental/Missing Link Dirty Instrumental/John Berry – DOA Mix
CD 2: THE ST LUKE MIXES/7″ Nero Mix/Disco Hospital Casualty Mix/Dodo Bassburger Escariot Mix/Missing Link Symphonic Mix/ 3 Over 3 Out Patients Mix/Monty's Full Up Pompeii Mix

Two CD single set (discs available separately) feature MES on vocals

Tackhead Dangerous Sex

SBK7014

B-side of single, Repetition, *features MES on vocals*

Long Fin Killie Heads Of Dead Surfers
Single features MES on vocals

Compilation LP **The Disparate Cogscienti** *features Mark E. Smith at the beginning of side 2*

A History Of Punk, Volume 2
Virgin CDOVD487, 1997 (CD)
Features Cruisers Creek

A History Of Punk
Receiver RDPCD11, 1997 (2 CD)
Features A Lot Of Wind

INCH feat. Mark E. Smith
Regal REG27CD, February 1999 (CD)
Single features MES on vocals. Also available on 12" REG27.

Elastica
Deceptive, 23 August 1999
Six track EP features MES on How He Wrote 'Elastica Man'/KB

The Clint Boon Experience
You Can't Keep A Good Man Down, 9 August 1999 (CD/7")
Single features MES on the B-side: I Wanna Be Your Dog *(live)*

Wire Magazine, October 2000
The accompanying free CD features: Dr Buck's Letter

Select Magazine, January 2001
The accompanying free CD Revolutions features: Two Librans

That Art Rocker/Rough Trade
2001 (MC)
Compilation cassette features: Totally Wired

Also

Cruiser's Creek/Couldn't Get Ahead/Barmy/Vixen/Petty (Thief) Lout

PVC PVC5909, 1985 (Widely available US import 12")

Totally Wired

Razor And Tie 1999 (CD)

US compilation CD features Totally Wired

VIDEOS

Perverted by Language Bis

Ikon Videos IKON8, January 1983

Wings/Totally Wired/Kicker Conspiracy/Hexen Definitive-Strife Knot/Eat Y'self Fitter/Tempo House/The Man Whose Head Expanded/Smile/Draygo's Guilt – Hip Priest (excerpts)/ Container Drivers

VHS8489

Beggars Banquet BB010, August 1990

Wrong Place, Right Time/Hit The North/Big New Prinz/ Mr Pharmacist/Lucifer Over Lancashire (edit)/Hey! Luciani/There's A Ghost In My House/Couldn't Get Ahead/Victoria/Cruisers Creek/ Guest Informant (edit)

Shift-Work And Holidays

Phonogram 083.590-3, June 1990

So What About It?/The Mixer/Error-Orrori/High Tension Line/ Pearson's Revenge/The Book Of Lies/Big New Priest/Shift-Work

Snub TV, Vol. 1

EMI MVP9912133, 1990

Compilation video features Dead Beat Descendant

Snub TV, Vol. 2
Virgin VVD837, 1991
Compilation video features Bill Is Dead

BOOKS

Edge, Brian. (1989). *Paintwork – A Portrait Of The Fall.* Omnibus Press.

Smith, Mark E. (1985). *The Fall Lyrics.* Lough Press, Berlin.

Garner, Ken. (1993). *In Session Tonight.* BBC Books. ISBN 0-536-36452-1.
Details all BBC Radio 1 sessions to 1992 and comes with complementary CD (Strange Fruit BOOKCD1) featuring Kimble *as the last track.*